SPIES, INC.

STACY PERMAN

SPIES, INC.

Business Innovation from Israel's Masters of Espionage

PEARSON
Prentice
Hall

An Imprint of PEARSON EDUCATION
Upper Saddle River • New York • San Francisco • Toronto • Sydney
Tokyo • Singapore • Hong Kong • Cape Town • Madrid
Paris • Milan • Munich • Amsterdam

www.ft-ph.com

A CIP record of this book can be obtained from the Library of Congress.

Editorial/Production Supervision: *Patti Guerrieri*
Cover Design Director: *Jerry Votta*
Cover Design: *Anthony Gemmellaro*
Interior Design: *Gail Cocker-Bogusz*
Manufacturing Buyer: *Maura Zaldivar*
Senior Editor: *Paula Sinnott*
Developmental Editor: *Russ Hall*
Editorial Assistant: *Richard Winkler*
Marketing Manager: *John Pierce*

 © 2005 Pearson Education, Inc.
Publishing as Financial Times Prentice Hall
Upper Saddle River, NJ 07458

Prentice Hall offers excellent discounts on this book when ordered in quantity for bulk purchases or special sales. For more information, please contact: U.S. Corporate and Government Sales, 1-800-382-3419, corpsales@pearsontechgroup.com. For sales outside of the U.S., please contact: International Sales, international@pearsoned.com.

Company and product names mentioned herein are the trademarks or registered trademarks of their respective owners.

Extract from *Under This Blazing Light* has been reprinted with the permission of Amos Oz and Cambridge University Press.

Printed in the United States of America

First Printing

ISBN 0-13-142023-2

Pearson Education Ltd.
Pearson Education Australia Pty., Limited
Pearson Education South Asia Pte. Ltd.
Pearson Education Asia Ltd.
Pearson Education Canada, Ltd.
Pearson Educación de Mexico, S.A. de C.V.
Pearson Education — Japan
Pearson Malaysia SDN BHD

For my father, Leonard Perman

Contents

Preface

I first came across unit 8200 when I wrote a magazine piece chronicling Israel's high-tech boom. It was 2000, and there was a cataclysmic buzz going on about this tiny, defiant nation that had in a very short period of time lept onto the global stage as one of the world's most dynamic technology clusters. At the time, Israeli startups numbered in the thousands, and the country placed third behind the United States and Canada in the number of companies listed on NASDAQ. There was something big going on inside of this small nation. Undeniably, the driving force behind much of this was the Israeli Defense Forces (IDF) and, in particular, its elite technological units. However, there was one that stood out—unit 8200—and although it had remained in the shadows for decades, it seemed to cast the strongest light over much of the dynamism that was happening in Israel.

The IDF plays a wide-ranging and singularly exceptional role in Israel, but there was something fundamentally unique and interesting going on in this secretive intelligence unit that has been compared to the National Security Agency (NSA) in the United States. While the list of world-class technologies and companies that could trace their lineage to the unit was certainly remarkable in its own right, it appeared to be just a small thread that was part of a longer string. Israel's particular set of geopolitical and historical circumstances had shaped a very distinctive kind of innovative thinking. The military was its most evident expression, and unit 8200 proved to be its most explicit example. This creative entrepreneurial character that had served Israel so well in war and defense was propelling the nation in a new direction. But the story didn't begin with the high-tech boom, and it didn't end with its crash. Actually, it seemed to me that the story began earlier. What were the forces at play? Here was a young immigrant nation, poor in every conceivable measure and surrounded by hostile neighbors. Yet, it had a deep and rich heritage of innovation. If Israel, under siege, could create world-class universities and research institutions and breakthroughs in the fields of medicine and science and technology, might there be lessons for the rest of us? (After all, in a 2004 *Forbes* magazine survey of the world's leading companies, broken down by region, the Middle East had nine— eight were Israeli.)

I was intrigued, and I found that there was a deeper and broader story to be told about this incongruous nation of innovators. A significant place to begin was with the military, which repeatedly led me to unit 8200. How did it come to pass that an intelligence unit sitting smack dab inside a military infrastructure turned out to be one of the nation's most distinctive schools for entrepreneurs and an incubator for innovative ideas? As the saying goes, business is like war, and in Israel, the unique intersection of surviving in a hostile region and the unrelenting pressure to innovate to defend itself had broader implications. As it turns out, espionage, counterterrorism, and defense had very real business lessons. It was worth examining this connection because innovation is one of the most important parts of business, and here it was found in a military structure.

This was not an easy subject to cover. For one, although unit 8200 has been mentioned more publicly in recent years, it remains, for the most part, classified. For years it was forbidden to talk about the unit, and the time it had spent in total secrecy continues to cast a pall over its public image. Although the high-tech boom cracked open the wall of silence that had surrounded this unit for decades, many of its former members remain reluctant to discuss their time in its service. One former soldier told me that one of the reasons so many unit alumni ended up working together after leaving the unit was simply because nobody could talk about what they did there to outsiders. There was a secret language among soldiers, and a resume was not part of it. To research this topic in any detail required the trust of several former members of the unit, and I thank them for handing over their stories to me.

The individual cases and stories (or rather, what can be told) are not meant to undermine state security, but rather are to illuminate the machinery, the cog behind the wheel. They are a metaphor for the way innovation has taken root in Israel through circumstance and history, and for a way of thinking and what it says about this place that continues to defy all odds and expectations. Since the subject was a sensitive one, I consulted with Israeli military authorities, and, as a result, some modifications to the manuscript were made.

A number of my interviews took place at cafés, others at company offices and boardrooms, and not a few at army bases and the Kirya, the Israeli defense complex in central Tel Aviv. Many individuals requested that only their first names be used, and others asked not to be identified at all. For the purpose of clarification, in the latter case I have given these individuals an assumed name. However, whenever possible, I have identified individuals in full. I spent almost nine months in Israel in 2003 and the early part of 2004 researching open source documents and conducting interviews, nearly 100 of them in all, for this book.

It was a surreal time. Suicide bombings continued apace, and Israeli military reprisals were a constant. War with Iraq loomed around the corner. I had my reporter's notebooks and a gas mask ready to go. A friend suggested that we time the sprint between my apartment and the nearest public bomb shelter, should Iraqi SCUDS start falling. Fortunately, they never came. However, in the midst of all the tension, there was a remarkable normalcy and vibrancy to daily life despite the fact that the economy had been decimated by the protracted and deadly conflict, and the gains made during the boom years had all but vanished. Israelis had already shifted gears to the new reality of life at war—again. I was struck time and again at how new ideas were taking shape—ideas that might become products and companies. It was astonishing how this nation refused to get mired in the difficulties of the time. Rather, it sloughed them off like old skin to start anew. The cafés and restaurants were full, and movie theaters and opera houses were packed. There was a fighting spirit that was palpable. Nobody surrendered to the distinct pressures and deficits that piled up each day. It became very clear to me that this was a place where the kinds of challenges and difficulties that would cause most to throw up their hands were perceived quite differently. They were viewed as challenges to be met head on, as opportunities to be uncovered through adversity. This is where innovation begins.

Acknowledgments

This is a book that required an open discussion in many ways on a subject that remained closed to the outside world. I am indebted above all to those who shared their thoughts and time with me—many over coffee at cafés all over Tel Aviv, Herziliya, and beyond.

There are those without whom this book would not have gotten off the ground. Firstly, I wish to thank Bob Slater, who opened the door and patiently answered all of my questions. A very special thanks goes to the incomparable David Rubin, a miracle worker in his own way whose assistance can never be fully measured and for whom adequate appreciation cannot be shown. For discussion and moments of clarity (although they may have been brief), my thanks to Gadi Ariav, dead of the High-Tech Management School at Tel Aviv University, and thanks also to Udi, for giving so generously of his time, our many meetings, and the eye-opening trip to the desert.

I wish to also give a nod of thanks for the support and help of Dov, Moshe, Hadassah, Hezie, the library at the Center for Special Studies at Glilot, and the IDF's spokesperson's office. A special thanks is reserved for the behind-the-scenes navigation and seemingly never-ending assistance from those who asked to remain unnamed.

For their generosity of friendship, hospitality, and endless rounds of discussion during the many months in Israel, I give thanks to Chana Arnon, Tamar Avital, Shira Richter, Janice

Wasser, and Daniel Savin. At home in the United States, my thanks go to Susan Scandrett, who provided the crucial pillars of friendship, laughter, unofficial manuscript reader, and comrade in the trenches; Riza Cruz, who, as always, provided friendship, wit, and support; Barbara Maddux, who contributed mirth and rallying words; and Sue Ruopp, who has been a friend for as long as I can remember. For giving me a place to land and taking care of the details of my life while I was away so that they would not totally escape me, I am grateful to Isabel and Howard Kosberg. For their smiles and hugs every time I leave and the same when I return home, I thank Lexie, Madeleine, and Hayden Sosa. Last, but hardly least, for her unwavering support, I must thank Esther Perman.

In the past, I've had the good fortune to work with editors who were as inspiring as they are talented: Bill Saporito, Charlie McCoy, Tim Carvell, and Susan Casey. Your imprint, I hope, presides in these pages. Additionally, I extend my appreciation to Karen Rothmyer, a wonderful teacher, who first opened my eyes to the possibilities of reporting while I was a student at Columbia University.

This book would not have been possible if not for my publishers at Prentice Hall: Tim Moore, who first believed in this book; Paula Sinnott, who took up the baton; and Russ Hall, my editor; all of whom displayed great patience and responded with much support and enthusiasm all along the way in this endeavor. And, finally, Patti Guerrieri, who brought this book to the finish line.

1 The Intercept

Off the coast of the Arabian Peninsula, January 3, 2002...

In the inky darkness of the predawn hours, the Red Sea had turned choppy. The sun had yet to bathe the sea, known in Arabic as *Al Bahr Al Ahmar,* in its winter light. Fishing boats moored in the waters surrounded by Yemen, Saudi Arabia, and the Sudan rocked in the stormy darkness. An old, blue cargo ship, sailing under the flag of the kingdom of Tonga, cruised northward, making its way toward the Suez Canal, while on board most of its 13-man crew slept.

Observing the situation from the sky above, in a Boeing 707 outfitted as a command and control craft, was Lieutenant General Shaul Mofaz, the Israel Defense Forces' (IDF) chief of staff. Just the day before, Mofaz, a military careerist and former elite paratrooper, cancelled a scheduled trip to Washington, D.C. Now he was high above the open water staring through the lenses of specially made high-powered field glasses from which he could make out the letters *K-A-R-I-N-E-A* painted on the side of the ship.[1] For three months, Israeli intelligence had been monitoring the freighter as it made its 3,000-mile journey from Lebanon to the Arabian coast. The 4,000-ton *Karine-A,* the Israelis quickly discovered, was a

1

gunrunner, carrying an illicit arms shipment from Iran. Its destination: the Palestinian territories.

The Middle East, a volatile slice of the earth in the best of times, had turned particularly ugly in the fall of 2000. The Palestinian *intifada,* or uprising against the Israelis, exploded in September, igniting shortly after the failure to achieve a final settlement on a Palestinian state at a Camp David meeting attended by Israeli Prime Minister Ehud Barak, Palestinian Chairman Yassir Arafat, and U.S. President Bill Clinton. The uprising turned lethal following the visit of retired general and Israel's soon-to-be next Prime Minister Ariel Sharon to the open plaza outside of the Al Aksa Mosque in Jerusalem. Accompanied by a cordon of Israeli policemen, Sharon's provocative display of Jewish sovereignty over the Temple Mount—a site holy to both Jews and Muslims—inflamed the Palestinians, who erupted in demonstrations. The entire conflagration went south quickly as stone-throwing Palestinians resorted to guns, escalating to a wave of human suicide bombers. Israeli reprisals added another violent stamp as they took to hunting down and assassinating suspected Palestinian militants. Now the intifada was raging well into its fifteenth bloody month. Despite diplomatic maneuverings, its end was nowhere in sight. A cycle of violence engulfed the region. It was a powder keg threatening to explode.

The *Karine-A* and its cargo hold full of weapons would do little to quell the unrest. Floating along international waters, it was both a potential match and fuse. Weapons smuggling was not a new twist in the decades-old Israeli-Palestinian conflict. The Palestinians had moved weapons into the territories in the past. Most often, according to the Israelis, this was done through a system of underground tunnels dug beneath the Israeli-controlled border that separates Egypt and the Palestinian-controlled town of Rafah on the southern edge of the Gaza Strip. But for the most part, efforts to channel large amounts of advanced munitions had failed. The intifada, with its withering spiral of attacks and counterattacks, had already pushed the prospect of peace under the Oslo Accords[2] from its fragile moorings. The possibility of adding a load of sophisticated new weaponry into the mix would do little to restore the peace.

In a secret meeting just weeks earlier, Prime Minister Sharon, a fleshy tank of a man who had fought in just about every Arab-Israeli war since 1948, met with Mofaz and the heads of the Israeli Air Force and Navy to discuss how to make sure the *Karine-A* would not make its final destination. The Israelis could simply sink the ship—unverified accounts had reported that the Israelis had engaged in sinking missions in the past. Or they could capture it. In the spring, eight months earlier, the Israeli Navy had seized a fishing vessel called the *Santorini* only a few dozen miles off of the coast of Haifa en route from Lebanon to Gaza. Its cargo held a load of anti-aircraft missiles, anti-tank missile launchers, artillery rockets, and mortar shells, intended, Israeli officials said, for the Palestinian territories.[3]

In operational mode, Israel's top military personnel began devising a plan for the *Karine-A* that would account for all contingencies. Whatever they did, however they did it, they would have to get it right. Certainly, the freighter, sailing in international waters in the busy shipping lanes of the Red Sea, would be an intricate target. First, the Israelis had to make certain the *Karine-A* was indeed the boat carrying the rogue arms shipment. Far from Israeli jurisdiction, the scheme would require a precise maneuvering of Israeli air and naval power. Complicating any operation, aircraft would need to be refueled mid-route, and naval patrol boats used to monitoring the 164-mile Israeli coast would be stretched beyond their usual operational limits. At more than 300 miles from Israel, the location posed its own dangers in attempting a commando mission. Then again, the distance also served as an advantage. It was too far at sea for anyone to suspect a surprise raid. An operation of this scale would set a new precedent.

There was, however, another troubling specter for the Israelis. Intelligence had found that the *Karine-A* stood in the middle of a new murky web that they claimed connected the Palestinians, Iran, and the Lebanese-based terrorist organization *Hizbollah,* or Party of God. In seizing the ship, the Israelis could not only disrupt the delivery of arms but also, just as importantly, expose this disturbing relationship. It would be a political triumph for the Israelis as much as a military one. It was an opportunity to deal a crushing blow to Palestinian Chairman Yassir Arafat, who as the ship moved toward its final destination was publicly denouncing violence and declaring his commitment to eliminate terrorism and revive the peace process. Indeed, the captain of the ship, Omar Akawi, later told western reporters in a jailhouse interview that he expected to be ordered to halt the mission after Arafat's public call for a truce.[4] The order never came, and the *Karine-A* stayed the course. As it passed through the Bab al Mandeb Straits on the tip of Yemen, Arafat offered a goodwill gesture to Israeli President Moshe Katzav: an invitation to address the Palestinian Parliament in Ramallah in the West Bank.

Aboard the Boeing jet, keeping track of the operation and monitoring the internal communications among the commandos at sea, Mofaz sat with the top ranks of the IDF: Navy Commander Major General Yedidya Ya'ari, Air Force Commander Major General Dan Halutz, and the head of *Aman,* Israel's military intelligence, Major General Aharon Ze'evi Farkash. Cruising high above the ocean, they posted frequent updates to Prime Minister Sharon (himself a veteran of many Israeli undercover operations and the man who had most likely green-lighted the mission) back in Israel. In a second Boeing jet, representing the rear command, sat Deputy Chief of Staff Major General Moshe Yaalon, the deputy commanders of the Navy and the Air Force, and intelligence agents. F-15A fighter jets provided additional cover.[5]

As dawn broke, the *Karine-A* was positioned between the coasts of Saudi Arabia and the Sudan. The mission, codenamed Operation Noah's Ark, was a go.

At 4:00 A.M., under the cover of Apache helicopters, Israeli Navy Dabur patrol boats raced toward the ship. Appearing in the sky above, Sikorsky CH-53 transport and Black Hawk helicopters released rubber boats, which naval commandos from the elite Flotilla 13 unit scrambled after. At the same time, more commandos stormed their way onto the *Karine-A* from a naval command ship deployed nearby. Within a minute flat, they had climbed up the hull of the ship, entered its control room, and overpowered two crew members before they had a chance to reach for their guns. Unaware of the scuffle on deck, the remaining 11 crewmen were handcuffed as they slept in their bunks. They weren't the only ones caught off-guard. As the *Karine-A* was intercepted by the Israelis, Palestinian officials, including the PLO's ambassador to Cairo, were said to be waiting for the ship where it was expected to dock on the Egyptian Coast.[6] The entire operation took eight minutes. Not a single shot was fired. When it was over, the chief of staff placed a phone call to Tel Aviv. "It's in our hands," he reported to the high-level government officials awaiting news of the mission.[7]

Under a pile of clothing and toys, the Israeli commandos uncovered wooden crates marked "fragile" and packed in waterproof plastic sleeves. They held some 80 submersible containers packed with 50 tons of Iranian and Russian-made weapons and explosives. The Israelis put a price tag on the weapons in the tens of millions. The arsenal was enough to supply a small army, which was fitting as Israeli intelligence had determined the *Karine-A* and its lethal cargo was bound for the Palestinian Authority. The haul included dozens of 122-mm and 107-mm Katyusha rockets with ranges of 20 and 8 kilometers, hundreds of shorter-range 81-mm rockets, numerous mortars with hundreds of bombs, SAGGER and RPG 18 anti-tank missiles, sniper rifles, AK-47 assault rifles, and anti-personnel and anti-tank missiles.[8] Most of the weaponry uncovered from the *Karine-A* was in violation of the agreements signed by the Palestinian Authority under the Oslo accords. The scope, magnitude, and long-range capability of the arms bore little justification, said Mofaz later, for use in self-defense or law enforcement.[9] Most alarming was the 3,000 pounds of C4 explosives found on board. It was enough to manufacture hundreds of suicide bombs, making them a much deadlier and sophisticated batch than the kind of improvised explosives studded with nails, nuts, and bolts for maximum impact—the bomb of choice for Palestinian suicide bombers.

According to the plan, as it was later reconstructed, the *Karine-A* would have sailed to port in Alexandria to transfer the weapons to smaller ships that would then dump the floatable canisters off the Gaza coast, where fishing boats would pick them up and send them to the Palestinian territories. If the plan had been successful, the weapons would have enabled Palestinian militants to escalate the already deadly intifada, perhaps even spiraling it into a regional war. As it was, the intifada by this point had claimed more than a thousand Palestinian and Israeli lives. But with this new cache of weaponry, cities and towns all over Israel would have been made vulnerable and would have been within striking distance from attacks coming from well within Palestinian territory. "If warfare equipment of this kind had reached the hands of terrorists acting against us," Mofaz exclaimed after the raid, "it may have dramatically altered the security of the citizens of the State of Israel and the soldiers of the IDF, and drastically increased the terror activity against us."[10]

Immediately, Operation Noah's Ark was announced as one of risk, brilliance, and imagination. For the Israelis, it was another accomplishment in survival. It was also, more bluntly, a spectacular triumph of military daring—another in a long line of movie-worthy Israeli special-ops victories such as the kidnapping of Nazi Adolph Eichmann from Buenos Aires, Argentina, to Israel; the hostage rescue operation at Entebbe, Uganda; or the bombing of the Iraqi nuclear reactor at Osirik, north of Baghdad. But it was no less a success, although a deliberately less trumpeted one, of Israeli intelligence. Every operation of any magnitude depends on accurate, timely information. And Operation Noah's Ark was no exception. Yaacov Erez, editor-in-chief of the Israeli daily *Ma'ariv,* summed up the enormity of the operation in an editorial in which he wrote, "Uncovering the cargo aboard the *Karine-A* was the primary goal of the military raid, but the significance of the operation, which was carried out flawlessly, was that it demonstrated impressive operational capabilities by the IDF, far from Israeli territory, while using intelligence methods in an awe-inspiring fashion."[11]

Indeed, in a briefing following the successful raid, Israeli Navy Admiral Ya'ari congratulated the efforts of the Air Force and the Naval commando unit before giving a brief if oblique acknowledgment, saying only that the mission "...began with intelligence...."[12] And he left it at that.

Thanks to the information collected by intelligence, the Israelis knew precisely when the ship was purchased, who purchased it, from whose courtesy its lethal cargo had originated, and its final destination. The only question left for the Israelis was what to do about it.

A year earlier, Israeli intelligence had picked up signs that the Iranian-backed Hizbollah was aiding the armed uprising against the Israeli occupation by bringing weapons and know-how into the Palestinian territories. In October 2000, they learned that Adel Mughrabi (also known as Adel Awadallah), who is the head of the Palestinian Authority's procurement department, Palestinian Naval Police Commander Juma'a' Ghali, and his deputy Fathi Ghazem were in touch with Iranian and Hizbollah agents.[13] The following August, Mughrabi purchased the 4,000-ton merchant ship in Lebanon for $400,000. Arafat's senior finance officer, Fuad Shubaki, funded the deal. From the time the ship set sail from Lebanon, it was under surveillance.

On the heels of the terrorist attacks on the World Trade Center in New York City and the Pentagon in Washington, D.C., the boat was registered with the kingdom of Tonga on September 12 and given the name *Karine-A*. It then sailed for Aden, Yemen, where Akawi took command, along with a crew of four armed Palestinians and an additional group of Egyptians and Jordanians.[14] Although the Egyptian and Jordanian sailors thought they might be part of some smuggling adventure—possibly trafficking in stolen stereo and other electronic equipment—they were evidently unaware of the exact gravity of the freight with which they were sailing. The Israeli press reported that when a crate broke apart during the loading of the ship and exposed its true cargo, some of the Egyptian and Jordanian seamen requested to leave—only reportedly to be told that from that point on, "There is only one way to get off the ship—with a bullet in the head."[15]

In early December, the ship arrived at the Iranian island of Kish in the Persian Gulf, where it was met by a ferry said to be carrying Iranian intelligence officials and the weapons. Shortly after the operation, published reports suggested that Israeli intelligence had implicated senior Hizbollah operative Imad Mughniyah in the operation. Long suspected as the mastermind behind the 1983 U.S. Marine barracks bombing in Lebanon that killed 241 Americans, as well as the 1985 hijacking of TWA flight 847, in which a U.S. Navy officer was killed, Mughniyah was on the FBI's most wanted foreign terrorist list. The Israelis also wanted him, as Mughniyah was considered to be responsible for the 1992 terror attacks against the Israeli embassy in Argentina that killed 29 and the one against the Buenos Aires Jewish community center two years later. More recently, reports surfaced linking Mughniyah to Al Qaeda.[16]

With the weapons on board, the *Karine-A* left in mid-December for Dubai, where it collected a bogus cargo designed to hide the stash of weapons. Then, after an unscheduled week's pause in Hodeida, Yemen, to repair the engine, it resumed its journey sailing around the Arabian Peninsula heading for the Palestinian territories. On January 3, as U.S. envoy retired General Anthony Zinni was to meet with Arafat and begin a four-day series of talks between the Israelis and Palestinians in an attempt to put together a cease-fire, Israel authorities announced that its commandos had stormed and seized the *Karine-A*. Now traveling under an Israeli flag, the ship sailed north, to the southern Israeli port of Eilat. When it arrived there two days after the raid, hundreds of beachgoers on the rocky shore erupted in applause.[17]

The Israeli government invited journalists and diplomats to Eilat to see for themselves what Prime Minister Sharon called "a ship of terror," "a ticking time bomb," and "this Trojan horse by sea" at a press conference shortly after the seizure, where the IDF displayed the captured arms organized in rows, each marked and labeled. Amid the display of weaponry, Sharon said the *Karine-A* proved "once again that the Palestinian Authority has been focusing all its efforts on terrorism and preparing the operational infrastructure for the next waves of terror."[18] Soon after, the IDF put up a streaming video of the arms cache on its own website.

The Palestinian Authority denied any involvement in the episode at first (as did the Iranians), accusing Israel of manufacturing the whole thing. Later they said the shipment was headed for Lebanon. Indeed, some U.S. officials expressed their own doubts about the Israeli claims in initial reports, raising the possibility that the arms were actually intended for Hizbollah in Lebanon. For their part, the Israelis claimed irrefutable evidence that the arms shipment was organized by Palestinian Authority officials with the aid of Iran and Hizbollah and was earmarked for the Palestinian territories.[19] Washington, however, was not totally in the dark, as American intelligence was also said to have been following the ship and even to have shared strategic information with the Israelis. The Israelis, however, denied it.[20]

Although no direct line of evidence surfaced linking Arafat to the *Karine-A*—at least not publicly—such a large purchase would not likely go unnoticed by Arafat given his ironclad hold on the Palestinian Authority's coffers. And, too, the men implicated in the scheme were not marginal to the Palestinian Authority—they were quite close to the chairman's inner circle. Omar Akawi, the ship's captain, did little to quell the connection. In interviews he gave with Israeli TV and western journalists following the seizure, he identified himself as an officer of the Palestinian Authority and a 26-year member of Arafat's own Fatah group. Akawi referred to Arafat as his "commander and chief," calling him by his *nom de guerre*: Abu Amar. Describing himself as a soldier who must obey orders, he said the operation was organized and supervised by senior Palestinian Authority official Adel Mughrabi, and he affirmed that the munitions were indeed headed for Gaza and for the Palestinian Authority. As for the weapons' provenance, he told an Israeli journalist in a television broadcast, "I received [the cache] near Iran, so where could it have come from? You're smart and can understand on your own."[21]

The event was greeted somewhat ambivalently by a conflict-weary world that viewed it with what was becoming the increasingly jaundiced prism with which they looked at the growing tensions in the area. However, back in Israel, there was much backslapping and congratulations. The operation was a perfectly executed combination of military might and intelligence prowess. The naval commandos under air force cover had stormed the ship, arrested its crew, and secured the dangerous cargo. Of course, the entire mission was predicated on information, and that information came from intelligence. After all, as one former high-level intelligence officer explained, "You can't just go in and take over a ship in international waters." Intelligence had to piece together that an illicit arms smuggling operation was in progress. It had to determine that the *Karine-A* was that ship and not simply a merchant vessel transporting T-shirts to Egypt. It was a complicated affair, logging 3,000 miles and crossing a considerable number of countries—most of which are hostile to Israel.

In Israel, there were a select few who knew exactly what was needed to support such an operation. Sitting deep within the furtive Israeli intelligence complex exists an agency until recently little known outside of the intelligence community. It's an ultrasecretive unit without a name—just a number: 8200. Pronounced *shmone matayim* in Hebrew, it is known as the ears of Israeli intelligence. As the former intelligence officer continued, "Important information came from this unit. A military operation is the last step based on intelligence." The Israelis could not afford any kind of mistake. They needed to be sure it was the right ship, where it was going, and when. In concert with several organizations, unit 8200 played a significant part in teasing out the kind of information needed to put together the intelligence puzzle. Thanks to 8200's high-tech ability to listen, intercept, and mine thousands of pieces of information, it was able to help build the kind of portrait needed.

Technological intelligence units in the IDF were established in order to greatly enhance the kind of instant intelligence needed to provide early warning of the impending actions of its enemies. Such units are also an important tool to provide the raw data necessary to form policy, strategy, and, ultimately, the basis of a military operation. Ringed by its Arab neighbors, and for most of

> *"Technological intelligence units in the IDF were established in order to greatly enhance the kind of instant intelligence needed to provide early warning of the impending actions of its enemies. Such units are also an important tool to provide the raw data necessary to form policy, strategy, and, ultimately, the basis of a military operation."*

its history in a state of war with them, Israel needed not only real-time intelligence but the means with which to collect and interpret it just as instantaneously. From its rudimentary beginnings during the early years of the state, 8200 was made up of an enormously gifted brain trust of mathematicians and engineers. It is they who are said to have created and analyzed much of the super-secret technology of Israeli intelligence sleuthing. Manipulating huge amounts of information, it plumbs through an endless skein of intercepts from phones, faxes, and all other types of electronic communications to extract the vital signs and form the abstract links that connect the dots. The unit is also the producer of the kind of sophisticated systems that capture and decrypt these enemy transmissions, unraveling their signals, turning them into comprehensible messages, and ultimately exposing their hidden meanings. The unit sits squarely at the center of Israel's defense and security.

It has been described as perhaps more important to Israeli espionage in recent years than its better-known counterparts like the Mossad. The men and women who toil inside of unit 8200 are in large part responsible for the long and penetrating reach of Israeli intelligence. "Reuven," a former 17-year veteran of the unit, related, "Every step in the process, one way or another 8200 is involved. 8200 is responsible for every significant event in the life of this country, whether it's war or the odd event of peace. A considerable amount of all information is first received by 8200."

Until recently, when the unit was mentioned in public, if it was mentioned at all, it was referred to innocuously as the Central Collection Unit. Little is known about 8200 outside of the clandestine intelligence community. Its members work in tight groups, and their contributions are known only among themselves. Perhaps the best-known example of such eavesdropping took place more than three decades ago during the Six Day War in 1967, when intelligence intercepted and recorded a radiophone conversation between Egyptian President Gamal Abdul Nasser and King Hussein of Jordan on June 6, the second day of the war.[22]

> *Nasser:* Does Britain have aircraft carriers?
>
> *Hussein:* (Unclear)
>
> *Nasser:* Very well. So King Hussein will publish and we shall publish an announcement.
>
> *Hussein:* Thank you.
>
> *Nasser:* Yes, Yes.
>
> *Nasser:* Hello, good morning my brother, be strong.
>
> *Hussein:* Mr. President, if you have any request or idea...at any time.
>
> *Nasser:* We are fighting with all our forces. The fighting goes on all fronts. All the night, and if there was anything at the beginning, never mind, we shall overcome and Allah

will be with us. Will his Highness publish an announcement concerning British and American participation?

Hussein: (Answer not clear)

Nasser: I swear to Allah that we shall publish an
announcement, and you will publish and we shall see to it
that the Syrians will publish an announcement that American and British aircraft are participating against us from
aircraft carriers. We shall announce it and emphasize it.

Hussein: OK.

Nasser: Your Highness, do you agree?

Hussein: (Answer not clear)

Nasser: Thousands of thanks, be strong, we are with you
with all our heart. Our aircraft are over Israel all [day]
long today, our aircraft are pounding the Israeli airbases
since this morning.

Hussein: Thousand thanks, good bye.

Two agents listening at a base near Tel Aviv, using unso-
phisticated, old World War II equipment, caught the exchange.
Recognizing its political cache, Israeli Prime Minister Levi Esh-
kol and Defense Minister Moshe Dayan insisted that the conversation be made public, broadcasting it in Israel, Great Britain,
and the United Nations Assembly. It was a rare exposure of
Israeli intelligence capabilities, and it was done despite the
vehement protestations of military intelligence. The discussion
came to be known as "The Big Lie." The fabrication of an
American-British conspiracy humiliated both Nasser and Hussein, hurting for a time their relations with the western powers.
Its consequences, however, had a much greater impact. Despite
the fact that the Israelis had pummeled most of the Egyptian
Air Force, Nasser neglected to mention this important detail to
King Hussein. With his back against the wall, the Jordanian
monarch, in a face-saving move, joined forces with Nasser and
entered the war. He lost half his kingdom, the West Bank, to the
Israelis, radically altering the shape of the geopolitical map of

the Middle East. The consequences of this episode reverberate to this day, remaining a source of heated conflict, putting millions of Palestinians under Israeli occupation.[23]

It is a general rule of thumb that intelligence organizations are loathe to make public much of the information they collect in order that they not expose the sources and methods with which they obtained it. This reluctance to make information public was one major reason why the United States failed to produce a smoking gun during the great Iraqi weapons of mass destruction debate at the United Nations in the early part of 2003. (Of course, the vexing question of whether such weapons existed at all would emerge later and haunt the Bush Administration following the invasion of Iraq.) Indeed, the famous exchange between Nasser and Hussein had great short-term effects, but it also upped the ante for Israeli intelligence. Immediately the Arabs took greater measures to secure their communications, eroding a significant portion of Israeli SIGINT (signals intelligence) capabilities against their neighbors at the time. On the other hand, the Arabs were no longer so sure when, where, or how they were being monitored. Indeed, as a result of this breach, six years later, as the Egyptians and Syrians prepared their surprise attack in what would become the Yom Kippur War of 1973, they were notably cautious regarding Israel's SIGINT capabilities. They avoided communicating between themselves on telephones, cables, and radiophones.[24]

It would be almost another 20 years before the Israelis would exchange such deep intelligence activity for political gain, at least publicly. They did so on October 16, 1985, after members of the Palestinian Liberation Front (PLF), an offshoot of the Palestine Liberation Organization (PLO), had hijacked the Italian cruise ship *Achille Lauro* in the Mediterranean en route to the Israeli port of Ashdod. When the hijackers were discovered by a crewmember, their plans went awry. Most notably, they shot an invalid passenger, 69-year-old Leon Klinghoffer, and dumped his body and wheelchair overboard. They then tried to sail to Syria but were refused permission to enter. Ultimately, the ship pulled into Port Said in Egypt, where the hijackers surrendered to Egyptian and PLO officials. However, almost from the moment the ship was taken, Israeli intelligence had electronically intercepted and monitored Egyptian communications and recorded ship-to-shore conversations between the hijackers and PLF guerilla leader Mohammed Abbas, also known as Abu al Abbas and reportedly on the executive committee of the PLO. Shortly after the incident, no less than Ehud Barak, then head of *Aman*, released a portion of the recorded transcript. The PLO, which had tried to distance itself from the hijackers by calling attention to its diplomatic efforts in resolving the matter, was now publicly implicated in the affair.[25]

In the cat and mouse game of intelligence, special electronic and technological units like 8200 spend their existence exhaustively inventing new and ingenious ways to intercept enemy transmissions and decipher and analyze signal communications however they were transmitted and from wherever they originated. From its earliest days, the insular world of electronic intelligence was kept in almost complete secrecy. Due to the clandestine nature of intelligence, the unit could not make large acquisitions, and instead it came to rely on developing its own technologies and solutions, customized and suited to the unique challenges of fighting terrorism and a war that at times seems endless. The result has been a kind of innovation engine that has driven the development of some of the most advanced commercial technologies in a number of areas that would later find applications in the civilian world, such as the areas of wireless telecommunications, encryption, search engines, firewalls, data security, data and voice compression, streaming technology, DSP chips, and virtual networks, to name a few.

From the beginning, faced with a host of unique geopolitical challenges, Israel's founding fathers knew it would have to depend on knowledge, cunning, and imagination to sustain the nation. This feverish environment gave birth to military and intelligence units like 8200, which would wage an unending war. The byproduct of unceasing security and defense had also become an engine for ingenuity

From the beginning, faced with a host of unique geopolitical challenges, Israel's founding fathers knew it would have to depend on knowledge, cunning, and imagination to sustain the nation. This feverish environment gave birth to military and intelligence units like 8200, which would wage an unending war. The byproduct of unceasing security and defense had also become an engine for ingenuity that would permeate outside of the tiny country.

that would permeate outside of the tiny country. These individuals, indelibly trained in the notion that innovation serves as a fundamental pillar of national security, would go on to help establish an entire high-tech industry as civilians. The impact of this industry would stretch beyond the narrow geographical borders of Israel.

2 In the Beginning...

British Mandate Palestine, 1948...

In the spring of 1948, nearly 30 years after its inception, the British Mandate over Palestine had ended. Battered and weary from ruling over the antagonistic and increasingly bloody aspirations of Zionism and Arab nationalism, and unable to implement a solution satisfactory to either side, the British finally gave up. On the morning of May 14, the last vestiges of British civil and military authority withdrew from their remaining positions in this ancient land. The Union Jack, flying over Jerusalem, was lowered for the last time. And at 4:00 in the afternoon, David Ben-Gurion stood under a large photograph of Theodore Herzl, the founder of modern Zionism, and announced the establishment of a Jewish homeland in Palestine. Except for Jerusalem, which was without electricity at the time,[1] the entire Jewish population listened as the soon-to-be Israeli prime minister broadcast his proclamation of the new state. "By virtue of our national and intrinsic right," he announced from the Tel Aviv Museum on the grand tree-lined promenade of Rothschild Boulevard, "and on the strength of the resolution of the United Nations General Assembly, we hereby declare the establishment of a Jewish state in Palestine, which shall be known as the State of Israel."[2]

17

Egyptian air raids over Israel began that night. The following day, the Arab armies of Syria, Transjordan, Iraq, and Lebanon joined Egypt in invading the new Jewish state. It was never a contest of equals. Vastly outnumbered, Israel's ragged army with little in the way of heavy weapons, artillery, armored vehicles, or planes faced the better-armed, combined attack of their British Arab Legion-trained neighbors. Over time, many of the fine points of the war have been exhaustively argued, but in the end the fledgling Israeli army exploited its significantly smaller numbers into a quick, flexible, and disciplined group of fighters to beat back the disorganized, decentralized mass of Arab armed forces. In short, the Israelis improvised.

During the battle of Jerusalem, for one, the Jewish forces drove Iraqi troops from the western part of the city using a homemade mortar called the *Davidka*. Named after David Leibovitz, the engineer who built it, the Davidka possessed a roar that was worse than its ability to inflict any real damage. The primitive gun wasn't rifled, so when it fired off shells, they were uselessly inaccurate. What the Davidka could do was to burst in the air with a terrifying thunder. Only a handful were built. The Israelis would mount them on a vehicle, fire off a few rounds, and then transport them to another location, creating the illusion that there were many of these powerful mortars ringing the city. The bluff worked, and the strategy was repeated in the northern town of Safed and the coastal city of Tel Aviv. The boom so frightened the Arabs that they beat a hasty retreat and were unaware that they were victims of nothing more than a grand noisemaker.

The war lasted nearly eight months, punctuated by long periods of intense fighting and temporary cease-fires. By the time the hostilities finally ended, Israel had not only defended the 5,600 square miles allotted to it under the United Nations Partition Plan—which the Arabs had rejected a year earlier—but they had also conquered another 2,500 square miles in the Negev and western Galilee. Against near-impossible odds, the Israelis had won a remarkable victory. It came at a steep and bloody price. More than 6,000 people, 1 percent of the Jewish population, were killed in the fighting,[3] and the battle they had just concluded had really only just begun.

Looking at maps delineating the region over time, there appears not so much a defined state as a geographical tangle of borders, partitions, enclaves, and passageways outlining and separating the various ruling entities, tribes, and populations. The 1948 map, carved out of what the Israelis refer to as the War of Independence—and the Arabs call *al Nakba*, the catastrophe— was no different. Jerusalem was a city divided. The Israelis ruled over the western part of the city, and the Jordanians annexed the eastern half, including the Old City and its holy sites as well as all of the West Bank to the Jordan River. Egypt held the sandy ribbon of land called the Gaza Strip. An Arab Palestine was never established. The Palestinians who fled the battle zones, either by force or voluntarily, became refugees in Arab lands or remained inside the cease-fire lines as Israeli Arabs. The newly demarcated frontiers would remain in dispute for decades. The animosity they would engender would fuel a twofold legacy for the Israelis: an unceasing need for defense and vigilant innovation in which to maintain it.

For such a highly contested piece of real estate, the country now called Israel was hardly much of a prize. Its precarious security was only one among many piercing and immediate issues. Barren and impoverished, with a paucity of natural resources, the small slice of land was hemmed in by the Mediterranean Sea on one side and hostile Arab neighbors on the other. Exhausted by war and neglect, the place had yet to recover from the four centuries spent as a dreary backwater in the disintegrating Ottoman Empire. During this period, the Ottoman Turks cut down entire forests to build a railway into the Arabian Desert, emptying the region of vital timber and vegetation, and eventually desiccating the soil. Villages were laid to waste and citrus groves destroyed. Hunting expeditions nearly blasted indigenous wildlife, such as ibex and antelope, into extinction. By the time the first wave of Jewish settlers arrived in the 1800s, it was little more than a malarial swamp in the north and a desert dustbowl in the south.

There is a sepia-toned archival photograph taken sometime after the founding of Tel Aviv in 1909 depicting a bleak stretch of uninhabited sand dune north of the Jaffa port. Gathered there and seemingly out of place, dressed in their buttoned-up formal suits and hats despite the stifling Mediterranean heat, is an odd collection of new European arrivals about to draw lots for the plots on which they will build their new homes. This group of idealists, poor in practically every conceivable measure, did not, it would appear, suffer a poverty of imagination. At an accelerated pace, the new arrivals transformed this desolate sandbox into a thriving modern city—a center of culture, education, and business. The International building style influenced by the Bauhaus school and others soon overtook the sand dunes, as did a seaside promenade lined with luxury hotels and cafés. In time, glass high-rises would house Israel's world-class diamond exchange. Later, industrial parks—miniature Silicon Valleys—would emerge, transforming Israel into a high-tech economy. For Israelis, the creation of the state was a quantum leap forward, and Tel Aviv represented the forward march toward progress and modernity.

Israel was based on an idea: Zionism—a utopian-socialist idea in which the state would be founded by Jews from all over the world who sought refuge in their historic homeland. Put forth in the Balfour Declaration in 1917, it was an answer to the problems arising from 2,000 years of exile. It was a solution to the past, and Israelis would become seasoned problem solvers. The first wave of Jewish settlers, called the *Yishuv*, left their homes in Russia and Eastern Europe in the 1800s and lit out for Palestine. They established agricultural communities in Rishon Lezion, Rosh Pina, and Zikhron Ya'akov. They joined a smattering of Jews who had lived in the holy cities of Jerusalem, Hebron, Safed, and Tiberias and the desert Bedouins and Arabs who lived mostly in villages spread across the landscape. Motivated by ideology, these early pioneers were consumed with the notion of national fulfillment. Many decided that the difficult life that they now faced was preferable to what they left behind. Others did not. Between 1904 and 1914, several thousand returned to Europe or immigrated to America within a few years of their arrival.

From the outset, the Israelis faced daunting challenges at every possible turn in geography, sustainability, boycotts, embargoes, and security. They ran against the near-impossible odds that informed the rhythm of life there. The nation of Israel had not existed for thousands of years; modern Israelis had to reinvent it. And they did, simultaneously developing the country and defending it under massive economic burdens. Israel was little more than an immigrant encampment in the guise of a modern nation struggling to build itself up out of very little. Settlers drained swamps and reforested the land, built roads, and set up educational and government systems. They revived a moribund language—Hebrew—turning it into a modern living tongue. Israeli author Amos Oz once described the new nation as "...the state of Israel: a refugee camp thrown together in a hurry. A place of wet paint. Remnants of foreign ways from Marrakesh, Warsaw and Bucharest and the godforsaken shtetls drying in the sun among the sand in the wretched new housing developments."[4]

Unlike many of their neighbors, the Israelis couldn't simply drill underground for oil; they had to reach above ground, tapping their primary resource: brainpower. From their earliest days as citizens of the new state, the Israelis combined science with the concept of nation-building. This, of course, also set the foundation for self-sufficiency and significant breakthroughs. In Israel, hardship, defense, and innovation would be locked in a fateful and seamless embrace.

In its short history, Israel would absorb continuous waves of immigrants: Russian émigrés fleeing the privations and horrors of life in the Pale; European Jews escaping the Nazis; Holocaust survivors abandoning what was left of their communities; Ethiopians, isolated for centuries, rescued in secret from squalor and a brutal regime; Latin American Jews leaving economic hardship and military dictatorships; and refugees from Egypt, Iraq, Yemen, and Syria, who were cast out as their host countries and neighbors to Israel weren't exactly thrilled at the prospect of the new

Jewish state next door. Added to this assortment was an infusion of immigrants from relatively well-off situations in Europe and North America. It became a melting pot like the United States, except that Israel would have to integrate large numbers of newcomers that would constantly shift the population balance, challenging the resources of an already stretched society. Between 1948 and 1951, the population nearly doubled with the influx of some 700,000 people. In the 1990s, almost one million people arrived from the former Soviet Union.[5] The sounds of this immigrant nation gathered from more than six dozen countries are clearly audible. Israel hums like a linguistic symphony, where Russian, English, Arabic, French, Spanish, and many other languages can be heard switching back and forth into Hebrew.

Immigration was the crank that turned the wheel of Israeli society, evolving into a kind of methodical chaos. The constant flow of immigration meant a culture in constant movement. This collection of different skills, backgrounds, and abilities gave rise to a vibrant mosaic of influences. Indeed, Golda Meir, who was Israel's prime minister from 1969 to 1974, was born in Kiev, Russia, grew up in Milwaukee, Wisconsin, and came to British Mandate Palestine in 1921. Israel's eighth prime minister, Moshe Katsav (elected in 2000), was born in Byzad, Iran, in 1945 and immigrated to Israel six years later. In Israel, diversity became an asset, producing an outpouring of viewpoints and ideas. Jews from Arab lands would make a number of contributions, including those to Israel's intelligence capabilities; Russian engineers would help advance Israeli technological output; and Europeans and North Americans would supply know-how in scores of areas, including building the country and fomenting ties with the countries they left. This jumble forged a brashness—an innate sense of inventiveness based on a highly developed survival mechanism.

An intense contraction of time characterizes Israel. The sense of hurriedness is pervasive. Its survival has been utterly dependent on its ability to identify problems and to adapt and change quickly. History and geography have served only to heighten this sense of urgency and forged a deeply short-term outlook. Israelis talk fast. And they drive as if there is no tomorrow. Indeed, a paradox in a country not short on paradoxes is that more Israelis died in traffic accidents during the intifada in the year 2002 than they did from terrorist attacks.[6] Yet, for all its impressive accomplishments, the ability to develop a multinational company or the kind of large-scale project that is reliant upon long-term discipline is not at the top of the list.

Israel is a vibrant, difficult place. Continuously at war, it battles terrorism from without and a set of internal tensions from within: ethnic strife, social gaps, and religious-secular fissures that would tear apart most societies. At the same time, the country is in possession of an economy and a political system that appears on the verge of sinking under the weight of itself at any moment. This synthesis of dilemmas created a nation of problem-solvers and short-cutters. If a roadblock presented itself, it was not enough to remove it or find a way around it—the roadblock problem had to be solved in multiple ways and with multiple means. Sometimes this led to great achievements, and other times it simply caused problems: slipshod building, political miscalculations, economic misfires, and the unfortunate preference for expediency over pragmatism, to name a few. However, it always led to something new. Nothing is sacred here; everything is open to question and upturning. After all, this is a place where a group of Israelis and their Palestinian counterparts, who were all extremely dissatisfied with the slow progress of their respective governments in regards to the peace process, flew to Geneva, Switzerland, in 2003 and hammered out an accord among themselves, outlining a draft of permanent status between the two nations.[7] There is always room for improvement. A powerful dynamism of invention, ideology, and pluralism has taken root. Israelis like to point out that this is a place where the impossible is a way of life. A place described by writer Ephraim Kishon as "a country where nobody expects miracles, but everybody takes them for granted."[8]

Shimon Peres is one of Israel's most durable politicians, a visionary thinker and a crucial architect in the country's development. He arrived in pre-state Israel in 1934 at age 11, an émigré from Wolozyn, Poland. Perhaps the only visible mark left from his early years is his still detectable Polish accent. From the start, Peres developed a strongly held conviction that Israel's future depended upon its intellectual capital and the inventive application of science and technology. "Now somebody once said that the Jewish people have had more history than geography, and as a young man I thought, 'How do you compensate for that?' " Peres ruminated in his office in Tel Aviv on a sunny Friday morning, three days after his Labor Party was trounced in the national elections in January 2003. Asked to discuss the source of Israeli innovation, the silver-haired elder statesmen started with himself. With the Nobel Peace prize that he was awarded in 1994 and shared with the late Prime Minister Yitzhak Rabin and Palestinian Chairman Yassir Arafat displayed behind him, he explained, "We have to rebalance and reconcile history and geography. I thought we could compensate for geography with technology. I thought it was here that lies the real compensation for our smallness as a people and the smallness of our land."

Peres has held practically every high-level office of the state: defense minister, foreign minister, finance minister, and prime minister (twice). Unlike the rough-around-the-edges generals who traditionally form the core of the political elite, Peres comes across more like a European scholar. Erudite, he wears nice suits and keeps a mountain of books waiting to be read on his desk. Moreover, he never served in the military. Instead, tapped by his mentor David Ben-Gurion at age 27, he masterminded a number of extensive arms deals with France, Germany, and the United States in the early war-torn years of the state. In fact, Peres, a man now indelibly identified with the peace process, was largely responsible for creating the country's fledgling defense forces. Israel would become a major military power in large part because of a number of arms acquisitions, joint weapons research, and production deals Peres hatched in the early years of statehood.

Even a short list of Peres's contributions and initiatives is impressive. Always the dreamer, he saw potential where others did not. In 1951, he convinced Ben-Gurion that Israel, though lacking in infrastructure and financially strapped, could develop its own aircraft industry. They paid a visit to Burbank, California, to see Peres's old friend, Al Schwimmer, who ran an aircraft maintenance business. A year earlier, Schwimmer had been convicted, fined $10,000, and had his U.S. citizenship revoked for purchasing the surplus U.S. military planes and weapons that helped secure Israel's independence in 1948.[9] "I was [considered] a laughingstock," he said. However, he convinced Ben-Gurion "why not Israel?" Schwimmer came back to Israel, and together they helped found what eventually became Israel Aircraft Industries (IAI). At first a refurbisher of old planes, IAI would later develop fighter jets and commercial aircraft, and its subsidiaries would develop an impressive scope of airborne electronic warfare systems. Today it is the country's largest employer, with $2 billion in annual revenue—80 percent of which comes from exports.[10] Despite overwhelming odds and opposition, Peres orchestrated the construction of a nuclear reactor near the southern Negev desert town of Dimona in 1958, bringing this small and economically poor country a nuclear deterrent. "There are no small lands," he said, "only small minds." And pleased with his turn of phrase, he wrote it down in a small leather-bound notebook, to remember later.

Now in his eighth decade, Peres's work is far from finished. He negotiated the Oslo peace accords with the Palestinians, but the stretch of violence of the second intifada has practically rendered his dream of a "New Middle East," one of harmony and free trade between Israel and its Arab neighbors, at best an anachronism and at worst a remote fantasy. At the moment, Peres may be more popular abroad than at home, and the grasp of his renewed political leadership may appear elusive, but his vision today is not so different from the one he held when he first preached the necessity of the "scientification of the country." Israel is a country that will and must survive on its innovations. "Israel is a producer of ideas, and the world is poor in ideas," he explained, and then leaned forward into his oversized wooden desk and presented a few ideas of his own. At the top of his list is nanotechnology, the emerging field that draws on the disciplines of biochemistry, physics, materials science, and electrical engineering to create apparatuses the size of molecules. "We can produce a computer unit that fits on the head of a pin. Forty-five years ago I thought about nuclear power; now I think about nanotechnology." He also outlined a world 10 years in the future in which the global war on terror will stimulate a need for new kinds of weapons. "We will be able to paralyze communication systems with invisible anti-communication instruments." Rounding out his list of problems to be tackled is the desalination of the oceans and, of course, peace.

If there is one thing that Israelis do not lack, it is problems. At the hub of Peres's discussion was simply that circumstances have forced Israel to come up with a host of solutions to survive. Peres shrugged, "We don't have anywhere else to turn. We have no land, no water, so what else are we going to do? Our compass in society is to the west but we don't have the same resources. Instead we have a lot of enemies." In his anecdotal style, Peres went on to recount the story of the young boy who went on to win the Nobel Prize. "Each day after school his mother said to him, 'Did you ask a good question today?' This is at the heart of why we are good problem-solvers."

Besides, he said, change and innovation are a deeply ingrained part of the Israeli psyche. "Generally, the Jewish people are never satisfied with their existing situation," Peres continued. "Israel was a nonconforming nation all the time, from the days of Moses and Abraham. Whatever they got their hands on they wanted to reform. Even these days when we buy a piece of equipment in America, we want to improve it. There is this joke I like about the Israeli translator who translated Chekov from Russian into Hebrew. When he was done he presented the book, saying, 'Here is Chekov, translated and improved.' " Peres laughed, "That is generally our nature. We are translating and improving."

In essence, in many ways Zionism translated European concepts, and adapted and improved upon life in the diaspora in the form of a new enterprise: nation-building. The Jews of Palestine pioneered new techniques in a number of areas: they created a national health and education system, and they developed a socialist economy. And hand in glove with these new enterprises they built a people's army, the *Haganah,* with which they defended themselves. One of the first enterprises was the agricultural collective, known as the *kibbutz.* Based on socialist principles, it was a socio-economic innovation in communal living. Russian-born immigrants in the Jordan Valley, where the Sea of Galilee receives the Jordan River, founded the first, Kibbutz Daganya, in 1909. Located at strategic outposts, they helped shape the borders of the new state and provided a way to merge scarce resources and mobilize a workforce. They played a significant role in reclaiming the land, defending against Arab enemies, and absorbing immigrants.

In response to harsh landscapes and a shortage of everything from arable land to water, the kibbutzim spawned a number of important developments of their own. Coming up with new methods in agriculture based on technology and science, the kibbutzim converted barren fields into green, lush, and abundantly productive land. With neither the space nor the water to produce large quantities of crops, the kibbutzniks, those who work in a kibbutz, devised ways to create more out of very little. They developed strains of fruits and vegetables with longer shelf lives than previously existed, and they learned to breed cows that produced the highest milk yields and chickens that laid the largest quantities of eggs possible.

The oft-quoted cliché of making the desert bloom owes a debt of gratitude to Kibbutz Hatzerim, which created an opening in the harsh and unforgiving ecosystem of the desert that covers more than half of the country. In the early 1960s the kibbutz developed the system of drip irrigation. Located in the Negev Desert near the city of Be'er Sheva, it is an area where the severe conditions of dry climate, poor water resources, low rainfall, and dry soil with high saline content conspire to render traditional irrigation methods ineffective. Out of necessity, members of the kibbutz created a system based on a network of pipes that uses small amounts of water that are absorbed into the soil. The early and simple systems were based on a timeclock, but over time they came to develop an expanding line of advanced irrigation systems and products based on the same principle. Drip irrigation became a mainstay in Israeli agriculture, and in 1965 the members of Hatzerim founded a company, Netafim, to market and develop the systems abroad. By 2001, Netafim had sold 30 billion drippers to more than 100 countries, bringing the kibbutz total sales of $250 million.[11]

While the kibbutz movement always represented only a small percentage of Israeli society, and its numbers continue to dwindle, its ethos formed an influential basis of a particular way of turning adversity into a virtue. In the same vein, Israel's significant talent pool of scientists and engineers proved remarkably imaginative. They found incredibly resourceful ways of mining and utilizing minerals from the Dead Sea, which at 1,300 feet below sea level is the lowest spot on the planet. They harnessed the sun, becoming world leaders in solar energy. In 1983, they built one of the largest solar ponds in the world, which ran a turbine-powered 5-megawatt powerplant on the shores of the Dead Sea. Even as early as 1954, the Weizmann Institute of Science in Rehovot built one of the world's first electronic computers, the WEIZAC. It was used to carry out complex mathematical computations, one of which predicted the exact location of an amphidromic point, the spot at which high and low ocean tides never occur.[12]

In time, this small country would command a long list of accomplishments (in all fields—from agriculture to science to medicine to technology) disproportionate to its size and population. Drawn by the amount of immense talent, a number of big U.S. companies have set up extensive research centers in Israel. Motorola has one of its largest development centers outside of the United States in Israel, and Intel's Israeli subsidiary created a number of computer chips, including the high-speed Centrino mobile technology processor. Ehud Avner, who spent 23 years as a field security officer in the Israeli army before going on to found his own IT security consultancy, said the following on the subject:

We have a relational advantage. We have relatively
advanced science, a well-educated people relative to any
other country with no land, water, natural resources, or
oil. The land is not going to get any bigger, and we are not
going to have more rain than we have now. Do we breed
new types of tomatoes or develop a treatment of seawater
because we love it? No, we have no other choice, and we
should do it. What we can do is use our brains and
develop. That's what you can see in Israel. What is Israel's
contribution to society? Knowledge. We can bring knowledge to new heights. We have nothing else except knowledge in many subjects.

The pursuit of knowledge and education is fundamental to
Israeli society. It is an extension of the importance that Judaism
has traditionally attached to learning. This preoccupation with
education has produced and developed world-class institutions
of higher learning and research centers. Twenty percent of
Israel's workforce has university degrees. Per capita, Israel pub-
lishes the most scientific papers in the world (109 per 10,000),
and its citizens are said to buy the most books, read the most
newspapers, and listen to the most radio and TV news broadcasts.[13] Israelis have an enduring love affair with gadgetry and
adopting new technology. Its population has one of the world's
largest penetrations in mobile phone and personal computer
ownership. Israel has more engineers per capita (135 per
10,000) than any other nation (the United States has 85 per
10,000).[14] The country spends 4.2 percent of its gross domestic
product (GDP) on civilian research and development. By contrast, the average Organization for Economic Cooperation and
Development (OECD) country spends 1.9 percent (Sweden is at
3.6 percent and Japan at 3 percent).[15]

In some five decades after the country was founded, Israel
placed fifth (behind the United States, Finland, Singapore, and
Sweden) in the World Economic Forum Economic Creativity
Index, a measure of technological innovations and conditions
for startup activity. At the peak of the new economy in the year
2000, this nation with a population of six million had roughly

4,000 startups (ranking second after Silicon Valley) and trailed only the United States and Canada in the number of companies listed on NASDAQ. Battered by the intifada and a global economy in decline, those numbers have contracted, but the number of new ideas has not. Israelis have proved resilient in their capacity to manage with little capital in times of crisis, to react quickly, to adapt to a constantly changing environment, and to shift focus accordingly.

A case in point is Gennadi Finkelshtain, who arrived in Israel in 1990 as part of the massive wave of Soviet immigration that took place in the 1990s. Trained in the Soviet Union as a power engineer, Finkelshtain spoke Russian and French, and was virtually unemployable in his new country. "I had limitations, I came from Russia, I had an accent, I didn't know Hebrew or English, and I didn't know business," he explained from his windowless basement lab in the industrial town of Yehud, outside of Tel Aviv. "I worked at many manual jobs. I worked as a shepherd for a few months and as a construction worker for 18 months." Not that he let that stop him. Later, he found work as an engineer at the Hadera Power Station and as a production manager at a kibbutz factory.

Finkelshtain had dreams, and he dreamed big. He wanted to develop a clean, efficient technology that didn't use oil. "I decided to establish a fuel cell business. Nobody believed in a fuel cell company created in Israel because there was no knowledge or tradition of the technology in such a small country." Despite the fact that major car companies and governments had been working on the very same thing for decades, Finkelshtain remained undeterred. Instead of following the route of others and going big, the poorly funded Finkelshtain decided to go small, developing portable fuel cells for electrical devices like mobile phones and laptops.

Eight years after arriving in Israel, he brought in other Russian immigrant engineers, and with a small investment they established More Energy, which became a wholly owned subsidiary of Medis Technologies. Unlike most fuel-cell developers that use hydrogen, Medis came up with a proprietary direct liquid methanol fuel cell, which Finkelshtain unveiled at a fuel-cell conference in Tokyo in 2001. Today, Israel Aircraft Industries has a 22 percent stake in Medis, and Finkelshtain is confident that by 2005 Medis will produce a fuel-cell charger for between $20 and $25 that can power 8 to 12 hours worth of energy. According to Finkelshtain, Medis is in discussion with a number of companies, including General Dynamics, for military applications. And Finkelshtain, who taught himself English and Hebrew, no longer works in construction.

Then there are the 22-year-old identical twins Michael and Alex Bronstein, from the northern city of Haifa, who made headlines in 2002 because the brothers, both studying for their master's degrees in electrical engineering at the Technion University, had developed a highly touted facial recognition technology that potentially can be used for security at airports and other high-risk installations. It began when their professor challenged them to come up with a system that could differentiate between their faces. In exchange, he would give them a 100 percent in his computer science course. The pair's professor and another student had already come up with the algorithms necessary, and the Bronsteins built a three-dimensional scanner that checks and records the surfaces of the face by light patterns and storing the raw information as a 3-D image. The system uses mathematical algorithms, measuring the distances between several points on the face's surface. Reconstructed as straight lines in 3-D configurations, the new image is built on a very specific mathematical calculation that mimics the unique facial signature of an individual and is apparently more accurate than current systems that are based on two-dimensional images. The Bronsteins have already registered for a patent in the United States.[16]

Perhaps most crucial to understanding the Israeli penchant for innovation and the entrepreneurial spirit is to recognize that Israelis have developed a highly evolved ability to outwit the system. "This is a culture that is trying to circumvent; it does not accept rules and regulations," explained David Rubin. "This is what being an entrepreneur is all about." Rubin, the son of famed Israeli painter Rueven Rubin and a former systems analyst, spent three years in the late 1990s as his country's economic minister to North America. Rubin began by comparing Israel to a country that is almost certainly its complete opposite in culture and mentality: Japan. "The Japanese excel where Israel fails—in discipline. They do everything by the book. For many years Israel had no book. In recent years people have said that we need a book. Now we have a book but we don't read it." To clarify his point, Rubin recalled a visit to South Africa. "I was driving on the highway between Johannesburg and Pretoria with a South African driver. He was going 50 miles an hour, and the highway was empty. I asked him, 'Why are you going so slow?' And he said, 'That's the speed limit.' I said to him, 'So what?' This is the Israeli point of view. First figure out if the law is good or bad; we don't circumvent all laws, only those that are bad, and we figure a way to get around them."

Honed by centuries of living as minorities in the diaspora where they were subject to the vagaries and strictures under the governments of those countries they lived in, Israelis developed all sorts of methods to get around these limits. During the Mandate, the Jews found myriad ways to evade the British and defend themselves against the Arabs. There are hundreds of stories in which fighting units had no guns or food or uniforms and their commanders would tell them to go get them. They would, of course, return in a few hours with the requested items. They had no procedures to do so—they either stole them, borrowed them, or convinced people to part with them. This would set the stage for the kinds of activities for which the IDF and its intelligence apparatuses would become famous. In one classic early operation, an Austrian Jew hid 60 pistols loaded with bullets in concrete grinding stones and sent them to port in Beirut, where they were transferred by carts to Kibbutz Kfar Giladi in the north. After they arrived, members of the kibbutz broke open the stones, uncovered the weapons, and sent them to members of the Haganah.[17]

Nowhere was this ingenuity more evident than in the enormous amount of energy that was invested in resisting the British White Paper, which strictly limited Jewish immigration to Palestine during the Mandate. In response, the Jews developed underground networks that organized a campaign to rescue illegal immigrants, called the *bricha*, and bring them to Palestine. What stood between boatloads of *bricha* and Palestine were thousands of British naval troops who patrolled the coast. In order to get around them, the Haganah ran covert intelligence operations to learn of British interception plans. Armed with information lifted by monitoring radio transmissions between the police and British Criminal Investigations Department Headquarters and between coast guard stations and navy patrols, they ran elaborate schemes of distraction. This allowed several boatloads of illegals to slip through the British cordon. While not always successful, during the autumn and winter of 1945–1946, 4,000 refugees landed in Palestine.[18]

Although a fledgling country with limited means and no strategic depth, Israel's intelligence became a fine art. Early on, rudimentary but highly effective wiretapping became an essential tool. Later, eavesdropping would become a sophisticated and highly technological asset. The *Shai*, the precursor of today's *Mossad* intelligence agency, set up a comprehensive wire-tapping operation on phone conversations coming in from Amman, Damascus, and Beirut between British officials and Arab leaders, and they even tracked the British government's own tapping of leading Arab and Jewish Agency officials. In one instance, they intercepted information of an incoming convoy of arms and ammunition from Beirut in March 1948. As a result, the convoy was ambushed and its leader Muhammad ibn Hammad al Huneiti, the commander of the Haifa Arab militia, was killed.[19]

Unlike most western cultures (like those in America or Germany) or a country like Japan, where citizens grow up learning their place in the system, Israelis learn how to beat the system. Buky Carmeli spent almost two decades in unit 8200. He left in 1998 to found his own company, Spearhead Technology. On a white board in his office in the industrial zone of Rosh Ha'ayan north of Tel Aviv, he made a crude graphic of lines going from a to b to c to z. "People in America follow this system," he said, pointing to the letters on the board. "They go from a to b, and if they don't stop they go all the way to z. Israel is a culture in which we educate our kids by encouraging them to be very creative. To find different solutions to the same problem." Then he marks up the straight-line path from a to z with lines jutting from different directions. "What we really encourage is creativity, and that starts in the initial feedback stage. We don't give feedback on progress; we don't see it as a target but a tool. When a kid gets to z we say, 'Well done,' and when another kid gets to z another way, we say, 'Wow.' "

Innovation is not a science of discipline. It flies in the face of conventional wisdom. It is messy, flourishing in an environment of chaos and paradox. It feeds on risk and boldness, diversity and instability, and constant movement and change. It measures success in its own way. It discounts specializing and favors the wide spectrum

> *Innovation is not a science of discipline. It flies in the face of conventional wisdom. It is messy, flourishing in an environment of chaos and paradox. It feeds on risk and boldness, diversity and instability, and constant movement and change.*

of diversity. It encourages new ideas even if they fail. Indeed, it needs failure. It rejects the status quo, embracing change. The wrong answer is not frowned upon because it could lead to the right answer or a new spectrum of getting to a right answer or a different one altogether. Perhaps through no divine plan of its own, this is the kind of environment in which Israel finds itself: a country that carved out for itself an advantage out of constant turmoil and disadvantages. "To be bold is built into our heritage,"

Major General Isaac Ben Israel, the retired head of MAFAT, the directorate of the IDF's and Ministry of Defense's research and development branch, explained. "And innovation is being bold. It is being daring and not afraid of change, and then being able to change. This is what Israel is based on."

That is to say, Israel became a place in which its turbulent past would be supplanted by a tumultuous present. It is a place not without its shortcomings, but a place where the impossible is viewed as a problem to be solved, born of necessity and the need to survive.

3 Security Is the Mother of Invention

Southern Tel Aviv, February 6, 2003...

A month after a double suicide bombing savagely disrupted six weeks of relative quiet—killing 23 people and wounding another 120 near Tel Aviv's old central bus station—Israel's security forces closed off a busy section of Highway 57 that stretches between the coastal city of Netanya and the West Bank town of Nablus. On high alert, the army had received what it called "very accurate" intelligence reports warning of possible suicide bombers in the area, and the IDF closed in, setting up a surprise roadblock near the village of Talusa, just north of Nablus. Caught in the clot of traffic that ensnared travelers for hours late into that Thursday afternoon was a taxi carrying five Palestinian passengers from the West Bank into Israel. Before they got there, soldiers from the Haruv battalion ordered the taxi to stop. Two of the men inside were, according to the Israelis, wanted members of the militant group Islamic Jihad en route to carry out a terrorist attack inside of Israel.[1]

Shin Bet, Israel's formidable internal security apparatus, also known as the *Shabak*, took over from there. The captured militants, later identified as Shadi Bahalul and Tareq Baslat,[2] were turned over for interrogation. That evening, police uncovered an explosive belt hidden in the toilet of a mosque in the Israeli-Arab town of Taibeh, just inside the Green Line that separates Israel from the West Bank. In general, suicide bombers conceal belts or vests packed with explosives hooked up to a detonator under their clothing to avoid detection as they approach their designated targets. This belt, thought to belong to the two men apprehended hours earlier, never made it to its intended target. It was removed and detonated by police bomb squad sappers. In doing so, an attack thought to be only one or two days away was prevented.[3]

That Thursday in February was not a good day for would-be suicide bombers. In the morning, security forces moved into the al-Aida refugee camp near Bethlehem and arrested Ihab Issa al-Saizer Omar, who was allegedly planning to carry out a suicide attack against Israel. And in Bethlehem, IDF special forces arrested a man who was reported as a senior *Tanzim* commander, one of the fugitives who was said to have barricaded himself inside the Church of the Nativity the previous March.[4] The Tanzim is the armed wing of the *Fatah*, the largest faction of the PLO, headed by Yassir Arafat, and this suspect was wanted by Israeli authorities for his alleged participation in assisting Tanzim suicide bombers, including one who blew up a bus in Jerusalem a year earlier. That Thursday was just one day of one week of many months in which Israeli authorities were trying to stay one step ahead of danger and catastrophe.

During 43 months of the ongoing intifada that began in September 2000, Israel was on the receiving end of some 111 terrorist attacks—specifically, suicide bombers.[5] The tactic of suicide bombs became a regular form of terror against the Israelis starting in the mid-1990s. However, during the period of this intifada, suicide bombings had become a pervasive form of warfare, responsible for killing 942 Israelis and wounding hundreds more.[6] (Israeli military reprisals had claimed more than 2,900 Palestinian lives.)[7] Nowhere in Israel felt safe. A visit to the local café or shopping mall, or a ride on a public bus, could be lethal.

In particular, the year 2002 marked a grim season of death in Israel. Barely a week went by without the shrill sirens of

ambulances piercing the air on their way to some new yet eerily
familiar scene of torn limbs and twisted metal. In the month of
March alone, there were 12 attacks. Ten people were killed and
50 injured in one instance when a terrorist pulled the trigger on
himself next to a group of women waiting with their baby car-
riages for their husbands to leave a synagogue after a bar mitz-
vah celebration in Jerusalem. A week later, a suicide bomber
blew himself up at the crowded Moment Café in Jerusalem on a
Saturday night, killing 11 and injuring 54. Eleven days after
that, a suicide bomber blew up a bus traveling from Tel Aviv to
Nazareth, killing 7 and wounding 30. The following day, 3 people were killed and another 86 seriously hurt when a suicide
bomber wore explosives packed with metal spikes and nails and
then detonated himself in the middle of a throng of shoppers on
King George Street in downtown Jerusalem.

Six days later, as 250 people sat down for their Passover
holiday Seder at the Park Hotel in Netanya, a suicide bomber
walked into the banquet hall and blew himself up, killing 29
and injuring 140 others. The bomber, a member of the militant
Islamic group Hamas, was on a list of wanted terrorists whom
Israeli officials had asked the Palestinian Authority to arrest.[8]
Shortly after this episode, which quickly became known as the
Passover Massacre, the IDF launched Operation Defensive
Shield, a massive deployment of tanks and troops into the West
Bank to root out the bomb-makers and their workshops and
disrupt and dismantle the terrorists' infrastructure.

Israeli officials had repeatedly insisted that the Palestinian
Authority crack down on the violence. For their part, the Palestinians insisted that Israel's military actions made it nearly
impossible for them to do so; furthermore, to dismantle the
militant groups would be to invite civil war. Unimpressed with
the Palestinian Authority's progress, the IDF took matters into
its own hands. It brought the war into the Palestinian territories, sealing borders, arresting militants and demolishing the
homes of their families, placing strangulating curfews on them,
and sending tanks and dropping covert special-ops units into
the West Bank and later the Gaza Strip. More controversially,

the Israelis had stepped up their policy of killing militants they held responsible for suicide bombings and terrorist attacks against their citizens. This was a tactic they had deployed over the years as a weapon in extremely specialized cases, but it had steadily increased as a strategy during this period. During the three-and-a-half-year stretch of the intifada, it was reported that the Israelis had assassinated more than 100 Palestinian militants.[9] While the Israeli operations did little to incur international sympathy or convert the motivation of would-be Palestinian terrorists, the Israelis contended that they dramatically reduced the number of attacks on Israel.

In the ebb and flow of terror, there began a relative slide in the number of episodes. As the intifada dragged on during the first four months of 2003, there were *only* five successful suicide attacks, compared to the same period a year earlier when there were four times as many.[10] When one would open the newspaper or listen to a radio or TV broadcast, rather than daily tallies of the dead and wounded from suicide bombers, dominating the news were stories of Israeli helicopter gunships firing into the cars of wanted Hamas leaders or destroying Gaza bomb factories, and of special undercover forces arresting militants. Just past midnight on one Saturday late in January, elite Givati troops, backed by helicopters, were sent on a raid into Gaza City to end rocket and mortar attacks on the Negev and Israeli settlements within the Gaza Strip. Dubbed Hot Iron, the fight lasted well into the morning. When it was over, 13 Palestinians were dead. There were no Israeli casualties.[11]

In Israel's war on terror, it is generally the heavy hardware incursions, the tanks, the gunfire, and the missile strikes that claim the most attention. Yet, it is the nation's proficiency in electronic warfare that has played an important role in the battle. In concert with the nation's intelligence agencies, sophisticated electronic intercepts, monitoring systems, and underground informants have allowed the Israelis to cast a wide net on the Palestinians and to smash terror. As of April 2003, more than 1,100 Palestinians were in jail.[12] Scores of top militants had been hunted down and killed. A season of death had come inside the Palestinian territories as well. Hamas militant Ibrahim Odeh was killed when a bomb was detonated in the headrest of his car. Mohammed Abdel-Al of Islamic Jihad was killed by helicopter gunfire, and Salah Darwazi of the Hamas military wing was killed after four missiles were fired into his car as he drove through Nablus. Dozens more militants met equally brutal, quick, and decisive ends.

As the result of such operations, Palestinian terror cells were kept off-balance and under constant surveillance, and, in essence, were terrorized themselves. That was the intention—to severely hamper their ability to inflict harm. It did slow down the carnage; it did not, however, end it altogether. It could have been worse—a lot worse. According to many, the Israelis were preventing 90 percent of all terrorist attacks on its citizens. In one day alone in February 2003, there were 47 terror alerts, and that was not even considered a record.[13]

According to "Leni," a former member of unit 8200, this was not because of luck: "Let's assume that someone was assassinated. The soldiers who did it know what he looked like, where he is living, what car he is driving, where he is going, and where he is coming from. This information came from somewhere—in real time. We provided the technology that provides them that information." He continued, "Before an operation, you have to make sure it's the right person, and afterwards you must collect information. If you eliminate the head it takes time before it grows a new head, and a lot of information is free and unprotected." In the final analysis, he said, "In 90 percent of the cases a bomb didn't explode, and I know some very proud people within the unit who built the technology that got that information."

It was, however, exactly this kind of work that received unwanted attention at the end of January 2003 when the Israeli newspaper *Ma'ariv* first reported that an 8200 officer identified only as "Lieutenant A" had refused to obey an order. In response to the terrorist attack in Tel Aviv that killed 23 people earlier that same month, the Air Force was given orders to retaliate, bombing targets in Gaza and the West Bank. Lieutenant A, on duty at the 8200 base, was instructed to identify targets for reprisal attacks prior to the aerial assault. One of them was a Fatah office in Nablus. According to the published reports, Lieutenant A objected when he was asked to find out when people would be in the building rather than to provide information about the movements of known individuals. Thinking the operation would result in the unnecessary loss of innocent lives, he told his superiors the operation was illegal and refused to supply the information.[14] In this case, Lieutenant A withheld the information, delaying the operation, and it was eventually scrapped. Soon after, Lieutenant A was court-martialed and transferred to an administrative position.[15]

In the cat and mouse game of terror, prevention, and retaliation, the Israelis have learned that by killing one head of the Hydra, 10 others, less easily detected and more potent than the first, will emerge in its place. It is a seemingly never-ending operation. Just as the Israelis crack down on one particular strategy, the militants continue to up the ante, altering their modus operandi and shifting their strategy. Suicide bombers, generally the province of men, now included young women intent on blowing themselves up and taking many innocent lives with them. In their attempts at avoiding Israeli checkpoints and police patrols, the militants disguised themselves as Israeli soldiers and sometimes even Orthodox Jews. In one instance, a live donkey was laden with explosives to be detonated from a remote control. Following this transgression, People for the Ethical Treatment of Animals, the vocal American animal rights group, rebuked Chairman Arafat in a letter, imploring the Palestinian leader to keep innocent animals out of the conflict (no mention, however, was made about human victims). It was discovered that Hamas was planning on sending an unmanned drone packed with explosives into Israel when the six men preparing it were killed after it exploded prematurely at their home south of Gaza City.[16]

On unceasing military alert of some form or another since the country was founded, Israelis have forged an innate response mechanism to think beyond immediate circumstances and to stay ahead of the next potential strike. The Israelis have been locked in conflict—guerrilla warfare to all-out conventional battle—for more than 50 years. Every new situation presents a problem, and for every problem the Israelis must find some kind of solution. "Our security for the past 50 years is based on solving things we don't know," explained a former high-ranking intelligence officer and tank platoon commander. The result is a reflexive need to think creatively about ways to combat terrorism. Terrorism is a dynamic phenomenon. Terrorists adjust, evolve, and improve their methodology constantly. The tactics deployed against them must be more potent and resourceful. It is this continuous stream of threats that has piloted a number of developments and innovations in military weaponry and technology that have had a far-ranging impact.

On June 6, 1982, Israel invaded Lebanon in response to years of PLO attacks against Israel's northern frontier. Dubbed Operation Peace for Galilee, Israel intended to wipe out the PLO presence in southern Lebanon and set up its own security zone. Twenty years later, the PLO was gone from southern Lebanon, but Hizbollah had filled the vacuum, striking at Israeli troops stationed in the 328-square-mile security zone it carved out to buffer northern Israel from Lebanon. In 1998, Shaul Mofaz, then the vice chief of staff, called a meeting and formed a committee of a few generals representing all IDF divisions. He wanted to change the way the IDF was fighting in southern Lebanon. IDF patrols, with their heavy hardware of weaponry, were easily spotted—as were their movements, which could be monitored for routines, making them extremely vulnerable targets. The Syrian-sponsored Hizbollah took advantage of the craggy and hilly terrain and launched a steady barrage of rockets, ambushes, and roadside bombs against Israeli soldiers. Some 20 to 30 soldiers were killed each year. In the four-year stretch between 1995 and 1999, 123 Israeli soldiers were killed in the security zone.[17]

The committee concluded that a large portion of the problem was intelligence, specifically the ability to anticipate and prevent such attacks. A second committee composed of the various intelligence organizations was formed to find a way to fix it. "The main emphasis was to use technology to clean up Hizbollah and stop its infiltration," Major General (retired) Isaac Ben Israel explained in his Tel Aviv University office, which was filled with models of small missiles and posters of Albert Einstein, one of which reads, "Imagination is more important than knowledge." Shortly after retiring from the military, Ben Israel became a university scholar of the philosophy of Immanuel Kant and of security studies, and at the time of the meeting, he was the head of MAFAT. Something of a legend in the IDF, Ben Israel earned a PhD with degrees in physics, mathematics, and philosophy while moving up the ranks of the IDF, where he served in a number of positions, including the head of Air Force intelligence. In 1972, at the age of 22, while ranked only a second lieutenant, Ben Israel won the nation's highest defense prize, given by the President for developing a bombing system for the Israeli Air Force's newly acquired Phantom F-4 planes.

The IDF committee had gone up to Lebanon to see the situation for themselves. After another meeting on the subject held at intelligence headquarters north of Tel Aviv, Ben Israel was walking down a corridor on his way out to his car when, as he explains:

> I was ambushed by a young captain in the unit. He said, 'Can I show you something interesting? Can you spare me five minutes?' I entered the room, and he said, 'I will show you something that will change your work in southern Lebanon.' He had a vision on the blackboard, not even a prototype, and he described what he believed he could do if only we could give him $5 million to develop his idea. I listened, and I met with the commander and asked

about him. He was a very bright guy with good ideas. The idea was good, but who was going to give him $5 million?

One of the deeply ingrained notions in the Israeli military is the respect for ideas—no matter where they come from. It was a lesson learned from experience, and Ben Israel had his own. After only two years in the operations department of the Air Force, he confronted his superior officer and told him that the Air Force's strategy to destroy Syria's air defense was wrong and, moreover, would lead to disaster. Ben Israel did some mathematical calculations and predicted that under the security concept then in place, the Soviet-installed SA6 surface-to-air missiles (SAMs) would destroy six-and-a-half Israeli planes. His superior told him to write up his theory, and a special meeting was called to discuss it. It was rejected, and one week later, on October 6, 1973, the military forces of Egypt and Syria launched a surprise attack on Yom Kippur. Indeed, one of the first things the Israelis did was to try and destroy Syria's air defense. "We failed, and we lost six aircraft," Ben Israel explained. "One more plane was hit, the navigator jumped out, and the pilot was able to regain control of the plane. In the Air Force we say this was the half in the six-and-a-half planes. I realized that I understood this problem of air defense better than all the generals." He also realized he couldn't leave the Air Force. "I was going to stay on for two more years—I stayed 35."

> *One of the deeply ingrained notions in the Israeli military is the respect for ideas— no matter where they come from.*

Ben Israel took the young captain's idea to experts in MAFAT for discussion. They figured out that they could buy off-the-shelf equipment for $2 million and try out the idea first in a kind of a test lab. "It was an attractive idea; if it worked it would change our capabilities against Hizbollah, and it had universal applications." Ben Israel refused to discuss the details of the system, so as not to compromise Israeli security. (However, there have been analyses suggesting the hand of electronic monitoring and SIGINT at work.)[18] A year later, Prime Minister

Ehud Barak announced that Israel was finally pulling out of southern Lebanon—which it did in May of 2000. Months later, the second intifada began, and the Israelis were presented with a series of blinding and vicious suicide attacks against their civilians. So the IDF shifted gears and turned its attention to a new fight: anticipating and averting terrorist attacks coming from Palestinian militants, and deploying its new systems to do so. By the spring of 2003, Israel's security authorities had foiled more than 150 suicide bombers, catching them and jailing them before they were able to do any damage.[19]

As for the young captain who came up with the concept, today he is a lieutenant colonel.

The lynchpin of Israel's security has been its ability to quickly identify a host of very specific problems and develop solutions for them. The Arrow Missile, one of the most advanced anti-tactical ballistic missile systems in the world, was developed in response to the 39 Iraqi Scud missiles that rained down on Tel Aviv during the first Gulf War in 1991, exposing Israel to a new threat of a long-range missile attack. Largely funded by the United States, Israel Aircraft Industries developed and deployed the Arrow at a cost of about $2 billion with state-of-the-art ballistics and radar systems that can detect and track an incoming missile as far as 300 miles away. It can reach a height of 30 miles, travel at nine times the speed of sound, and intercept as many as 14 missiles at one time.[20] The initial concept for the missile system was developed in a

> *The lynchpin of Israel's security has been its ability to quickly identify a host of very specific problems and develop solutions for them.*

week.[21] It was built and operational in an astonishing 10 years, and the Arrow was deployed and ready on the eve of the second Gulf War in March 2003. However, this time, Saddam Hussein never fired a shot into Israel.

Likewise, the world's first operational Unmanned Aerial Vehicles (UAVs) were the result of the Egyptian deployment of Soviet surface-to-air missiles (SAMs) during the War of Attrition in 1969. The Israeli Air Force, which had laid waste to the Egyptian Air Force only two years earlier in the Six Day War, was suddenly made vulnerable to the advanced Soviet weaponry. An intelligence officer came up with the idea of a pilotless drone equipped with surveillance cameras to pinpoint the SAMs without exposing pilots to ground fire. It was based on remote, radio-controlled airplanes that the officer had once seen in an American toy shop, the kind flown by weekend enthusiasts in public parks. He figured that the model airplane could be reconfigured to hold and operate a 35mm camera with a zoom lens. After some initial skepticism, military intelligence dispatched someone to buy three model toy planes from the United States, each costing $850. They were outfitted with cameras and tested in battle conditions. Their performance was better than imagined.[22]

Moreover, today the UAV is considered one of the most valuable assets of modern warfare, playing a huge role in Israel's fight against terrorism. Israeli UAVs have been deployed to track down suspected Palestinian militants in real time before Apache helicopters come in for the precision kill, hitting their targets in cars, in apartment buildings, or on the ground. Palestinians say that when they hear the distinct lawnmower-like sound of a UAV's engine high above, they know that an Apache helicopter is on its way. During the battle in the Jenin refugee camp in the spring of 2002, UAVs played a major role in reconnaissance and in providing the military with the precise eye it needed to locate its targets in the close quarters of the city.

"We were the first Israeli startup," said Yair Dubester, now general manager of MALAT, the IAI division that designs and manufactures Israel's UAVs. Dubester was part of the first group of engineers who worked on the UAV program in the early

1970s. "We were talented but inexperienced; we made mistakes and took risks. We used the most advanced microprocessor at the time. The way we designed the system was a breakthrough." It was a breakthrough that came about because of very specific requirements. "We had a customer with a real and defined need. First we developed something to go 200 kilometers and send real-time video, then the customer wanted it to stay up longer and take pictures in the day and then pictures at night."[23]

Eventually, the first basic squadron of UAVs advanced from simple monitoring capabilities to provide sophisticated real-time battlefield intelligence day or night and in all types of weather. Built with redundancies, their payloads have complicated avionics systems and data communication systems capable of compressing and decompressing a host of electronic signals, and they can provide electronic capabilities and laser designators for laser-guided weapons. In the future, the size of UAVs will shrink considerably. In the spring of 2004, it was publicly announced that a new miniature UAV with a range of 300 meters, designed to give over-the-hill coverage to ground forces, had been developed. Weighing less than a pound, it is launched from a rifle barrel, holds a digital camera that takes 25 pictures a second, and can be downloaded to a PDA.[24] Also said to be in development is an even smaller drone, the size of a credit card. It is nearly invisible from the ground and undetectable to radar. It carries a miniature camera that transmits images to a laptop or a palm-sized computer and can be launched by hand.[25]

The United States is in possession of Israeli-made Hunter and Pioneer UAVs that it has deployed over the years. For instance, using an Israeli-made UAV during the first Gulf War in 1991, U.S. forces caught sight of a truck in the desert. In real time they followed the truck's route and noticed a hole in the earth in which people were seen passing supplies to men inside. This is how Iraqi bunkers were reportedly discovered along the Kuwaiti border.[26] And later, in 1999, UAVs were used to identify targets and assess bomb damage, and for reconnaissance missions in Kosovo.

Having developed its own fleet of advanced UAVs with lethal payloads, the Americans, on at least one known occasion, apparently emulated the Israelis in terms of counterterrorism strategy. In November 2002, an unmanned American Predator drone equipped with a Hellfire missile blew up a car in Yemen, killing six suspected Al Qaeda operatives, including Qaed Senyan al-Harthi, who the CIA had linked to the bombing of the *USS Cole* two years earlier.[27] U.S.-made UAVs, "the Predator, the Tactical Shadow, and the Global Hawk," explained Dubester, "all have Israeli DNA."

From its earliest days, Israel had the budget of a small country but the defense and military problems of a superpower, and so the Israelis improvised, innovated, and invented their way to security. During World War II, Jewish agents intercepted one of four Sten machine guns in the middle of a transport to Egypt. They examined its parts, made sketches, and came up with a variation using a simple tempered casting of iron from old guns. In the same way, engineers developed a flamethrower, replicating it from a British training manual that had no technical drawings, only photographs.

Israel simply has had no other choice. Smaller than the state of New Jersey, at its widest point (from the Mediterranean Sea to the Jordan River) Israel is only 85 miles across. Lacking strategic depth, a fighter jet can rip across the country in mere minutes. Even on world maps, the six letters it takes to spell out I-S-R-A-E-L are bigger than the country itself and almost always spill out into the Mediterranean. The surrounding 22 Arab countries are 640 times bigger than Israel, and Israel's population is eclipsed by that of the Arab countries 50 to 1. Early on, Israelis realized that, in order to survive, they had to maintain a qualitative edge over their enemies. Israelis learned the hard way that they had to develop that edge to a large extent independently. Technology became a substitute for brute force. Arms embargoes and living under a near-constant state of war catalyzed the country's drive for technological superiority and self-reliance. Shifting battlefields, combatants, and methodology pushed the Israelis to continuously come up with new and alternative approaches and weapons to match and best those of their adversaries.

For better or worse, Israelis possess a duel-edged mentality. They have an unflagging sense of mortal danger in which they fear being pushed into the sea and at the same time a confidence in their ability to shatter their opponents. The idea of survival is an extremely potent motivator. A common adage crops up in which Israelis say that they have to win every day, but that their opponents need only to win once. Unlike most nations' military doctrines, which are based on the concept of defense, the IDF expresses its primary defense as ensuring the country's very existence. Israel's security doctrine maintains that it cannot lose a single war. It has developed a defense policy based on a quick and decisive defeat of its enemies, preventing them from penetrating Israeli territory. With such a small population, Israel doesn't have the capacity to assemble a large standing army and instead relies on its reserve forces. What it lacks in size, the IDF must make up for in superior maneuverability and firepower, and to support the military's top-notch intelligence.

Over the years, Israel's ingenuity has helped it win many battles. Driven by security concerns, the Israelis developed an impressive military force with all of the conventions of a traditional armed service, and yet, unlike most armies, it is entrepreneurial in nature. Expediency over design has forged one of Israel's strongest values: improvisation. The IDF is an inculcator of a spirit of creativity and independence to a degree perhaps not in evidence anywhere else in the world. Boldness, imagination, agility, inventiveness, and self-reliance as Israeli characteristics are reinforced in the IDF. The distinct military culture threads itself within the national fabric. The army, and, by extension, Israeli society, places much value on these very qualities.

"We've been in a permanent war for the past 120 years," explained Uzi Arad, the former deputy director of the Mossad and a foreign policy advisor to Prime Minister Binyamin Netanyahu. Now head of the Institute of Policy and Strategy, a policy and security think tank at the Interdisciplinary Center Herziliya, Arad sees this as a circular discussion. Israel developed a powerful military force because it has powerful security concerns. "The other side always enjoys more: population, geography, oil, and money," he said. Arad continued, "We had to develop a defense industry. We couldn't practice economy of scale, and we had serious handicaps coping under overwhelming odds." And, he added, "We've had the bad luck of this happening in a bad neighborhood, the worst neighborhood in the world. It forced us into allocating an inordinate amount of energy and talent into self defense, and the by-product has been some industry."

Even before the state was founded, self-defense was a crucial component of Israeli culture. It started with the underground Haganah, which was established during the British Mandate to defend Jewish settlements against frequent Arab attacks. Originally, it was a kind of loose association made up of local defense groups that protected towns, villages, and settlements. But after the Arab riots of 1929, which left hundreds dead, the Haganah transformed itself into a serious military fighting force. Its operating style, dependent upon a complete mobilization of men and women to fight, an inexhaustible need for new weaponry and techniques, and a reliance on young commanders to lead and take responsibility well beyond their years and experience, formed the backbone of today's IDF. The Haganah came up with increasingly bold and inventive ways to resist the British and defend itself against the Arabs. It operated clandestine networks in Palestine and abroad, and these networks obtained intelligence, transmitted messages, and smuggled arms and people.

Within the Haganah was an elite commando unit called the *Palmach*. Ill-equipped and outnumbered, the Palmach (a Hebrew acronym that means "strike force") compensated for what it lacked by instituting an improvisational model that relied on agility and outsmarting the enemy. This, of course, would become institutionalized in the IDF. While the Haganah called up its members on an as-needed basis, the Palmach was fully mobilized at all times. Made up of nine assault companies in the northern, southern, and central Galilee and in Jerusalem, the Palmach often used Jewish members from Arab countries who spoke fluent Arabic and sent them behind enemy lines on sabotage and reconnaissance missions disguised as Arabs. The unit became permanently etched in the fledgling country's spirit, and many of its leaders, such as future Prime Minister Yitzhak Rabin and IDF Chief of Staff David Elazar, would eventually become a who's who of Israel's political and military leadership.

In the early days of Israel, David Ben-Gurion made a propitious decision that the country's security and economy would be based on science. He started the Science Corps that later became RAFAEL, Israel's Armament Development Authority. The corps invented new arms and explosives and electronic devices suited to the growing and intensive needs of the army. Internal development has always been crucial, particularly since the military's needs have always outstripped its ability to obtain weaponry overseas. An informal estimate put the number of IDF officers who have university degrees in science and engineering at 30 percent. Not surprisingly, every Israeli government has spent a significant amount of its GDP on defense, channeling large sums into technological research and development. In 2002, according to published reports, Israel spent $8.97 billion, or 8.75 percent of its GDP, on its military.[28] In contrast, Egypt, with a population nearly 10 times that of Israel, spent roughly half as much ($4.04 billion, some 4.1 percent of its GDP) as its neighbor to the east.[29] Israel's security needs have eclipsed almost everything else. During the 2003 elections, while the economy continued to sputter in a death spiral and unemployment hit nearly 10 percent, it was security issues above all else that helped to propel hawkish Ariel Sharon into the prime minister's office.

As a result, the IDF transformed itself from a poorly supplied, amateurish fighting force into a potent military, earning a reputation for being swift, exacting, and spectacularly unpredictable. It has also evolved into something well beyond a powerful army—it defines a national ethos. The IDF is referred to, without question, as a people's army. Most of the population (including women) is expected to serve at the age of 18, with women required to serve two years and men three, followed up by *miluim*, or reserve duty, of several weeks a year until the age of 50 plus. Perhaps no force in Israel is more unifying than the military. More than religion or a shared history, it is the military that has fused Jews from every corner of the earth and every income and social group into one nation. This army's deeply embedded culture of self-reliance, teamwork, innovation, and boldness is evident throughout Israeli society.

Whereas for most college-age individuals in the United States the all-volunteer army is rarely even an afterthought, in Israel the best and brightest enter the military, joining the most difficult combat and intelligence units and becoming officers. Perhaps the best of the best is the elite *Sayeret Matkal*, better known as "the unit." One of the most effective special-ops forces in history, it is responsible for some of the most spectacular counterterrorism operations in the world. Most famously, the unit was behind the rescue of hostages in Entebbe and the hunt for and assassination of the members of the PLO splinter group Black September, which massacred the Israeli Olympic team at the Munich Games in 1972. When Prime Minister Sharon, himself an alumnus of the unit, announced his government's intention to hunt down those responsible for both the terrorist attacks on Israelis at the Paradise resort and the attempt to shoot down an Israeli charter plane, incidents that took place in Mombassa, Kenya, in the winter of 2002, it was very likely that it would be this unit that would do the hunting. Only a rare group of individuals make it in the Sayeret Matkal, and the group has formed some of the most powerful leaders of the nation. Former Prime Minister Ehud Barak, the most decorated soldier in Israel, came from the Sayeret Matkal, as did Binyamin Netanyahu.

Terrorism first struck Israel in the 1950s when Egyptian, Jordanian, and Palestinian guerillas called *fedyaheen* made frequent cross-border attacks. In response, the IDF formed small and nimble commando units like the Sayeret Matkal to strike back in punishing raids. In one particularly brutal attack in October 1951, Sharon led his commandos into the West Bank town of Qibya, where they blew up dozens of houses and killed 69 civilians. Sharon has said the killing of civilians was a mistake, but the event, like several others during the course of his career, would cling to him, indelibly marking him as a brutish hawk in world opinion.

Twenty years later, border infiltrations gave way to more sophisticated attacks on a global scale. In the 1970s, a series of dramatic hijackings became the terrorism of choice, but Israeli counterterrorism rose to the challenge. In 1972, members of Popular Front of the PLO hijacked a Sabena aircraft and forced it to land at the airport in Lod. As it sat on the tarmac—filled with passengers—members of the unit stormed the plane disguised as mechanics, rescuing the passengers, killing two of the terrorists, and capturing two others. The first operation of its kind, it could never be repeated. Danny Yatom, one of the members of the Sayeret at the time who was involved in the rescue and a former Mossad chief, once compared these kinds of operations to a tailor who must sew a new suit for every customer.[30]

The Israelis became so adept at attacking and preventing hijackings that the security measures they take at their airports and national carrier El Al are considered the gold standard. Long before September 11, 2001, El Al made sure that its cockpits were secured with special security and that its passengers were pre-profiled, and some of its planes have been reported to be outfitted with special anti-missile deflection flares. Indeed, the first and last hijacking of an El Al plane took place in 1968 when Popular Front for the Liberation of Palestine terrorists took over a Rome-bound flight and forced it to land in Algiers, holding the crew and passengers hostage for weeks in exchange for Palestinian prisoners. Thirty-four years later, an attempt to broach the cockpit of an El Al plane in November 2002 by a knife-wielding passenger on a flight to Istanbul was thwarted when two undercover Israeli marshals immediately overpowered and disarmed the would-be hijacker.

Although it could be said that El Al may be one of the world's biggest targets for terrorism, the kinds of thorough and measured security procedures it has established over the years have also made it one of the safest. Its security detail is always on the lookout for all potential threats and attacks, in addition to hijackings, before they occur. That became clear on April 17, 1986, when El Al agents at Heathrow Airport in London were screening 375 passengers waiting to board a Tel Aviv-bound flight and came across a pregnant Irish woman named Anne-Marie Murphy who was carrying 1.5 kilograms of Semtex plastic explosives and an altimeter detonator in the false bottom of her suitcase. As it turned out, unknown to Murphy, Nezar Hindawi, her Jordanian-born Palestinian fiancé, had sent her off with the lethal baggage and the promise of meeting her in Israel. Hindawi, reported to be a Syrian Intelligence agent, was arrested shortly afterward. As a result of this incident, for a time Britain broke off diplomatic relations with Syria.[31]

On the edge of Jaffa, where the old seaport meets Tel Aviv, in an area filled with small streets lined with even smaller industrial shops and gas stations, there is a large metal gate. The site, situated off the corner of Eilat Street, was once an Ottoman railway station and later it was used as a British military camp during the Mandate period. A motley collection of a few dozen metal sheds lined with old armored vehicles and mortars and set amid palm trees and pebbled walkways, it is the Israel Defense Forces museum. The collection is a tangible record of the emergence of the IDF and the military struggle for Israel's existence. Among the collection is the "Monster," a homemade armor-plated vehicle used in the War of Independence in 1948 to break through the stone barricades the Arabs set up on roads. One shed displays captured vehicles from Israel's various wars, and another displays weapons used by various Arab terror organizations against Israel. Also on exhibit is the original halftrack commanded by Colonel Motta Gur, which broke through the Lion's Gate of the Old City of Jerusalem in the Six Day War. Even the official cars used by David Ben-Gurion, Menachem Begin, and Moshe Dayan when each served as minister of defense are on exhibit.

In the shed marked Pavilion #16, under Plexiglas, is the console of a Philco 211. It is marked by the caption "The IDF's first computer, 1963," and the caption also contains a quote from *Psalm 44.2*: "We have heard with our ears, our fathers have told us." At a time when few nations were in possession of computing capabilities, the IDF created *MMRM*, the Hebrew acronym for the Center of Computers and Automated Recording, better known as *Mamram*. Mamram is set up around the Philco mainframe, the IDF's main computer unit. Costing somewhere in the millions, the mainframe was an expensive acquisition for an economically strapped country that was barely 10 years old, still absorbing thousands of new immigrants and building a national infrastructure. But in 1959, four years before the army received the giant computer unit, a few men like Yitzhak Rabin, then Israel's deputy chief of staff, recognized that a computer was a weapons system and that if Israel were to realize itself as a modern army, it must computerize to keep its edge over its Arab neighbors.

Mamram stands off of a busy street on an army base in the Tel Aviv suburb of Ramat Gan, its perimeter flanked by large stone walls left over from the British Mandate period. Hung on the wall in the stairway leading to the basement floor of Mamram's nerve center is an Israeli newspaper article from the early 1960s. The article criticizes the defense establishment for spending so much money on a computer thought big enough to power the entire Middle East. Colonel Avi Kochba, Mamram's commander, pointed out the headline: "The army is a head with no brain." Born in Little Rock, Arkansas, and raised in Brooklyn, New York, Colonel Kochba immigrated to Israel at the age of 10.

At 18, he enlisted in the Nahal infantry but transferred a year and a half later to Mamram (where he started as a computer operator) after his parents, who are Holocaust survivors, objected to their only son serving as a combat soldier. Moving up the ranks over 20 years, he was appointed to run the unit in 2002. Rereading the headline, he said, "It's ridiculous if you think about it today."

Indeed, Mamram came to play one of the most important roles in the technological advancement of the IDF and helped to convert this country of kibbutzim and diamond polishers into one of the most vibrant high-tech economies of the world. The IDF is arguably one of the most computerized armies in the world. All branches of the military have computer and research and development centers that are staffed by soldiers who received their computer training at Mamram. Except for military intelligence, Mamram is in charge of the IDF's software, hardware, and data communications infrastructure and the introduction of new technology.

In the beginning, Mamram used the Philco mostly for data processing and logistics. Still, it needed experts to keep it up and running and, in the hot and humid Tel Aviv summers, to take care that insects didn't get inside the mainframe (which, by the way, is the original literal meaning for the phrase "computer bugs"). Because the unit was established several years before computer science became an established academic discipline and because the IDF had very specific needs (such as large-scale data processing and simulations), Mamram created its own internal training school for computing. This in turn spawned the country's impressive IT community of software engineers trained to identify specific problems and to come up with a solution quickly and innovatively.[32] "If you look around Israel, most of the information technology leaders in the industry came out of this unit," Colonel Kochba said. It is one of the most coveted units in the military, and its soldiers have become some of the most sought after when their service is completed. Its style of commando problem-solving in which soldiers tackle complex problems, finding inventive solutions through quick and original routes, has embedded itself deeply into society and industry.

Mamran's reputation in the civilian world was helped exponentially in 1998 when two of its former soldiers, Israel Mazin and Eli Mashiah, sold the information security firm they founded, Memco, to Platinum Technologies for about $550 million.

After parsing out the top tier of incoming conscript soldiers, Mamram puts them through a grueling battery of tests. Mamram candidates go through seven months of an intensive basic training course that starts at 7:30 in the morning and ends at 10:00 at night. Those who are left standing must serve an extra three years of military service. Most of the learning is on-the-job training, explained Colonel Kochba:

> We put a problem to our soldiers. This is a situation: compute it down, and we need it in 30 minutes. They have to figure out what to do at a young age. They are decision-makers. At 21 years old, an officer may lead a team of soldiers on a program. He could be in charge of infrastructure at night or the end of the week. Sometimes there is no other officer, and a whole installation is on his shoulders. If something goes wrong, he must take care of it. As time goes by and the older they get, the more responsibility they get. This is a young army, and it develops and teaches soldiers to take responsibility when they are young.

At about the same time that Mamram was formed, the beginnings of what would eventually become unit 8200 were formally taking shape. Recognizing the importance of wiretapping and code breaking, the Jews of Palestine had earlier set up a unit in what they called Intelligence Service 2, which was tasked with monitoring enemy transmissions. Within Intelligence Service 2 was another unit called Rabbit that was responsible for breaking codes. Only a handful of countries, the United States, Great Britain, Germany, and the Soviet Union among them, had sophisticated code breaking and monitoring capabilities in the 1940s. But the Jews of Palestine, many of whom had worked closely with the British during World War II, understood the advantage in listening to their enemies and acquired the skills to do so. They would leave little to chance. During the Mandate, British military headquarters at Jerusalem's Palace Hotel were bugged.[33] Decades later, the importance of electronic surveillance only intensified. "By the time you can see your enemy coming, it may be too late," said "Eban," a former intelligence officer. "It's better to know what they are thinking and what are their intentions first."

Prior to the founding of the state, Israelis learned the art of cryptography from an American lawyer named Nachum Bernstein, who was approached in 1947 to teach intelligence-gathering to members of the Haganah. Bernstein had learned the craft of bugging, wiretapping, and surveillance in gathering evidence for insurance fraud claims, and he later applied his specialized skills at the Office of Special Services (OSS) during World War II. Toward the end of the war, he had learned how to use a one-time pad cipher, a device that he and a colleague later translated into Hebrew and used to secretly teach his recruits cryptography in a lower Manhattan synagogue.[34]

From the beginning, the unit was involved in developing many of the technologies needed to capture intelligence. Many of its members spoke Arabic. At the time the unit was established—or, rather, the origins of the unit were established—it often relied on improvised and amateurish tools to get the job done. In time, the unit's technology would become increasingly sophisticated, but the methodology in getting there would be rooted in the same kind of dynamic creativity. Its engineers and analysts and their handiwork would evolve to develop sophisticated communications systems that could intercept, decipher, encrypt, and break enemy lines.

Being embattled and suffering years of isolation forced the Israelis to become proficient in weapons development. The

French, the country's main weapons supplier, imposed an arms embargo on Israel following the Six Day War in 1967, hastening the establishment of Israel's own military industrial capacity. Its answer to the embargo was to manufacture its own fighter jets, the first of which, the Nesher, was an improved version of the embargoed French Mirage 5. This shift greatly influenced the advancement of Israeli high-tech industry. It was during this period that Israel's first generation of high-tech companies, such as ECI, Elbit, and Tadiran, emerged.

While the United States filled the vacuum left by the French to counterbalance the Soviet supplies to the Arab states, it has, however, restricted its transfer of weapons platforms and technology to soften Israel's edge over its neighbors. In response, Israel has come up with a number of technologies that either mirror American systems or best them altogether. Recognizing the potential economic calamity in producing large systems, Israel became proficient at adapting the platforms it acquired from the United States (like fighter jets) and outfitting them with its own software systems. The number of tank casualties during the 1967 and Yom Kippur Wars spurred the development of the Merkava, a tank now in its fourth generation and considered one of the most impregnable tanks in the world. As well, Israel became so adept at modernizing and utilizing old military equipment, particularly the huge amount of Soviet weaponry it captured from Arab nations in its many wars, that after the Soviet Union, Israel was for a period the world's second-largest exporter of Soviet arms.[35]

There is an expression in Hebrew: *rosh gadol*. Literally, this expression means "big head." But to Israelis it has a deeper implication; it is a call to think in broad terms. To outsiders, it may sometimes be interpreted as arrogance, but not to Israelis. They are tasked from a young age to be inventive, to consider new ideas, and to take ownership of them. In contrast, to be called *rosh katan*, or literally "little head," is the equivalent of calling someone small minded—and in Israel that is a grave insult. In the military, *rosh gadol* is the mandatory operating procedure at any rank and at any age—all soldiers are expected to think big, to come to their own conclusions, and to take ownership of tasks.

"The military is a unique education. You are taught to think differently, to come up with new proposals and new ways to do things," Shimon Schocken, dean of the computer science school at the Interdisciplinary Center Herziliya, said. "This is probably unique to the Israeli military system." Schocken went on to describe the experience of his 19-year-old son in the officers' course:

> They do case studies of the legacy of major battles. There was a famous battle in 1973 when the Syrians managed to take the peak of Mount Hermon, and then Israel took it back. One battle failed, and one succeeded. My son has only been in the army for eight months, and at the end of basic training exercises he has to plan to take back the Hermon as if he were a platoon commander. He has to come up with a strategy and explain how he will do it. Then he is asked to play the role of the Syrians and defend the Hermon and explain how. These young kids are asked to strategize, and, even if their thoughts are useless, that's OK. He is predisposed to think this way.

On the surface, the IDF looks like any other military force, but, in fact, it has become one of the most important innovation incubators in the country. In many ways, the IDF takes the country's smartest, boldest, and most creative 18-year-olds and exposes them to huge challenges, overwhelming responsibility, and state-of-the-art technology. The military itself is entrepreneurial in character. The demand to be innovative is constant; the country's very existence is at stake. "We have 20-year-olds responsible for producing huge systems," explained Professor

Schocken. "If you compare that to a Microsoft [employee], a 20-year-old here has the same responsibilities as a 30-year-old [in the United States]. Here he gets a jump-start. It's as if Microsoft suddenly went into colleges and picked the best and the brightest and gave them huge budgets—which simply wouldn't happen."

Formidable as a series of dramatic victories have proven it to be, the IDF remains extremely flexible. Like most areas in Israeli life, soldiers learn that rules are made to be broken. Officers are rarely saluted, and it is a soldier's right to question his or her superior officer's orders. Rank is merely a formality. Soldiers are expected to think and act independently, but within the context of a team. Israel's ability to survive is predicated on its ability to react quickly to changes. Threats are immediate—in some cases the enemy is literally just over a fence. The IDF does not have the luxury of working in the theoretical; often stretched of both time and resources, it is not part of the everyday routine to simply drum up massive projects that might see the light of day several years down the road. A premium is placed on creating new solutions to immediate needs. And there is an extremely close cooperation between the developers of those solutions and the end users. In the space of one year, Colonel Boaz Hayek, who heads the electrical optics system of the IDF's technology division, said his engineer-soldiers had been to the West Bank and Gaza Strip 4,000 times to see for themselves how their equipment was holding up in the field.

When the intifada broke out in the fall of 2000, it imposed a new set of problems on the IDF. The Israelis were now engaged in urban warfare in which militants and suicide bombers regularly attacked civilians by sneaking into Israel's porous borders with the Palestinian territories and then quickly returning to these border areas, where they could easily disperse, camouflaged by the densely populated Palestinian towns and refugee camps. In response, the Israelis mounted their own counteroffensives, penetrating deep into the West Bank and Gaza. But between the IDF and those they were hunting down stood houses, towns, and people. Jeeps patrolling the area came upon a veritable obstacle course that posed potential hiding spots.

"We needed observation capabilities to look beyond houses and over fences," Colonel Hayek explained at Tel Hashomer base near Tel Aviv. "We needed to think. I had some officers, colonels and sergeant majors, in my office, and we started by thinking about what the units in the West Bank and Gaza needed. The problem was they couldn't see. If they came to a city near a border, they couldn't see if people were coming to the border or if they were in the valleys." Within three months, Hayek's division—along with Israel Aircraft Industries—had developed an operational, optical payload that rests on a retractable pole. Installed on IDF patrol jeeps, the system transmits images on a monitor to the soldiers sitting inside. The system, capable of operating during the day or night, offers a 360-degree perspective within a scope of several miles. It also takes only five minutes to raise automatically—without endangering soldiers who don't need to leave the jeep to manage or fix it. In many cases the solution need not be complicated to be effective. Hayek said the inspiration for this payload came from the automatic collapsible poles used to fix traffic lights.

Unlike traditional military culture, the IDF is not unquestionably dogmatic; when circumstances change, so does the military—and quickly. "The IDF is a very flexible organization," explained Brigadier General Shmuel Yachin, acting head of the research and development branch of the Ministry of Defense. "We learn to change priorities very fast; threats change on a recurring basis. We created a special system of command to deal with these things. The bigger the organization, the slower it moves." Indeed, when the intifada broke out, the IDF and security apparatuses had to quickly shift gear from a focus on long-range threats and the promise of peace to guerilla warfare next door. Due to sheer numbers, IDF infrastructure is smaller and flatter than the American armed forces. The highest-ranking general has three stars, and there is only one: the chief of staff; following him are 20 two-star and 100 one-star generals. A special forum of brigadier generals, largely stripped of layers of decision makers, meets regularly in the face of new and existing threats to sort through ideas that are actively promoted at all levels within the army. The flexible, informal military culture that is responsive to bold ideas gave birth to some of the military's most innovative initiatives and some of its more spectacular episodes.

In the early 1950s, the IDF needed a light submachine gun to take on mobile patrols. The regularly used Sten jammed frequently, had a short firing range, and was inaccurate and difficult to reload in the dark. The army commissioned its Science Corps to come up with a new design. At the same time, a young kibbutz member and soldier named Uziel Gal, who had a knack for weapon design, submitted his own ideas for a new type of submachine gun while participating in an officers' training course. Gal's design had a small number of parts, could fire in dusty and sandy conditions, was easy to assemble and disassemble, didn't jam, and had a high degree of accuracy. His plans were approved, and the military named the new submachine gun after him: They called it the Uzi.

Or, take the case of what became known as Operation Rooster. In 1969, the Soviets had helped the Egyptians build up a massive anti-air defense based on surface-to-air missiles and early-warning radar. For Israel, which used its air force both as attack and defense, this was troubling—particularly since the Soviet-built P-12 early-warning radar was the eye that could locate and shoot down Israeli aircraft. Whatever qualitative edge the IDF had in understanding the weaknesses of the Egyptian air defenses, its ability to trick the enemy and to operate were quickly being rendered futile with the new sophisticated radar systems. RAFAEL determined that the Israelis could probably bomb 1 or even 10 of the early-warning radar systems. But the Egyptians had installed 300 to 400 of them on the Suez Canal. While high-ranking intelligence officers plotted out ways to destroy the radar, an intelligence analyst, a young sergeant, came up with a plan of his own. Israel would steal it.

During the last week of December 1969, Sergeant Rami Shalev was reviewing post-strike aerial photography when he noticed that a target the Israelis had hit was actually a dummy radar site. Perhaps more importantly, the reconnaissance film also revealed that an authentic radar site was located only a few miles away. Shalev also saw that this site, located on the beach at Ras-Arab, was completely vulnerable, unprotected by anti-aircraft guns. Shalev brought his proposal to steal the radar to his commanding officer, and the scheme ran up the chain of command. Training on radars captured during the Six Day War began immediately, and two days later, the operation was launched.

While A-4 Skyhawks and F-4 Phantoms attacked Egyptian forces on the western bank of the Suez Canal, three Super Frelons helicopters dropped Israeli paratroopers on the site, a small peak, to secure the target. They dismantled the system and swiped the radar system. The commandos attached the disassembled system underneath two CH-53 Sikorsky heavy-lift helicopters and returned to Israel.

Not surprisingly, the radar itself proved remarkably valuable. The military thoroughly examined the system, giving the Israelis another technological trick in their electronic warfare arsenal and allowing them to jam every Soviet-made system that was installed in much of the Arab world for some 30 years.[36]

Since its founding, Israel has never experienced a single era of peace, and every war since its birth was considered nothing less than a war of survival. Israelis tick off the string of regional conflicts like Americans recite memorable World Series baseball championships: the War of Independence (1948), the Sinai Campaign (1956), the Six Day War (1967), the War of Attrition (1969–1971), the Yom Kippur War (1973), Lebanon (1982), the first intifada (1987), the Gulf War (1991), and the Al Aksa intifada (2000). Perhaps to its own discomfort, security and defense have become a national legacy and industry. From the time Israel was founded, its leaders made a conscious decision: Israel would need to create for itself one of the best secret services in the world. Surrounded by powerful enemies, Israel would have to compensate with the only resource it had—its people. It would assemble a quick and effective army. For the army to be successful, it would have to develop the best intelligence. Its defenses would be built on the ingenuity of its people.

Closing in on the end of his military career, much of which has been spent in the never-ending search for new weapons and methods to fight a battle seemingly without an end, Brigadier General Shmuel Yachin explained it rather simply: "Out of necessity, innovation is connected to security. A clear and present danger is the mother of all necessity."

4 Brains

Not far off the coastal highway north of Tel Aviv, a small but significant display of objects is housed with little fanfare. The objects are exhibited in a tiny, unmarked museum that is located beyond a shopping center near the Glilot Junction. It is housed within the Center for Special Studies, which itself is situated among one of those rambling military compounds where the civilian and military worlds sometimes intersect. The complex is part of a knot of Israeli intelligence. There is a boot camp, a training school, and, within eyeshot, large satellite dishes and communication Radomes that dot the sky like giant golf balls. The museum is kept under lock and key and is accessible only by prior consent from its curator, a small, wiry man rarely without a cigarette in his mouth who himself is a former intelligence member. It is a room really, separated in part by a slight partition, that can't be more than 20 × 30 feet.

Its contents are an odd assortment of items that on first glance look quite a bit like dusty old props from B-movie spy flicks. Suspended from the ceiling near the entrance is what appears to be a remote-controlled toy airplane. White with a thick red stripe painted across it and a camera positioned underneath it, it is, in reality, one of Israel's first unmanned drones.

The rest of the items, arranged in no particular order, include a crude wooden model (it is of the Entebbe Airport in Uganda) and a miniature camera that fits in the palm of one's hand (its parts can be quickly disassembled and easily stowed away undetected). Under Plexiglas there is a makeshift, stiff black mask—it was placed on Adolph Eichmann's face as he was spirited away to Tel Aviv from Argentina. Also displayed in the small exhibit is a simple signal transmitter hidden in the base of a flatiron, invisible ink disguised in bottles of Old Spice and Aqua Velva cologne, and a recorder concealed inside a brass Bedouin coffeepot. Set back in the rear portion of the room is an Akai 51 S receiver, the size of a small refrigerator, with large reel-to-reel tapes. It contains the actual recording of the now famous conversation between King Hussein of Jordan and President Gamal Abdul Nasser of Egypt that Israeli intelligence intercepted on the morning of June 6, 1967, during the Six Day War.

This small collection represents some of the earliest espionage artifacts of Israel's five-plus decades engaged in intelligence gathering. Not unlike uncovering an anthropological cache of tools that helps to shed light on a community, these objects demonstrate ingenuity even in the most rudimentary of gadgets. While seemingly improvised and even amateurish at times, they reveal the kinds of characteristic traits that have long dominated the Israeli intelligence machine: creativity, innovation, aggressive intelligence, and surprise.

To say that Israel has remained embattled and on war footing ever since it was first established is to tread a well-worn groove of thought. However, as such, the role of intelligence has always been crucial because the stakes have always been so high. Although at times predisposed to alarm, it is not simply a paranoid adage for Israelis, who have come to believe that the first war they lose will be their last. Israel has a well-developed siege mentality. In 55 years, Israel has fought seven major regional wars, two Palestinian intifadas, scores of terrorist attacks, and countless battles and skirmishes. The place that intelligence has in Israeli life and by extension in the Middle

East is not insignificant. During the Cold War, when the intelligence communities of the East and the West battled each other, it was a highly politicized war of brinkmanship and one-upmanship to defend their respective superiority and hegemony. In the Middle East, a region of constant strife and conflict, intelligence has taken on an amplified sense of importance. For many, it is considered the tether between life and death.

Created in a relatively short period of time and without the benefit of a long-held tradition of its own, intelligence developed in part by absorbing the conventions of long-established services but also, in good measure, it built methodologies and a philosophy that was decidedly independent. As such, it has become a repository for all the dynamic forces at play in society. It's like a gathering of every extreme Israeli impulse: entrepreneurship, boldness, creativity, risk, and an innate craving for change. Responsible for protecting the nation, intelligence has also had a hand in shaping Israel's very nature.

Although small in size, Israel's trio of intelligence bodies is widely acknowledged as among the most effective in the world. The Mossad (*Hamossad le modein u le tafkidim meyuchadim*), perhaps the best-known branch of intelligence, is responsible for foreign espionage and is often compared to the American CIA. The General Security Services, more commonly referred to as either Shin Bet or the Shabak (*sherut hatiachon haklali*), is Israel's domestic counterespionage force likened to the FBI. It has operated an exhaustive campaign of intelligence gathering in the West Bank and Gaza since these areas came under Israeli occupation in 1967, and it is said to have penetrated nearly every strata of Palestinian society through informants and special undercover units. The third branch is Aman (*Agaf modein*), the country's military intelligence arm. It is directly connected to the IDF and is involved in many areas, including preparing the annual National Intelligence Estimate to the prime minister, and is responsible for intelligence-gathering methods such as signal, communication, electronic, and visual intelligence.

In all its facets, intelligence provides a barometer of war and of peace. At the same time, the role that it plays in the country may be categorically unique. At times, it squared off against the sum of the intelligence capabilities of the entire Arab world (and during the heyday of the Cold War, the Soviet secret services as well). However, it also serves as the compensating mechanism for the significant gap that stands between Israel and a host of geopolitical realities. This is the strategic core of the Israeli survival instinct. Like a tightly wound coil, Israel must be prepared to battle for itself at a moment's notice. At the same time, for a country in a permanent state of war, there is a remarkable regularity to daily life. Perhaps it is for this very reason that the Israelis have veered toward the unconventional and the unusual. This approach is defined by ingenuity. Rather than relying solely on either the desk-bound analyst or the orbiting satellite, Israeli thinking in this area has constantly sought to create new openings, new opportunities, and new ways of doing things.

In his office at the Center for Special Studies in Glilot, Major General Meir Amit sat under a blown-up black-and-white photograph of himself and the late General Moshe Dayan taken at the Wailing Wall not long after Israeli troops reclaimed the Old City of Jerusalem during the Six Day War in 1967. For Amit, the only person ever to have headed up both Aman, or military intelligence, and the Mossad, it simply comes down to this: "Israel is a very small state with no depth. The German forces came into the heart of Russia [in World War II], and they were still defeated," he offered by way of comparison. "We have no place to go in this kind of position. The value of intelligence is a much more important matter of fact. Intelligence," he insisted, "is the eyes and ears of the state, and this is not just a phrase. In our case it is a substitute for depth. It is a substitute for many things that we lack. This is for us a matter of life and death." In the vernacular of business, intelligence is Israel's core competency.

A small but sturdy figure, with the years clearly visible on his face, the long-retired general remains one of the seminal figures in the annals of Israeli intelligence. For Amit, the greatest tools of spy craft are imagination and creativity, and both marked his tenure. He is credited with running a ring of agents behind enemy lines in Egypt and Syria. In a business in which most of the details are kept under wraps, one of Amit's most spectacular feats of espionage is one of his most publicly celebrated. It was Amit who famously orchestrated the theft of a Soviet MiG-21 from Iraq in 1966 and the defection of its pilot and his family. At the time, the MiG was one of the most advanced fighter jets in existence. Israel's possession of the jet's inner workings played a huge role less than a year later in its stunning victory in the Six Day War against the Soviet-supplied air forces of Egypt and Syria. His vision of intelligence has had a profound and far-reaching influence.

A field commander and former deputy to Moshe Dayan, Amit was tapped to run the Mossad in 1963 while studying business administration at Columbia University in New York City. A parachuting accident left him in crutches, and the IDF sent him to New York to study. While there, he came into contact with a Philco computer. "It was the size of a room," he recalled. Very quickly he realized the significant role that modern technology could play in intelligence gathering. When he returned to Israel, he was one of modern technology's most vocal advocates. Moreover, he saw the technological capabilities and human endeavors not as separate competing units but as complimentary entities. "Everything," he exclaimed, "is man and machine." He initiated a working relationship between the two sides: the military equivalent of the customer and supplier. "The people in field operations must understand the technical side, and technicians must understand the operations," he said. Of his many accomplishments, not least of which was to amass an amazing amount of intelligence on the Egyptian Air Force (down to the minutest of details) that proved instrumental in Israel's smashing of it in the June 1967 war, Amit says that establishing an integrated relationship between operations and technology was "one of the wisest things I did."

The weight of Amit's experience (he went on to help initiate Israel's satellite program) still commands attention. Although long retired from active service, at 82 he continues to come to his office at the Glilot intelligence hub weekly, maintaining his intricate ties to the community, but in a decidedly different manner. In the spring of 2000, he co-founded Spark Enterprises, a small venture firm that invests in new Israeli innovations in software applications, optics, information technology, and biotechnology. "These are civilian ideas," he said, "but many come out of intelligence backgrounds." Amit relies on what he calls his "brain trust of ex-intelligence officers" as consultants. "I say, 'Listen, I need someone, the best man in this field, about a project.' I get an opinion." After all, he reiterated, "Intelligence has the most creative minds."

From the start, Israel has been consistently adept at marshalling its human and technological resources into a proficient defense mechanism. This is a country that maintains a high state of alert 24 hours a day, seven days a week. Unable to maintain a large standing army like its opponents, it is dependent upon a swiftly mobilized military reserve force that needs 24 to 70 hours of notice for a call-up. There is the potential threat of its immediate neighbors: Syria can strike at the country in just minutes by air and by land in a matter of hours. There is also a constant shift in a cast of prospective dangerous players coming from peripheral Arab and Muslim countries hostile to Israel. As the first Gulf War in 1991 demonstrated, Iraqi Scud missiles landed in Israeli population centers in less than seven minutes. Finally, Israel is engaged in the static war at home. Needing less time than an Iraqi Scud and wreaking considerably more damage in recent years are a number of hostile Palestinian and Islamic militant groups. Embittered and emboldened over the years living under Israeli occupation in the West Bank and the Gaza Strip, they have shown time and again their ability to slip into Israel proper and strike.

All of the hardware and the firepower at one's disposal can provide the upper hand—initially. They do not, however, give one the ability to peer into the motivations, the movements, or the minds of one's adversaries. For that, one needs intelligence. Besides, the enemy eventually gets wise to the infrastructure and adapts.

If the IDF has played the singularly potent force in ensuring the nation's existence, it is Israel's intelligence bodies that have been the crucial connection behind many of its successes (and at times withering failures). Like every nation's intelligence services, its fundamental mandate is to uncover the activities, strengths, weaknesses, and intentions of its enemies and provide a bulwark of early warning against attack. From its earliest days, the Israeli approach has stood apart from the classic functions of spy craft. In Israel it is also the heavily weighed evaluation upon which policy and tactics are based. A theme repeated in Israel with frequency is that the country's unique circumstances have always called for extraordinary measures.

Good intelligence involves both collection and action. It is an innately difficult and unscientific endeavor. Its battles go on for the most part unknown to the public at large. It exists in a kind of twilight world and communicates in a language all its own. Its collection has been compared to finding a needle in a haystack, and its successful analysis and interpretation have been described as putting together a puzzle without all of the pieces. It involves going to places most people would rather not be and discovering solutions to problems that have yet to emerge. Indeed, precisely how this information is captured and how it is used has formed the basis of a series of dramatic operations that have become the calling card of Israeli intelligence.

Some of these operations have deployed stunning technological prowess, others have involved stealth undercover commandos, and others still have consisted of the simple execution of a clever idea. The Israeli Air Force's destruction of the Iraqi nuclear reactor at Osirik in 1981 and, 13 years earlier, the mission during which Israeli soldiers commandeered a German ship and absconded with its cargo of 200 tons of uranium oxide in 560 sealed oil drums are calculated episodes and not random exercises in brute force.[1] The long striking arm that made them possible was linked to some wily brains back in Israel.

Although usually quite capable, Israel's formidable intelligence agencies are not, however, invincible. In a biting reminder of the difficulties and limitations of intelligence, a subcommittee of the Israeli Knesset, its parliament, made partially public a highly critical 81-page document compiled in the spring of 2004 that censured military intelligence's failure to properly assess Iraq's capabilities in the run-up to the U.S.-led invasion the year before. It also pointed out a gaping absence of information on Libya's attempts to acquire nuclear weapons. As well, the committee recommended that Aman's unit 8200 operate as a civilian organization instead of as a military one.[2]

This parliamentary report could be added to a catalog of some embarrassing and bitter missteps that have come to light over the years that have put into perspective some of Israel's agencies' hallmark successes. Standing among them is the failure to properly assess Egypt and Syria's moves toward war, resulting in the bitterly fought Yom Kippur War that nearly ended in disaster for the Israelis. It remains a national trauma. Moreover, there was *l'affaire Pollard*. In 1985, a Jewish-American naval intelligence analyst working for the Israelis, Jonathan Pollard, was caught passing on classified documents. This event badly bruised not only the reputation of the intelligence services but for a time damaged relations with Israel's greatest ally, the United States.

Another embarrassing incident is the 1997 episode in which two Mossad agents traveling under Canadian passports attempted to assassinate Hamas leader Khalid Meshal in Amman, Jordan, by spraying him with some kind of lethal poison. The attempt was made following a spate of suicide bombings in Israel said to be orchestrated by Hamas. The operation, later called "amateurish" in an internal inquiry, was a fiasco. The agents bungled the mission and were caught. The Jordanians put the screws to the Israelis, who were forced to dispatch an antidote that was administered to Meshal. Moreover, the Jordanians, with whom the Israelis had signed a peace treaty only three years earlier, successfully demanded release of imprisoned Hamas leader Sheikh Ahmed Yassin, who was sitting in an Israeli jail.[3] This turn of events would have wide-ranging repercussions for years to come. Less than a dozen years later, Yassin's name would surface frequently when he was accused by the Israelis of being a major instigator of suicide attacks during the second intifada, which took place between the years 2000 and 2004.

Yassin was a marked man, and the Israelis wanted him. After a failed attempt to eliminate him in 2003, when the Israeli Air Force dropped a 550-pound bomb on a building in which Yassin and Hamas leaders were said to have convened, he was killed in a missile strike on the morning of March 22, 2004, as the wheelchair-bound cleric left a Gaza mosque following his morning prayers. Afterwards the Palestinians vowed nothing less than violent revenge against the Israelis.

For an intelligence service that tends to move along the outer reaches as a matter of course, Israeli intelligence has maintained a tradition of unorthodoxy. In addition to its roles as defender of the state and safeguarder of early warning, it has anointed itself with the responsibility of protecting Jews throughout the world. For instance, it is the Mossad that is widely credited with secretly airlifting thousands of Iraqi and Moroccan Jews to Israel in the 1940s, '50s, and '60s. Two decades later, it was again Israeli intelligence that was behind the secret flight of 8,000 Ethiopian Jews over a six-week period in 1985 from an undisclosed location in the Sudan, dubbed Operation Moses. After news leaked of the mission, however, Arab states pressured the Sudan to cease aiding the Israelis, the flights stopped, and 15,000 people were left behind. The flights resumed under Operation Solomon in 1991 after political and diplomatic wrangling. During a 36-hour period starting on Friday, May 24, 34 El Al jumbo jets and Hercules C-130 transport planes flew non-stop and ferried 14,324 Ethiopian Jews to Israel.[4]

It is the unrelenting demands of security that have spurred Israel's intelligence agencies to use every ounce of its human resources and to develop sophisticated intelligence systems, the source of many technological innovations that would not only radically transform intelligence-gathering but would greatly impact the information age. This situation, resembling a spinning top rotating counterclockwise within another spinning top that is turning clockwise, has created a razor-sharp reflex to adapt and to consider the improbable. "When there was the Cold War between the East and West you saw everything. You could tell each other what the other was doing," said retired Brigadier General Elie Barr, who commanded unit 8200 between the years 1987 and 1990. "Here the situation is different. Today it is Hizbollah, tomorrow Iraq. There is relative peace with Jordan but you can't overlook it, and the Egyptian situation may change tomorrow. It is topsy-turvy, and it calls for creativity combined with restricted resources."

That defining ethos is perhaps why Israel has been at the vanguard in stretching its human and technological assets beyond the customary confines of espionage. Beyond having to innovate to survive, Israel must innovate to stay afoot. There is a continued pressure to increase layers of security and options in meeting new and unseen threats, and in doing so defining a way of thinking instilled in generations of Israeli innovators. One of its basic advantages is its predilection toward the unconventional and audacious. "The way I was trained when I was an intelligence officer was to think like my opponent," said "Eban," who served in the field as a platoon commander and received the Israel Security Award and Intelligence Prize for Creativity. At one point in his career, he was sent on an exchange to the United States Army Intelligence Center at Fort Huachuca in Arizona. "I was involved in several exercises in which we would act in several military situations. For every situation there were two, three, or four possibilities from the most reasonable to the other side. At Fort Huachuca they only went with the ways that were written in the book. But there are ways of doing things that are not in the book." He adds that while some look for a lost coin at night under a street lamp, "we are looking for it in the dark where it's more frightening and more difficult."

Just weeks after U.S. Armed Forces captured Saddam Hussein in December 2003, Israeli newspapers revealed an Israeli plot, ordered by the late Prime Minister Yitzhak Rabin, to assassinate the Iraqi dictator in 1992.[5] The planned operation, in retaliation for the 39 Scud missiles that Hussein fired at Israel during the first Gulf War in 1991, intended to land members of Sayeret Matkal, the elite Israeli commando reconnaissance unit, into Iraq and fire custom-made missiles that would home in on Hussein during the funeral of his father-in-law. The mission, however, was scrapped when five soldiers from the Sayeret were killed after live missiles were mistakenly used during a training exercise at the Tze'elim base in the southern Negev.

Despite the tragic training mishap, there are two important points to note that underscore the intrinsic Israeli approach. The first is the relative daring of the plan itself. It required covertly landing the commandos into enemy territory at least 400 miles away from Israel and flying them out on an Israeli plane from a temporarily built airfield in Iraq. Secondly, and more importantly, the intelligence information needed to pinpoint Hussein, a peripatetic dictator who was widely reported to not sleep for more than a few hours at a time in one location and to have deployed a small army of doubles during his reign, needed to be dead accurate. The Israeli commandos never arrived at the funeral, but as it turned out, Saddam Hussein did indeed attend it—just as intelligence predicted.[6]

As with audacity, the Israelis are known for their painstaking attention to detail and a singularly enterprising ability to ferret out even the thinnest of information to great effect. It's one thing to pick off information through conventional means such as monitoring the movements of an army, its weapons, and infrastructure and quite another to grasp intentions, motivations, strengths, and weaknesses that rarely venture out into the open. The notable failures notwithstanding, the Israelis have had remarkable success in finding and then connecting the dots. "We understand the importance of the small detail," said retired Brigadier General Pinchas Buchris, who commanded unit 8200 between 1997 and 2001. "We are involved in a lot of efforts to collect the small detail; nothing is too small." Through a combination of informants, deep cover agents, and technology, intelligence agents have become adept at marrying a little knowledge and a lot of imagination.

For instance, in the early part of 1999, the Israelis were involved in talks with the Syrians in an attempt to negotiate decades of enmity and disputed borders between the two nations. For their part, the Israelis wanted to know a little bit more about Syrian President Hafez Assad. Inscrutable, the autocratic Assad had run Syria for nearly 29 years since a bloodless coup installed him in power in 1970. But as the two countries engaged in unprecedented peace negotiations, it was clear that Assad was in ill health, the exact nature of which (like much about Assad) was not public. For the Israelis, it was urgent that they should know precisely what they were dealing with, as Assad was now in the mood to talk; whoever succeeded him might not be so inclined. The key question was when such a succession might take place.

According to published reports in Israel and abroad, the Israelis seized on the opportunity of the state funeral of King Hussein of

Jordan, who died after a lengthy battle with cancer in February 1999. Assad would attend Hussein's funeral in Amman. A special toilet was reserved for the Syrian leader's exclusive use, and the Israelis redirected its pipes to a jar. A urine sample obtained this way was sent to Israel, where doctors evaluated it and found that Assad was in the very advanced stages of cancer and diabetes. The doctors concluded that the Syrian dictator was not long for this world, and, indeed, he died 16 months after the episode.[7]

For many, the origins of Israeli intelligence go back to the days of the Old Testament when Moses sent 12 spies into the land of Canaan to report back on the strengths, weaknesses, and numbers of the Canaanites. The modern tradition of running agents across enemy lines began, in the early years before the state of Israel was established, with the *Palmach Mista'aravim,* a unit of Jews disguised as Arabs. That tradition continues in many forms, including the clutch of undercover units that operate within the Palestinian territories. Indeed, one of the hallmarks of Israeli intelligence has been its adroit use of human intelligence. This practice may be one of Israel's finest examples of mining a homegrown resource in a land where resources are always in short supply.

In running spies all over the world, Israel has prodigiously tapped into its deep and broad repository of immigrants from more than 70 countries, particularly those that originally came from Arab lands. Meir Amit recalled the first generations that arrived in Israel. They not only spoke fluent Arabic but also lived and breathed as Arabs and could easily be absorbed in any number of Arab cities without arousing many suspicions. "This was a very important asset for us in infiltrating without anyone noticing," he said. "It was not just teaching them the language but they knew Islamic habits. They could pray in the mosque, and even if they were woken up they wouldn't blow their cover." A testament to just how good many of them were is that many died while in the field and are buried in cemeteries in Arab countries, their true identities concealed. Perhaps the most famous Israeli spy of all time, however, was Egyptian-born Eli Cohen, a legend in the history of Israeli espionage who accessed the highest levels of the Syrian government. He spent two years establishing his cover as Kamal Amin Taabes, a businessman born in Lebanon of Syrian parents who had emigrated first to Egypt and then to Argentina. During his three years undercover in Damascus, he laid bare Syria's fortifications on the Golan Heights, exposed plans to reroute the Jordan River's headwaters away from Israel, catalogued Soviet weaponry sent to Syria, and detailed the relationship between Syria and the PLO, until he was found out and publicly hanged in Damascus in 1965.[8]

By comparison, the United States, an immigrant nation of the tallest order, found itself linguistically ill-equipped on a number of occasions. For instance, immediately following the September 11, 2001 terrorist attacks, the U.S. government was short on speakers in a number of Central Asian and Middle Eastern languages, and it put out a public call asking for native speakers of Arabic, Pashto, and Urdu. It was later reported that when American troops were deployed to Haiti in the 1990s, the National Security Agency had only one Haitian Creole linguist and suffered a similar dearth of linguists before entering into the conflicts in Somalia and the Balkans.[9]

A reminder of the significance that human intelligence has played in Israeli life is a tumble of sandstone walls that come together to form the shape of a human brain at the Center for Special Studies in Glilot. It is a memorial to those who died in the service of intelligence. Established in the mid-1980s, its walls are engraved with the names of the hundreds of men and women killed while serving their country's intelligence services. Still deliberately shrouded in secrecy, only the individual names and dates of death are recorded. A separate unmarked wall commemorates those who died and must remain under deep cover even in death. Here on Intelligence Day, the relatives of those whose names are represented on these walls come to remember them.

While Israel's use of human intelligence may be in a class by itself, the nation's unparalleled need for accurate and real-time intelligence spurred the move toward the development and deployment of electronic espionage methods. Like the IDF, which has served as an important

...Israeli intelligence has played a crucial role in the development of information technology, which in time would find its way into a number of commercial applications.

incubator in the development of technology in Israel, devising advanced electronic weaponry to offset its personnel deficit, Israeli intelligence has played a crucial role in the development of information technology, which in time would find its way into a number of commercial applications.

The brilliant mathematician and scientist Yuval Ne'eman is widely viewed as the individual who very early discerned the role that technology would play in intelligence-gathering. Born in Tel Aviv in 1925, he earned his bachelor's and master's degrees in engineering at the Technion in Haifa and his doctorate in science and technology at Imperial College, London. Nicknamed "the Brain," Ne'eman fought in Israel's War of Independence in 1948 and later joined Aman. He would make important contributions in the fields of particle physics, astrophysics, cosmology, and philosophy of science. Among his many illustrious achievements, he served as president of Tel Aviv University, Israel's minister of Science Development, and Israel's chief defense scientist, and he founded Israel's Space Agency. He was also director of the Center for Particle Theory at the University of Texas, Austin, where he resides as a professor emeritus. His idea of "instant intelligence," now a thoroughly routine concept in intelligence-gathering, was nothing less than a breakthrough when first introduced.[10]

It was the 1950s, a time when computer science was more fantasy than fact. Ne'eman, however, displayed a prophetic understanding that technology offered a way to sort and analyze the flood of information from existing methods to better anticipate and forecast future wars and attacks. The geopolitical realities of Israel meant that its traditional espionage techniques were not enough: the nation needed real-time intelligence. Although considered revolutionary, he believed this would give Israel a decisive edge against its enemies. Indeed, Ne'eman's work in advancing electronic intelligence by using computers to analyze and document intelligence was considered equal in significance, although not in scale, to the efforts of the Pentagon and the National Security Agency in the United States, and it is said even to have rivaled the European efforts at the time.[11]

The development of electronic intelligence took a series of giant leaps forward. The daily updates sifted, sorted, and analyzed by computers gave way to the development of electronic watch stations that allowed the Israelis to constantly observe their borders as well as enemy territory with electronic recording devices capable of picking up conversations and collecting and recording information. The course was set. Despite restraints in budgets and resources, Israeli techniques would support the highly imaginative, the odd, and the seemingly improbable. For instance, in the 1970s the Israelis tested a microwave respiration monitor on the thousands of West Bank Arabs who regularly crossed into Israel over the Allenby Bridge. The idea was to narrow in on possible suspects while allowing others to pass through as quickly as possible. As soldiers checked the incoming Arabs, a monitor directed at them would record the microwaves bouncing off of their stomachs. Those breathing faster than normal would be flagged for extra scrutiny.[12]

For many years, the Israelis have benefited from their strategic, military, and technical cooperation with the United States and its agencies. However, Ne'eman's work provided the foundation for numerous enterprising devices, systems, and inventions that refined intelligence. It expanded the scope of intelligence-gathering, providing the traditional agent with better, faster, and more sophisticated tools. It would lead to areas in communications, and radar and monitoring systems. In a career of impressive innovations, one of Ne'eman's most far-reaching was the invention of a computerized system to track submarines.[13] Over the course of time, Israel would create several technological units under the rubric of its intelligence umbrella to continuously create new methods and means to predict and prevent war and to protect the nation.

Israeli intelligence distinguishes itself on a number of fronts: in its approach, its methodology, and the use of its "assets." As such, Israeli intelligence has earned the kind of reputation that has inspired both awe and fear from its rivals and colleagues. Israel's intelligence community does not stand apart because it is better. It does, however, operate with one fundamental factor that cannot be underestimated—motivation. "Our folks are more dedicated. We believe in the struggle," insisted Uzi Arad, the former deputy director of the Mossad. "We are not in it for fun. The head of British intelligence once said to me, 'Isn't this a great game we are in?' Israel does not enjoy playing intelligence. What makes us different is the human resource. Our people have a more developed sense of purpose and drive, and we try harder. That's what differentiates us from the others."

The difficulty concerning intelligence is that it is not a science; it requires one to know as much as one can about the enemy, which is to say that there is always an inherent level of doubt, of uncertainty, and of the unspecified. There is a great deal of room for the unknown, and dealing in the unknown means that one is dealing with options.

> *There is a great deal of room for the unknown, and dealing in the unknown means that one is dealing with options.*

Israel's identity has increasingly been defined by conflict, first with its Arab neighbors and later with the Palestinian population. What has developed is a pervasive military-intelligence culture that is as much about military power as it is about national identity. It is impossible to separate the two. Like many nations where the military occupies a central role in the life of the country, in Israel, too, it remains the arbiter of power and plays a seminal role in the shaping of leaders and the networks that support them. Under the surface, however, resides a symbiosis that defies the customary relationship between power and leadership and the ruler and ruled in a society living under a heavy military presence. True, the merits of its place as the dominant regional military power may be open for serious debate. But what is evident is that rather than closing the spigot for change and openness to new ideas, this singular force acts as a channel for them. Israel's military culture is inextricable from Israeli society. And Israeli society is indelibly marked by a penchant for creativity, entrepreneurialism, and innovation.

5 Listening In

Central Tel Aviv, Israel, January 5, 1996…

Early in the morning, a moment of relief filled the Kirya, the dun-colored military defense complex that sits in the center of Tel Aviv. Israel's top military and intelligence echelons had learned that less then 50 miles away, in a squalid Gaza refugee camp, the man behind one of the longest and deadliest stretches of terrorist attacks in a land not unaccustomed to violence was dead. He was Yehiya Ayyash, Hamas's master bomb maker, at the time Israel's most-wanted terrorist. Over a three-year period, Ayyash's lethal occupation left more than 100 people dead and another 500 seriously wounded. During his reign of terror, Ayyash had managed to escape the grasp of the Israeli military, confound its intelligence agents, and nearly bring the Oslo peace process to its knees. Now, the exhaustive hunt for the man known all over the Middle East as "the Engineer" was over.

It had ended in an instant, and it began with a phone call.

The beginning of the end for Yehiya Ayyash came sometime around 1:00 A.M. on April 16, 1993. A bomb of his design traveled along the Jordan Valley Highway, undetected inside of a Volkswagen Transporter. A young Palestinian named Shahar al-Nabulsi drove the Volkswagen from Nablus to the Mehula Junction and parked it between two Israeli buses. Al-Nabulsi flipped the master control switch, igniting an electric charge that set off a mass of explosives attached to the car's fuel tanks. The force of the explosion burst upward, creating an inferno that made scrap metal of the Volkswagen and instantly killed al-Nabulsi. Following the blast, some of his body parts were found as far as a hundred yards away.

The explosion also killed an Arab worker who had the great misfortune of standing near the junction that morning. Twenty Israeli soldiers and a civilian in the immediate vicinity of the bomb were injured. But the impact of this particular terror attack hit deeper than just the immediacy of the injured and dead. It marked a significant turning point in the Israeli-Palestinian conflict. Ayyash had introduced suicide bombings as a weapon of terror to the streets of Israel.

On the heels of the Mehula attack came more suicide bombings, and the attackers operated with greater sophistication and frequency. A year earlier, Ayyash had booby-trapped a car in Ramat Efal, northeast of Tel Aviv, but Israeli police had discovered it and blown it up before it could harm anyone. Ramat Efal was just a test case, and Mehula was Ayyash's opening gambit. If there was any question as to the deliberate nature of the attacks or their origin, it was answered on April 6, 1994. Another young Palestinian, Ra'id Zaqarna, most likely drafted from one of the many mosques where Hamas and other militant organizations recruited potential suicide bombers, drove a blue Opel Ascona packed with Ayyash's bomb, made of gas cylinders and antipersonnel grenades and fortified with carpenter's nails, to the small town of Afula in the Jezreel Valley. Zaqarna parked the Opel in front of the No. 348 bus that had just picked up a group of high school students and hit the detonator. A thunderclap-like bang filled the area as the car burst into a cloud of black smoke and flames. The bomb killed 9 and wounded 55.

Just days later, a crowded bus leaving Hadera, a coastal town south of Haifa, was ripped apart by another suicide bomb shortly after departing for Tel Aviv. The toll this time was 6 dead and 30 seriously wounded. Another powerful blast in October sheared the No. 5 bus as it passed by the busy Dizengoff Square in Tel Aviv. This time the violent explosion took the lives of 21 individuals and injured 50, and it was so strong that it actually raised the bus from its chassis.

Very soon it was clear that these bombs were not the work of a rank amateur but suggested the handiwork of a skilled operator. Every bomb has what is known as a signature (a common denominator in how it is made), and these attacks had the insidious mark of one individual. Following a thread that wove its way through informants, interrogations, and electronic monitoring, the Israelis had narrowed in on the identity of the bombmaker. Yehiya Ayyash was the eldest of three sons from the West Bank village of Rafat. Both a pious Muslim and an honor student, he possessed an innate ability for anything mechanical and studied electrical engineering at Bir Zeit University. No doubt he was an embittered product of the Israeli occupation. He was dangerous not just because of his ability to make bombs but also because he had a gift for teaching, and he used this gift to instruct a number of young and eager Islamic militants in the art of bomb-making.

Ayyash posed a serious challenge to the Israeli authorities—especially the Shin Bet, whose agents blanketed the Palestinian territories with undercover squads and a network of informants. The Israelis spent three years chasing him down. He was clever and elusive, and he made few mistakes. As he became public enemy number one for the Israelis, he quickly became a legend among Palestinians, and his fame spread in the towns, villages, and refugee camps across the territories. Ayyash survived by his wits. He moved among a series of safe houses, flitting in and out of Gaza and the West Bank. He rarely slept in the same place for long and was a master of disguises. It was reported that among his favorite covers were those of an Orthodox Jew and an Israeli soldier.[1] Israeli agents doggedly pursued him. They maintained surveillance on his wife and parents. Still, Ayyash was able to slip through their net. More than once the Israelis missed capturing him, sometimes by mere minutes.

It had become clear that it wasn't enough just to catch Ayyash; he had to be cauterized in order to stem the flow of the small and destructive army of suicide bombers he was capable of unleashing. Several Israelis described the particular arc of terror that they were facing in the same manner: When somebody is willing to die, it changes the rules of the game. Several years later, when Israel was again seized by a series of suicide attacks, Brigadier General Schmuel Yachin explained that when it came to suicide bombings, "the threshold of humanity has been crossed." The ultimate disincentive, or leverage, of death no longer applies. Outsmarting the suicide bombers takes on a whole new dimension. Ayyash had changed the equation, enabling a more effective weapon that could terrorize and paralyze a whole society. It is nearly impossible to eliminate the motivations of terrorists. However, it is possible to reduce their capabilities to act on those motivations.

Ayyash was clever. The Israelis had to be smarter. They had fortitude; what they needed was a break. What they didn't have was time. Until he was caught, Ayyash was, as the Israelis say, "a ticking time bomb" before the next attack. The Palestinian Authority, which under the Oslo accords was ostensibly cooperating with Israel on security matters during this period, had repeatedly been asked by the Israelis to arrest Ayyash. At one point, Arafat told them that Ayyash was in the Sudan.[2] The Israelis would take matters into their own hands.

At the tail end of 1995, the Israelis caught their break in the person of Kamil Hamad, a wealthy Gaza businessman who was believed to have had links with the Israeli military and, according to reports, to have worked as an informant of some sort on Shin Bet's payroll. In the pursuit of Ayyash, the name Kamil Hamad turned up. Hamad's nephew, Osama Hamad, was a member of Hamas who had offered Ayyash, his old college friend, a place to stay. It was an apartment in one of the many cinder-block buildings in the refugee town of Beit Lahiya on the northernmost tip in the Gaza Strip. The hunt for Ayyash, which had been stymied, thwarted, and close to successful on many occasions only to turn up empty, had renewed momentum. Now the Israelis had a fixed location on Ayyash. Furthermore, a very clever headline-making plan to lock in on him was in motion.

Ayyash was scrupulously careful in all of his movements except one. His fatal flaw was that he maintained fairly regular contact with his family—usually by cell phone, although he switched it frequently to avoid detection by the Israelis. Osama worked for his uncle, and in the course of their business together, the elder Hamad purchased a cell phone for his nephew. On occasion Osama lent it to his friend Ayyash. At some point, apparently, Ayyash passed the number on to his father as a way to contact him. Somewhere along the way, however, the Israelis had apparently convinced Kamil Hamad to hand the phone over to them first.

On January 5, Ayyash's father tried calling the apartment's landline but got a constant busy signal. So he dialed his son on a cellular phone. What happened next is well documented. Not long after Ayyash greeted his father on the cell phone, it exploded, killing him instantly. The execution was so precise that when he was found, his body lay untouched by the blast's impact—except for the right side of his face, which was blown off.

Although Israel did not officially claim responsibility for Ayyash's execution, its government had engaged in a long-standing policy of eliminating and preventing terror when and however possible. Moreover, not long after Ayyash's body was discovered, reports of his death quickly erupted in the Israeli media, which strongly intimated that the work of Israeli secret agents was behind the hit.[3] In subsequent years, Ayyash's assassination by cell phone became something of a widely held secret, largely attributed to the Shin Bet. However, like most operations, this one was an intricately choreographed combination of Israel's intelligence and security resources. While most of the operational details remain under wraps, what is certain is that it required extraordinary intelligence. The operation obviously involved classic human intelligence, but it also involved a significant amount of electronic information and signals wizardry.

As a result of Israel's unceasing need for real-time intelligence, it has accumulated a voluminous catalogue of information on its adversaries. Such intelligence-gathering has

necessitated the creation and refinement over time of the technological means with which to analyze the compendious
amount of information it collects. So, when Kamil Hamad's
name emerged, a link was quickly established, and it was only a
matter of time before a plan would be set in motion.[4] The Israelis could manipulate Ayyash's use of a cell phone. In the best of
times phone lines in the territories regularly malfunctioned, so
it would not trigger any alarms if they didn't work on the morning of January 5. It is believed that intelligence jammed the
phone lines in the house where Ayyash was staying. This strategy was not new. In April 1988, when Israeli commandos
stormed the Tunis villa of PLO number two Abu Jihad and
killed him, telephone and radio links in the neighborhood were
also jammed and interrupted, preventing anyone from contact-
ing the authorities during the raid and ensuring the soldiers
time to escape following the hit.[5]

Perhaps the most critical segment of the operation, once the
cell phone was in use, was to make certain that it was Ayyash on
the line. In order to authenticate the caller, somebody first had
to be listening in. As Ayyash answered his friend's cellular
phone, a small, unmarked plane was reported to have flown
above Beit Lahiya with an Israeli agent on board, who was said
to be listening on a headset as Ayyash greeted his father. Almost
instantly after the elder Ayyash addressed his son, the conversation was over. As soon as "the Engineer" was identified, 50
grams of RDX explosives hidden within the battery cavity of the
cell phone were detonated by radio signal.

Unit 8200 may be considered the most powerful and far-
reaching espionage agency in Israel, and until a flood of its exiting soldiers turned into entrepreneurs, it was perhaps the least

known as well. Its existence has for decades been buried under a mantle of secrecy and anonymity. The Israelis have been so scrupulous in guarding the details of the unit that only a small group of individuals could accurately measure the significant part it has played in Israeli intelligence and operational successes. However, tracing the thread of unit activity backward, the striking influence it has had in the development of the high-tech industry in Israel is hardly a secret. As such an influential group, it is a notable example of the very specific brand of Israeli innovation that is formed by the convergence of security threats, creativity, determination, and the premium placed on science, technology, and education in Israel in order to compensate for its limitation of land, borders, and personnel.

In Israel's unrelenting hunt to obtain intelligence on its adversaries and allies, the nation recognized early on the need to supplement its highly effective human intelligence (HUMINT) capabilities with technology. A significant part of that need includes the technological means to eavesdrop. In foreign reports, it has been likened to the National Security Agency (NSA) in the United States, and the unit is tasked with protecting Israel's sensitive data as well as collecting, deciphering, and analyzing the millions (if not billions) of pieces of information it traps, intercepts, catches, and targets in its sophisticated electronic dragnet. It is an open secret that communications within the Palestinian territories and links to other Arab nations are monitored closely. It is this unit that listens in on the electronic communications, the voice and data traffic that runs across communication networks. Yossi Melman, inveterate chronicler of Israel's intelligence services as a correspondent with the daily newspaper *Ha'aretz* and co-author of *Every Spy a Prince,* calls the unit "the most important unit in the field of collection—full stop. It is the most important [in intelligence]; more than the Mossad or anything else really, it is way beyond military intelligence."

For most, the name Mossad—the formidable Israeli intelligence service—conjures up images of a fearless, ruthless, and, above all, cunning group of spies waging a secret war in the service of their country. After all, its motto is "By Way of Deception Thou Shalt Do War." And for decades, the Mossad has done just that. With a history of seemingly impossible exploits across the globe, it has taken on a mythic status in the high-stakes game of survival. Many of the kind of special operations—those that are known anyway—that have become associated with Israel have a deserved reputation for astonishing feats of ingenuity. Some involve elite undercover squads, and others require technological sleight of hand, but all require very specific and accurate information.

In terms of the kinds of problems and threats Israel must deal with, it shares those of larger and more powerful nations and their security agencies. Israel's intelligence agencies do not, however, have the same kind of budget or resources in order to acquire the kind of technological assets to deal with them. So unit 8200, much like the military it hails from, came to rely a great deal on its own ingenuity in developing and creating its own sophisticated systems. The unit acquires some of the smartest and most creative brains in the country and essentially gives them a highly charged, technological sandbox in which to play. In a vastly technological-oriented army, unit 8200 has become a not inconsiderable source of the IDF's research and development in advanced technologies.

In 1950, the unit was designated as a department of the electronic and communications division of the IDF and was given a budget of $15,000 and an additional $110,000 for making electronic purchases abroad. While the early modest sums were supplemented greatly over the years, the unit's budget reportedly eclipses that of the Mossad. Early on, it was apparent that its needs would always outstrip its budget, resources, and personnel. At the same time, the field of electronic warfare remained in the dark all over the world. Few sources were available for acquisition. Moreover, owing to the clandestine nature of intelligence, the unit could not make large purchases. Instead, it developed its own technologies and solutions and adapted existing systems for its own specific needs. "When it comes to intelligence equipment," explained "Reuven," a former officer who spent nearly 20 years in the unit, "you never want to expose your sources. If you buy them, you expose them. We are not allowed to buy core technologies. We develop them in-house."

Since its earliest days, the unit's existence has neither been publicly announced nor formally acknowledged, but the marks of its activities are as numerous as they are untraceable. Most of its pursuits remain classified, and yet over time rumors of its activities surfaced. Some of its activities have surfaced intentionally, as in the case of the Nasser-Hussein and *Achille Lauro* intercepts, but mostly they could only be hinted at. On occasion, the unit was referenced in public, but usually in oblique terms, such as identifying it as the Central Collections Unit or the electronic eavesdropping arm of Aman, Israeli military intelligence. One of the public outings in which the unit was named and linked to its activities came about in Victor Ostrovsky's controversial and disillusioned account of his time as a case officer in the Mossad. In his book *By Way of Deception*, he briefly noted an elaborate communications interference operated by unit 8200 that included pilfering Arab transmissions from a satellite system linked to a Mediterranean cable out of Palermo, Sicily.[6]

In time, while the tightly coiled rings of military intelligence later widened to a somewhat broader circle within Israel, the unit took on a kind of exalted status. It became the brainy equivalent of brawny elite commando units like the Sayeret Matkal. These individuals worked their own kind of alchemy, and their currency was not gold but rather the relatively more valuable property of information technology. They were the minds behind the state-of-the art electronic and communications technologies that served the IDF. As the Israeli economy began to accelerate, powered in large part by the high-tech explosion that began in the mid-1990s, this unit that had spent its lifetime in the dark was suddenly coming into the spotlight. That is because an improbably high number of commercial technologies began emerging out of the country, and an equally disproportionate number of their entrepreneurs seemed to come from the same four-digit unit in the military. At one point, the Israeli daily *Ha'aretz* called this military unit the most important force in the Israeli economy.

And the paper produced a short list of big deals that had come out of it including Oshap Technologies, a software company that was sold to Sunguard Data in the United States for $210 million.[7] Soon, venture capitalists from Silicon Valley to Japan would inquire of Israeli entrepreneurs, "Are you from the unit?"

Since the exact details of the unit (including its members) are shrouded in secrecy, a kind of fabled status has been projected onto it. That includes the origins of the name of the unit itself. Of course, like most legends, quixotic elements become burnished into their histories—a blend of myth and fact over time—and unit 8200 is no exception. The name itself is a simple four-digit number (although it has gone through different designations through the years; at one point it was called unit 848), but in all likelihood, the number was ascribed to the unit through the mundane process of a computer assignment. However, a more popular story attached itself to the unit. It goes that the electronic warfare unit got its name from its founding members: 8 Ashkenazi Jews and 200 Sephardic immigrants who came to Israel from Iraq, who were educated under the British in wireless communications and as Iraqi Railways radio operators, and who, above all else, had an intimate understanding of Arabic.

Actually, in some ways, that description is not too far off the mark in terms of sentiment—even if it is not exactly a perfect recounting of historical detail. The unit's origins, however, are a rather more practical affair. It began in the hodgepodge of pre-state agencies linked to the Jewish agents who learned the art of wiretapping and early signal intelligence under the British. Indeed, many of their early skills were learned in the days when the British ruled Palestine during the Mandate and the Jews worked closely with them, first against the Ottoman Turks and later Nazi Germany. In turn, the underground Haganah would utilize these skills against the British.

Following independence, the Israelis set up a small and secretive electronic warfare unit in a green villa that once belonged to an Arab sheik in the old port town of Jaffa, south of Tel Aviv. Codenamed Rabbit, it was part of Intelligence Service 2, the rather unimaginatively named agency responsible for monitoring enemy transmissions. Rabbit was tasked with breaking codes and intercepting the electronic communications of Israel's Arab neighbors. The premise was simple: Information about the enemy is essential. It dictates all other actions, and this was a unit that would get that information through technological means.

During the first years of Israel as a modern state, only a clutch of nations possessed the ability to break codes and had computerized systems to aid in intelligence. Among them were, of course, the United States, the United Kingdom, and the Soviet Union. Israel quickly joined this elite group because it had deduced early on the importance technology could play in its intelligence and defense capabilities. "Israel was at the forefront of all of these countries," said Yossi Melman, intelligence correspondent for the daily *Ha'aretz*. "It was in the top 10 in the world." According to Melman, the exposure in 1967 of the conversation between Egyptian President Nasser and Jordan's King Hussein revealed as much about the gap between the Arab nations' and Israel's thinking as it did about Israel's technical capabilities. "It shows Arab leaders as obnoxious and unaware of our technological capabilities," he explained. "They spoke on an open line. Israel's edge over them was not because Israel had advanced equipment, but in the idea that we would listen to them."

Despite its early awareness of the role that technology could play, Israel was still bound by significant constraints. Lacking in the kind of experience, traditions, and budgets allocated to the established secret services and the technological capabilities of other countries, in its place the unit developed a highly tuned method in the art of finding a way to succeed under extreme pressure. For instance, not long after independence, one of its earliest and most rudimentary attempts to monitor Arab communications involved rigging up an antenna made from a metal wire hundreds of meters long tied between two poles and connected to an old S38 receiver. Other initiatives required inventive skills of another sort. In 1949, the unit developed and built its first monitor based on plans stolen from the BBC.

The improvisational style that came to signify the unit appeared early and remained a constant. In the late 1960s, it used a large antenna called a *corpse* to capture signals that had to be carried into place on the back of a big truck. The only truck big enough was so old and broken down that a second truck had to follow it carrying spare parts in case it fell apart. Every time members of the unit would go out to receive signals, they needed to take two trucks—one to carry the antenna and the second to carry parts for the truck. In 1966, a year before Israel would take the West Bank in the Six Day War, the IDF purchased its first dirigible, or balloon, from the British. It would be used to monitor signals. The only problem was that the Israelis had no way to figure out where to receive the strongest broadcasts of their intended target. So a soldier in the unit took a small plane and flew around Jerusalem. In one hand, he held out an antenna to measure signals on a screen. Every time the plane changed direction, the soldier had to move the antenna to the opposite window. Each time he received a signal, he graphed it on a chart to determine where the most powerful signals were located in order to place the balloon there. This location turned out to be Neve Ilan. A year later, the Israelis captured the entire West Bank in the Six Day War and no longer needed to keep the blimp aloft in Jerusalem.

The unit's kind of rough and ready ingenuity also applied to where it set up its early listening posts. In the early 1950s, it moved out of the Jaffa house and established a foothold among the orchards in central Israel. Technicians laid wire antennas in the fields and began working on expanding the unit's efforts into a number of electronic, signal, communication, and other complimentary disciplines. By the mid-1960s, the unit had five bases in different parts of the country, including Be'er Sheva in the Negev Desert, the Galil in the north, and Jerusalem. The unit used a police vacation building in the Galil when it was empty in the winter. When the police returned in the summer, unit members had to remove the monitoring equipment and install it in the garden. Another base on the Mediterranean coast was set up in a kennel, but first the soldiers had to sell all of the dogs.

The sensitive early work the unit was engaged in also found its way beyond Israel's borders. Two early examples subsequently came to light because they were ultimately discovered—one with tragic consequences. In 1954, five Israeli soldiers were captured by the Syrians as they retrieved taping devices planted earlier on telephone lines between fortifications along the Golan Heights—then part of Syria. These devices consisted of a long black wire that transmitted signals to a receiver in Israel and a small transponder buried underground with a built-in explosive charge, for use if the devices were discovered. One of the soldiers, Uri Ilan, the son of a former Mapai Party member of the Israeli Knesset (parliament), committed suicide in his Syrian jail. When his body was returned to Israel a year later, they found a note he had written which read, "I didn't betray my country."[8] About 20 years later, during the early 1970s, the Israelis tapped into Egyptian military communications by replacing a telephone pole with a hollowed out one near one of Egypt's army bases along the Gulf of Suez. Inside the pole was a nickel cadmium battery-operated transmitter that picked up and rebroadcast communications from Egypt's main military line to its Red Sea outposts.[9]

Technological advances would lead to significant leaps in the ability to spy. It would be intelligence agencies such as those in Israel, the NSA, the General Communications Headquarters (GCHQ) in the United Kingdom, and the Glavnoye Razvedyvatelnoye Upravlenie (GRU) in what was then the Soviet Union that would increasingly play important roles in driving technological breakthroughs in a high-stakes competition. Major General Aharon Ze'evi Farkash, who was appointed as the director of Aman military intelligence in 2001 and who between 1990 and 1993 commanded the unit, explained that it was these organizations that had a considerable influence in the development of technology:

They dealt with the nucleus of high technology. To close the operational circle you need to build a prototype and make it operational in a very short period of time. SIGINT was built from ELINT [electronic intelligence] and

COMMINT from communications. VISINT [visual intelligence] burst out in the 1960s to 1970s because of the Cold War between the U.S. and the U.S.S.R. Intelligence satellites were launched, and it was the beginning of the race to develop more accurate images [with resolutions of] 10 meters to 5 meters to 1 meter [and even smaller].

According to Farkash, having this kind of satellite imagery for intelligence work became very important for building the kind of technology that later would have civilian applications. "But in the beginning," he said, "it was very important, and billions of dollars were spent in this arena."

Amassing knowledge in these areas increased the range of options available and subsequently the kind of operations that would stretch the imagination. To this day, Israel's most storied counterterrorist action is the one in which commandos rescued the Jewish and Israeli passengers hijacked on an Air France jet en route from Tel Aviv to Paris and held at Uganda's Entebbe Airport in 1976. The episode has been the subject of several films and much ink. One important aspect of the operation that made it possible was the development of a secure voice communication system that allowed the aircraft, including Boeing 707s that served as flying command and control centers, to fly from Israel to Africa undetected. "Generally speaking, the Entebbe operation would not have been successful without it," said a former colonel of the unit who served in it for more than 20 years. "[The operation] needed an elaborate communication system."

Signals intelligence would come to play an increasingly important role in time, as it did in a politically fraught dogfight during the War of Attrition between Israel and Egypt in 1970. The conflict, marked by constant shelling, commando raids, and counterattacks, stretched into three years, starting in 1969. The Soviets, who took a dim view of Israel's crushing victory against its chief Arab client in 1967, supplied the Egyptians with ammunition, surface-to-air-missile batteries, tanks, and MiG fighter jets, and they backed up the arsenal with a few thousand of their own military advisors and technicians. At one point, the Israelis unleashed their air force, and soon dogfights high above the Sinai Peninsula between Israeli pilots in American-made F-4 Phantoms and A-4 Skyhawks and Egyptians in Soviet-made MiGs resembled an airborne shoot-out in the Old West. Indeed, the span of brown desert above which they battled was dubbed "Texas."[10]

The situation escalated when the Soviets, who had helped to safeguard Egyptian air bases and Cairo's airspace with their own pilots, began flying combat missions edging closer to a full-fledged confrontation with the Israeli Air Force in the first part of 1970. In June, after an Israeli Skyhawk on the Suez Canal was chased down by two MiG-21s into the Sinai (where one of the MiGs launched an air-to-air missile that hit the Israeli fighter and forced the pilot to land), the Israelis formed a complicated plan in which the next confrontation would deliver the Soviet-piloted MiGs into an Israeli ambush.

Four Israeli Mirage IIIC fighter jets set off on July 30 to attack an Egyptian radar station on the west bank of the Nile. The Soviets scrambled eight MiG-21s to shoot down the Mirages. As the Mirages drew the MiGs westward, Israeli agents monitored the impending confrontation in order to identify that indeed the MiG pilots flying for Egypt were actually Soviets. Once identified, an additional four Mirages flying in wait at low altitude appeared east behind the MiGs. The Soviets responded, scrambling another dozen MiGs. As the Soviet pilots in the cockpits of their MiG-21s were about to face off with eight Israeli Mirages, four Israeli Phantom F-4s flying under radar detection appeared from below and entered the battle. In the dogfight that enveloped the summer sky, the Israelis shot down five MiGs, killing two of the Soviet pilots while three others parachuted to safety. The remaining MiGs broke off combat, and the Israeli fighters were called off.

A former high-ranking officer of the unit remarked that this operation was possible because "8200 identified the Russian pilots flying as Egyptians. This was a very sophisticated ambush because of the signals intelligence." The complex actionable intelligence allowed the Israelis to monitor cockpit communications and obviously cloak their own. "In 30 to 40 seconds you could hear the Russian pilots going down," he said. "[The mission] couldn't have been unveiled without signals intelligence."[11]

Essentially, unit 8200 came to play two fundamental roles in Israel. The most obvious, of course, is providing intelligence. This is a large unit operating in a variety of areas, and it is responsible for gathering and disseminating actionable intelligence that can affect Israel's security at a

Israel faces a kind of continuous security situation that requires looking at a continuous onslaught of problems without ready-made solutions.

moment's notice. The general picture that has emerged resides on the surface: a unit involved in information warfare. The specifics, of course, remain in the dark; however, despite all of the classified layers of secrecy, what has floated out in the open is the culture of the unit that has made an important imprint all its own. Israel faces a kind of continuous security situation that requires looking at a continuous onslaught of problems without ready-made solutions. Functioning in a compression of time, this unit operates in the self-described realm between the difficult and the impossible. As such, it has come to play a secondary unofficial role in Israel as an R&D engine and as one of its most important developers of innovators.

6 The Collection Agency

Ein Tzahab, Syria, October 5, 2003...

For the better part of three years, Israeli F-16 warplanes had been deployed in striking militant Palestinian targets in the West Bank and the Gaza Strip, and on occasion strafing Hizbollah targets on the volatile Lebanese border, but at 4:30 A.M., they expanded their scope of operations deep inside Syria. For some time, Israel's security apparatuses had collected information on Ein Tzahab, a camp 14 miles northwest of Damascus. They had observed, among other things, would-be combatants learning the art of guerilla warfare and bomb-making. It was, they determined, a terrorist training ground operating with the support of the Syrians. Moreover, they discovered that after receiving instruction and support at Ein Tzahab, several of its graduates then moved back into the Palestinian territories.

According to the Israelis, the short list of those who used the camp included the Palestinian Front for the Liberation of Palestine-General Command (PFLP), Islamic Jihad, and Hamas—the latter two of which had led the campaign of suicide attacks that had marked the Palestinian uprising that began in September 2000. Although in the past the Syrians had denied harboring such training bases on their soil, the Islamic militant groups Hamas and Islamic Jihad kept offices in Damascus. Now, Israel, under the Sharon government, wanted to deliver a message. It was prepared to hit terrorists and those they believed aided them, wherever they may reside.

Barely 24 hours earlier, Hanadi Jaradat, a 29-year-old female lawyer from the West Bank city of Jenin, strapped an explosive belt under her clothing, walked into a crowded restaurant in the port city of Haifa, and blew herself up. The suicide attack killed 21 people who were eating lunch at a popular place called Maxim's on a Saturday afternoon; more than 50 others were wounded. Islamic Jihad claimed responsibility.

Israel's reprisal was delivered straight to Damascus. For the first time since the 30-year-old Yom Kippur War, Israeli warplanes flew into Syria and dropped precision-guided bombs on Ein Tzahab.[1] As the fighter jets returned to their base, all that could be seen of the destroyed camp were plumes of smoke rising up out of the dry riverbed that had previously sheltered it.

Israel had repeatedly accused Syria of being something of a poison-stringed marionette for supporting terrorist organizations that operated out of the Palestinian territories and Iran-sponsored Hizbollah militants in southern Lebanon against Israel. For instance, Khalid Meshal, a Hamas leader (and the subject of the botched Mossad assassination attempt in Jordan in 1997), along with Ramadan Abdullah Shalah, a head of Islamic Jihad, were based in Syria. The United States had also, particularly following the September 11, 2001, terror attacks, taken a somewhat tougher posture toward Syria, calling on Damascus to end its support of radical Palestinian groups and crack down on terror cells operating within its borders. Both the Syrian government and Islamic Jihad denied Israel's accusations, claiming Ein Tzahab was a civilian camp housing Palestinian refugees. Even so, at the time, they refused to allow journalists to visit the site.

Following the cross-border strike, the IDF released undated TV footage that they claimed was of Ein Tzahab, taken from Iranian television. On it, a military officer is seen presenting a tour of the camp that included a room displaying weapons apparently seized from Israel and tunnels filled with a cache of arms and ammunition. Not long after, amid regional and international condemnation of the airstrike, information surfaced that verified to a degree Israel's description of the site. Leaked reports coming out of Washington said that American surveillance satellites had identified new construction activity at the camp.[2] Furthermore, *Time* magazine reported that members of Iran's military had gone to Ein Tzahab early that summer with the expressed purpose of equipping the camp for Islamic Jihad.[3]

What exactly was going on at Ein Tzahab may never fully come to light publicly. However, sitting across the border in Israel is some powerful electronic monitoring equipment. One of Israel's most strategically important signal intelligence (SIGINT) stations sits on Mount Hermon, overlooking Damascus only 21 miles in the distance. Operated by unit 8200, Mount Hermon is known as the country's electronic eyes and ears in the north, from which it monitors, intercepts, and deciphers communications coming out of the area. Since the Israelis captured the mountain in 1967 when they seized the Golan Heights during the Six Day War, it has served as the country's technological high ground. The Hermon and similar outposts are on the front lines of Israel's ongoing security war. The battle they are engaged in is information, and it is technology, deployed by Israel's corps of electronic soldiers, that lies at the core of that battle.

Mount Hermon, the snow-capped peak on the northern shoulder of the Golan Heights, rises some 9,230 feet above the Upper Jordan Valley. The tallest mountain in the region, it is divided among Syria, Lebanon, and Israel in a knot of demilitarized zones and international borders. On the Israeli side there is a modest ski resort nestled on its sloped plateau, and at its foot sits Majdal Shams, the largest of the community of Druze villages that populate the area. Beyond Majdal Shams to the south is the Ram Pool, a small lake formed over thousands of years from an extinct volcano. A formidable mass of basalt stone, the natural beauty of Mount Hermon is matched perhaps only by the historical cycle of battle and conquer it has endured since Biblical times. That is because its location, overlooking the Golani highland, has given whoever controls the Hermon an obvious geographical and strategic advantage.

Blanketed in antenna towers and a vast array of electronic monitoring and communications intercept equipment, the Israeli ground station is an impressive electronic surveillance fortress that pierces the sky two-thirds of the way from Hermon's summit. It has been said that on a clear day from the Hermon, it is possible to see the Syrian capital with the naked eye. From here, the Israelis are well-positioned to pick up and monitor all kinds of electronic traffic coming in or out of the area. It is the kind of activity that has not only formed the crucial backbone of Israel's intelligence early-warning systems, but has also created an assembly of mathematicians, engineers, linguists, and analysts intensely devoted to evolving beyond the borders of their respective disciplines.

Indeed, the importance of the Hermon to Israeli intelligence-gathering operations was greatly exposed when Syrian forces attacked it on October 6, 1973, the first day of the Yom Kippur War. In the first hours of battle, Syrian commandos, airlifted by helicopters onto Mount Hermon, stormed the unit's bunkers, killing more than a dozen soldiers and capturing a few dozen more that were caught on the mountain outpost. They were held as POWs for several months in Syria. The assault netted a hoard of Israeli military intelligence, including electronic eavesdropping equipment. A complete set of military codes was now in Syrian hands, giving the enemy an open channel to monitor Israel's air force communications.[4]

The more damaging loss from the seizure of the unit's intelligence base atop the mountain, however, was for many the capture of one particular member of the unit, a soldier who happened to be in possession of an encyclopedic memory. A veritable human database, he had decided to go up to the Hermon listening post that fateful day on his own initiative. Under the weight of barbed interrogation, the Syrians were able to extract valuable information from him. The crux of his disclosures would come to haunt more than just this one soldier since they were considered by some to have compromised Israel's security more than the cache of codes and electronic equipment that was acquired in the raid.[5]

Although the Israelis took back the Golan Heights and the Hermon five days later in heavy and fierce fighting, the breach reverberated for decades. The IDF took a number of measures following the war, including stationing an exclusive cordon of soldiers on Mount Hermon. The IDF established a separate unit called the Alpinistim, culled from the ranks of elite special forces and trained specifically to defend the intelligence-gathering installation in the kind of extreme weather conditions and the rough terrain posed by the Hermon's geography.[6]

In addition to Mount Hermon, several electronic listening posts are spread across strategic locations in Israel and manned by the unit. From stations on hilltops to craters in the desert, the Israelis set up an extensive monitoring system of ground-based stations in such places as the Galilee in the north, the Negev Desert in the south, and the Golan Heights. Equipped to pick up signals, such as those from telephone conversations and radio transmissions, that are released into the atmosphere from behind enemy territory, these listening stations provide Israel with a constant stream of crucial data in its infinite task of intelligence collection.

Israel's victory in the Six Day War of 1967 greatly extended the nation's borders to include all of the West Bank, the Gaza Strip, the Sinai Peninsula, and the Golan Heights. As a result, Aman took advantage of the new geopolitical depth to penetrate its scope of monitoring operations against its neighbors still technically in a state of war. The extended frontiers improved greatly the ability to listen in on its adversaries, as the Israelis now had a closer purview with which to pick up their signals. They established a series of secret electronic eavesdropping and early-warning stations along the new de facto borders with Jordan, Syria, and Egypt. Following the peace treaty with Egypt in 1978, the Israelis withdrew from the Sinai Peninsula, and that included pulling up its listening posts in the area. It did not, however, exactly maintain radio silence on its western flank.

The Negev Desert is a large expanse of Israel that covers almost 3,860 square miles of the country to the south. It is a triangular sweep of chalky dunes, dusty plains, and Wadis that narrows down to a point on the Gulf of Aqaba. Traveling along the rugged terrain of expansive brown emptiness one comes across seemingly incongruous agricultural settlements—Israeli towns and Bedouin encampments—and on close inspection some sophisticated listening devices. For instance, to the west near the Egyptian border there is a white balloon lashed to a platform, which is used as an airborne early-warning system. Once, after the balloon broke free of its tether and started to drift east into Jordanian airspace, the Israeli Air Force had to shoot it down. And among the agricultural fields and a shepherd tending his flock, a clutch of monitoring and listening systems stand in the arid desert air, presumably accumulating data like outstretched hands collecting manna from heaven.

Supplementing the electronic ears on the ground, a number of other methods have been deployed to fill in the gaps between stations in order to collect imagery and intercept signals and electronic intelligence. Like the surveillance balloon in the Negev, there is another watching the northern border with Lebanon. Israel is also believed to have at least one intelligence-collecting satellite flying above the earth's atmosphere and capturing information from its neighbors. Flying in at a closer range is Israel's well-documented fleet of UAVs that monitors in real time and with remarkable precision Israel's borders and the Palestinian territories. For instance, on October 20, 2003, Israeli Air Force helicopters fired two missiles about a minute apart into a silver Peugeot they said contained Hamas militants as it drove through the Nusseirat refugee camp in the Gaza Strip. According to the IDF, the car and its passengers were fleeing a failed attempt to drop off suicide bombers into Israel. The Palestinians said that the IAF deliberately launched a missile into a crowd of civilians, killing 8 and wounding 80 others. They called the attack a "massacre." Within 24 hours, the IDF publicly released videotape taken by the pilotless drone that filmed the entire episode in an effort to dispute the Palestinian claims. The footage showed the car hit twice, and the streets surrounding it appeared empty at the time the missiles were fired. It did not, however, entirely quell the competing versions of events.[7]

For all intents and purposes, unit 8200 functions like a giant electronic information collection agency. Every hour of every day its systems amass an infinite number of electronic signals captured from its ground stations and assorted listening posts. The unit is an assembly of engineers, mathematicians, scientists, and crypto-analysts involved in signals intelligence such as capturing signals coming out of communication emissions and electronic signals. In the simplest terms, this means monitoring telephone calls, picking up faxes and email, intercepting radio signals, and unscrambling encrypted messages. The information is transferred to the unit's intelligence Mecca in central Israel, where computers and sophisticated software sort it, scan trigger words, and bust through encrypted messages, and special analysts and linguists evaluate the information.

Unit 8200 plays the kind of role that GCHQ in the United Kingdom and the NSA in the United States do in terms of its daily business. However, unlike its counterparts, which are government-civilian agencies, unit 8200 is part of Israel's military infrastructure. Another difference is that while the unit is a formidable regional player, in all likelihood it does not equal the global scope of mammoth systems in the United States, such as the satellite-based Echelon. Echelon is the source of much speculation about the unfettered capabilities of the NSA and its abilities to intercept and analyze billions of electronic transmissions sent between the United States and abroad. However, what the unit lacks in resources and budget it has always compensated for in resourcefulness. Also, the Americans and the Israelis have traditionally had a close political and intelligence-sharing relationship over the years. Although the relationship is not without tensions, it is one that has at times developed into a working alliance, where mutual interests overlap.

For instance, in 1999, it came to light that the United States had for three years occasionally intercepted the encrypted radio communications of President Saddam Hussein's elite security forces. The *Washington Post* reported that UNSCOM, the United Nations' weapons inspectors tasked with scouring Iraq for weapons prohibited following the first Gulf War in 1991, used portable all-frequency radio scanning devices and digital recorders that picked up the coded communications. The scanners were provided by Israeli intelligence at the behest of former UNSCOM inspector Scott Ritter. The information collected was then relayed to either Israel, Britain, or the NSA in Fort Meade, Maryland, for decoding and translation.[8]

According to the intelligence periodical *Covert Action Quarterly (CAQ)*, when the United States announced in the late 1980s that it had proof of Iranian complicity in a series of events, including the terror attack on Pan Am Flight 103 (which led to the plane's explosion over Lockerbie, Scotland), it opened a small portal into the kind of electronic alliance the agencies reportedly had been involved in. The claim was based on alleged evidence taken by the interception of encrypted Iranian diplomatic cables between Teheran and Hizbollah from Iran's embassies in Beirut and Damascus. *CAQ* reported that it was unit 8200 that filched the coded communications and decoded them.[9]

The cables, sent between Iran's Interior Minister Ali Akbar Mohtashemi in Teheran and the Iranian embassy in Beirut, reportedly disclosed that Mohtashemi had transferred nearly $2 million used for the Pan Am bombing to the Popular Front for the Liberation of Palestine–General Command. In order to crack the code, the unit had to have access to its key. The ability to do so, it was alleged, was part of a larger scheme in which the NSA was said to have manipulated the cipher machines manufactured by the Swiss firm Crypto AG, which sold cryptographic communications equipment to the Iranians as well as to dozens of foreign governments. As a result, when an encoded message was sent, said to be hidden within it was the random encryption key, the tool that allowed the receiver to decode the message. The Iranians eventually became aware that their supposedly secure communications were compromised. They arrested the firm's sales representative to Iran, Hans Buehler, in Teheran on March 18, 1992, and they held him in solitary confinement for several months. For their part, Crypto AG denied the allegations as "hearsay" and "pure invention."[10, 11]

A dozen years later, amid the swirl surrounding Dr. Abdul Qadeer Khan's nationally televised confession that he had been responsible for passing on nuclear weapons materials to such nations as Iran and North Korea, and his subsequent pardon by Pervez Musharraf, Pakistan's president and a former army general, there were still a number of unanswered questions. Chief among them was how Khan, known as the father of Pakistan's nuclear bomb, was able to transfer nuclear weapons technology independently. The general public expressed surprise at both Musharraf's swift pardon and the Bush administration's equally fast acceptance of the explanation of the dangerous breach. Not long after, investigative journalist Seymour M. Hersh, famous for breaking the story of the Mai Lai massacre in Vietnam, wrote in *The New Yorker* that several years earlier, unit 8200 had monitored communications between Iran and Pakistan about the former's growing nuclear weapons program after breaking a sophisticated Iranian code. The intercepts reportedly exposed the connection and both nations' duplicity in not conveying the full extent of Iran's nuclear capabilities to the International Atomic Energy Agency, and they were, according to Hersh, in some part communicated to the United States.[12]

It is a complex art to exploit, capture, and analyze electronic signals. To the uninitiated, catching electronic signal beams would appear as difficult as attempting to collect water in one's hands. Retired Brigadier General Elie Barr, one of the unit's former commanders, described it as a very sophisticated process and one that is constantly changing. "It's like catching signals in a large net, and the width of the holes in the net keeps changing," he explained. To understand the language of signals and electronic emissions is to have a vital advantage in information warfare. For instance, having broken Egypt's military code just prior to the Six Day War, the Israelis used it against them during the war. SIGINT officers commanded an Egyptian MiG pilot on his way to attack Israel to drop his bombs over the sea. The pilot, certainly perplexed by the strange order, asked the Israelis to authenticate their command. They, in turn, gave the pilot details about his wife and children. His response was to ditch the bombs, eject from the fighter, and parachute to safety.[13]

The ability to communicate through a variety of means such as the telephone, cell phone, email, radio, cable, or satellite generates a wealth of signals that can be snapped up, providing a trove of both sensitive and significant information. The importance of information that is pried from enemy signals is that, unlike information gleaned from human sources (which can be obscured by a variety of competing agendas—not to mention human error—once it is unraveled), signal intelligence offers information straight from the source of the enemy or intended target. Also, even if the content is unintelligible, a considerable amount of information can be tapped from dissecting the communication patterns. Before the unit can break a code or convert the message cloaked within it, it must first track, seize, and record it. It is the job of members of the unit to do so, and, at the same time, they must continuously develop the kind of technology and solution-oriented methodology that gives them the kind of capability needed.

The unit is responsible for collecting a nearly infinite flow of information. Generally speaking, information comes in two streams: that which is out in the open and that which is encrypted (with signals hidden and messages concealed). One part of the unit monitors open source information, scrutinizing mosque sermons in the Gaza Strip, listening to Arabic radio and television broadcasts, or reading Arabic newspapers, for example. The unit has a number of linguists, not surprisingly, who are skilled, above all, in Arabic.

However, a good amount of information is encrypted in some systems, and most systems aren't so simple to crack. Barr described the practice as a sophisticated, constantly changing puzzle. "Once a signal is unraveled," he explained, "you have to produce a system to present it in a comprehensive way and to have the ability to read, understand, and act on that information—to say what is important and what is not, and to take the trivial information and form a picture that puts the puzzle together."

Advances in communication jump-started the world of technology and created new directions in which members of the world's intelligence community could pry and peer into the minds of their adversaries. This constant march forward propelled groups such as unit 8200 to maintain a quantum trajectory in technological developments. "Communications opened up technology," stated Israel's intelligence director, Major General Aharon Ze'evi Farkash. "It is the real origin of SIGINT. It began with the first radio and telephone. So, if we want to have intelligence information monitored by SIGINT, SIGINT must lead in technological innovation. Why? Because if someone wants the technological capabilities to monitor radio and telephone systems, we must have the technological capabilities that are higher than the systems that have been already built."

As a result, in the broadest sense, spies have always utilized the most advanced technology in existence. The chronic need to know more about the enemy in real time has often resulted in the development of advanced technology. Also, much of it would later find its way into consumers' lives: Wireless communications, global positioning systems, and digital photography all derived from the need to collect intelligence.

Displayed in the engineering pavilion at the IDF museum on Eilat Street in Tel Aviv are examples of some of the kinds of communications systems the Israelis have devised or adapted over the years for their information war. It is fairly common knowledge that public announcement of an intelligence asset is tacit acknowledgment of its obsolescence. Still, the small collection displayed in the museum presents a snapshot of Israel's technological leap into the future. For instance, there is a large color photograph of the troposphere antennas perched in Mitzpe Ramon, the rim of the world's largest natural crater, in the Negev Desert, 2,952 feet above sea level. The antennas provided communication between the center of Israel and the town of Sharm al-Sheik in the Sinai Peninsula between 1969 and 1982. There is the acknowledgment that as early as 1960, Israeli intelligence personnel had developed communication encryption systems. Shortly after that, they developed encrypted mobile voice communication systems that could transmit between field echelons and general headquarters. Also, there are scanning receivers with adaptable antennas that protected against jamming and long-range radio communications systems used in the Sinai Campaign of 1956 and the War of Attrition in 1969. These devices were used by ground forces and paratroopers, who could carry the systems on their backs.

In Israel, two constants have always been in play: limited resources and unlimited challenges. For instance, in the early 1970s, one particularly clever soldier from unit 8200 devised a way to accurately adjust an antenna without a computer or GPS system to lock on to the target. "When you use an antenna to triangulate a target like a missile or radar, you need to calibrate the antenna," he explained. "You rotate the antenna until it picks up the maximum strength of a signal. If the dial shows 173 degrees north, then you point the antenna at 173 degrees north. You try to locate the signal and adjust the dial to the signal." He continued:

> The problem is to know where to put the transmitter and from what direction the signal is coming. You are directing it at the enemy across the border, and it also has to be the same elevation as the target on the horizon—not above it or below it. That can be a problem if you are on a base perched on a cliff, for instance. Also, you don't want to tell the operator at what angle to direct the antenna because you don't want to bias him or her. It must be exact. If it needs to be at 173 degrees, then it should be at 173 degrees—not 174 or 172. Additionally, it must be calibrated at many frequencies because some targets run on multiple frequencies.

Without the benefit of a global positioning system or a computer, this soldier discovered that it was possible to quite accurately tune the antenna manually by using the energy of the sun. He realized that the sun gives off ultraviolet rays and radar frequencies that could be picked up, and he asked the mapping unit of the army to prepare a table for every day of the year at every base of the unit to give the correct angle of the sun. When the sun rose in the east, members of the unit used it to calibrate the antenna on the Golan Heights facing east, and when the sun set in the west, they calibrated the antenna in the Sinai Desert, which faced west.

From harnessing the sun, the unit has, over time, developed a slew of inventive and sophisticated electronic, communications, monitoring, interception, and information systems that would transform warfare by merging technology and intelligence. The continuous introduction of new methods and systems would improve Israel's operational capabilities. At times, the capacities of these complex and high-powered tools would ricochet in unforeseen directions.

For instance, there is the cellular phone. Cellular phones present a war all their own, expanding the wireless frontier in an area with an unreliable telecommunications infrastructure and where land line providers are encased in bureaucracy. Cell phone usage in Israel is seemingly ubiquitous, and cell phones have become both an electronic communications tool and a weapon used adroitly on both sides of the conflict. According to *Time* magazine, Jewish hilltop settlements bristle with $4 million worth of antennas, put up by Israel in 1996, that allow its intelligence to pick up all cellular calls made by Palestinians (and, of course, Israelis) in the West Bank.[14]

Cellular phones, the omnipresent accessory of our time, give off a constant flow of information. Subscriber Identity Module cards, or SIM cards, installed in the back of cellular phones contain information about the user and are needed to access a cellular network. Cellular services use radio frequencies between the phones and their antennas. When a phone is on, radio signals are sent to additional antennas as well as to the primary antennas, which allows someone to calculate the user's whereabouts within a very specific zone. Over time, this information is useful in tracking somebody's movements and providing links to whomever the target comes into contact with by tracing the calls.

This is not news, however, to Palestinian militants. After narrowly surviving an Israeli helicopter missile attack on his car as he drove through Gaza City in early June 2003, one of Hamas's founding leaders, Abdel Aziz Rantisi, a fiery, bespectacled physician, told a Lebanese newspaper that using his cellular phone to arrange a meeting probably enabled the Israelis to hunt him down. Rantisi called a friend on his cellular phone, asking him to meet at al-Shafa hospital at 11:00. He told the paper that the first missile struck his car at five minutes to 11:00.[15]

Rantisi's reprieve, however, had its limits. Following the Israeli air strike that killed Hamas leader Sheik Ahmed Yassin on March 22, 2004, Rantisi, who swore vengeance against Israel, assumed the mantle of the militant Islamic organization. His appointment did not last long. Within a month, on the evening of April 17, Israeli helicopter gunships fired missiles into his car just a block from his house, in the Sheik Radwan neighborhood of Gaza City, killing Rantisi, his driver, and a bodyguard. The attack came mere hours after a suicide bomber killed an Israeli border policeman and injured three Israeli civilians at the Erez checkpoint in Gaza. Both Hamas and Fatah claimed responsibility for the terrorist attack.

Perhaps it became most clear just how prominent the role of the cellular phone had become in the protracted Israeli-Palestinian conflict at the end of the summer of 2003. During the course of several weeks in August, the IDF unleashed a series of missile attacks against nearly a dozen specific leaders of Hamas and Islamic Jihad in retaliation for a suicide bombing in Jerusalem that killed 23 people. Shortly after the strike that killed Hamas's deputy political chief Ismail Abu Shanab and four others, Hamas leaders and fighters went underground and instructed members to watch out. They said they were being monitored and marked for death, and advised these potential targets to curb their cellular phone use or to shut off their cell phones altogether.[16]

For their part, Palestinian militants have deployed cellular phones as remote bomb triggers, wiring detonators to explode when the ringer goes off. In July 2001, members of the PFLP claimed to have planted two car bombs in the Israeli town of Yehud and detonated each by cellular phone. A year later, in September 2002, Israel security forces thwarted what would have been a massive bomb when they intercepted a pickup truck near the northern Israeli town of Hadera. The truck was booby-trapped with 1,300 pounds of explosives, two barrels of fuel, and metal fragments. Attached was a cell phone set up to detonate the explosion.

Then, in March 2004, IDF soldiers stopped an 11-year-old Palestinian boy who reportedly had been offered a sum of money to carry a bag across the Hawara checkpoint into Israel. Apparently unknown to the boy, the bag he was carrying held a 10-kilo bomb. When the IDF stopped him, his handlers, said to be Fatah Tanzim members from Nablus, tried to set off the bomb using a cellular phone detonator. A technical glitch, however, prevented a potential tragedy, and the bomb never went off.[17]

For their part, the Israelis are said to have developed electronic jamming technology that can disable cellular phones and other devices. Indeed, an Israeli outfit, Netline Communications Technologies, a developer of commercialized cellular jamming and mobile phone detection technologies, was founded in 1998. According to the company, it was started by a group of former communications and electronic warfare experts from the ranks of the nation's military and defense industries.

However, triggered-cellular phone bombs are not indigenous to the Israeli-Palestinian conflict, as a number of events at the turn of the century would prove. Terrorist attacks in Spain, Indonesia, and Saudi Arabia were later found by investigators to have been detonated by mobile phones, as were several ambush attacks against U.S. troops in Iraq following the 2003 war.

As the number of remote-triggered bombs has grown, so too has the use of jamming technology. Reportedly, the United States has tested and deployed its own techno-version to disable

cellular phone traffic in combat zones in order to better protect
its troops in Iraq by shutting down remote-controlled signals.
Notably, it was jamming technology that was said to have prevented an assassination attempt on Pakistani President Pervez
Musharraf on December 14, 2003.[18]

While there are number of technological units in the IDF, unit
8200's sphere of influence in the art
of electronic warfare and its muscle
in devising and using complex and
sophisticated systems have created
a kind of influential template within

> *"What is unique is
> the kind of practical
> creativity we have."
> —former unit
> member*

Israel. The particular set of circumstances created a nexus of
security problems that converge with intelligence and spy technology to produce a major innovation crucible. Much like the
kibbutz, which represents only a tiny fraction of Israel's population and yet has provided an enduring blueprint in terms of the
nation's character and ethos, unit 8200 serves as an influential
metaphor for a highly charged way of thinking. As one former
member put it, "What is unique is the kind of practical creativity we have."

A unit like 8200 evolved as a technological response to the
geopolitical realities of the Israeli security situation. As it
turned out, the rise of the information age and the telecommu-
nication revolution coincided with the entry into the civilian
world by a number of the unit's soldiers. Their *raison d'etre* had
been information technology, albeit in a military context, but
their background in wireless communications and encryption
inventing (or improving these technologies) suddenly made
sense in a world that has been transformed in a relatively short

time into one in which there are tens of millions of computers (many of them networked), millions of fax machines, several million cellular phones, mainstream Internet access, the growing use of wireless data phones, and wi-fi networking chips in laptop computers and PCs.

Suddenly, the world-wide flood of information transported by means of fiber-optic cables, microwave relay stations, and the Internet posed new problems and new opportunities. One of the core requirements of the unit is managing, processing, and making sense of the massive amounts of data it collects on a continuous basis. A former officer of the unit who is now the CEO of an

With the swell of powerful microchips that powered personal computers and the emergence of the Internet and the telecommunications industry in the 1990s, many of the processes and applications that the unit used in intelligence became a tremendous asset in the civilian world—applications for a civilian society which was now itself in need of ways to manage, process, and protect information on the kind of scale it had never experienced before.

information service provider remarked that the unit was doing things 25 years before there were words for them. With the swell of powerful microchips that powered personal computers and the emergence of the Internet and the telecommunications industry in the 1990s, many of the processes and applications that the unit used in intelligence became a tremendous asset in the civilian world. There were applications for a civilian society that was now itself in need of ways to manage, process, and protect information on the kind of scale it had never experienced before.

A concentration of innovations developed wherever the IDF's needs were greatest. Innovations were particularly prevalent in the areas of communications and security, as the ability to protect and break into secured systems became increasingly important. "The Israeli Army has numerous units that must communicate," explained Shimon Schocken, the dean of the computer school at the Interdisciplinary Center Herziliya. So, for instance, when the Internet was designed, it was done so with little forethought regarding the need for security. As Schocken said, "The World Wide Web brought the Internet to everyone. You could buy and exchange information, and all its weaknesses were exposed in scalability and security." He continued, "By a tremendous fluke, most technology developed in the Israeli Army was relevant." Schocken said that the army had an acute need to multiply bandwidth. The army also led in algorithm compressions. "These were built for military purposes, but the Web immediately exposed weaknesses. All these guys in the military systems said we have solutions."

Now, software developed to search for links to terrorists could be used to shop online more effectively. Digital recording systems that helped eavesdrop on enemy targets could be used to transform the antiquated magnetic recording devices of Wall Street. Artificial intelligence used to anticipate the behavior patterns of, say, Saddam Hussein or Yassir Arafat could now be applied as a model to divine shopping habits of consumers and increase sales. Technology used to secure classified information and communications could be used to protect Internet and fax transmissions, as well as computer networks, from outside infiltration.

In short order, a number of companies with the unit's imprint developed. Whether the companies were stand-alones or acquired by larger American or western companies, they all had one thing in common: They found an important niche that was attractive to the market, the consumer, or a large company, and this niche served as the basis for innovation. A small sampling provides a brief glimpse. AudiCodes is acknowledged as a world leader in voice compression technology, and Jacada is a leading producer of legacy integration and Web-enabling technology. PowerDsine delivers technology that integrates the transmission of data, voice, and electricity on a single network through giants such as Avaya, 3Com, Nortel, Siemens, and Ericsson. CTI2 develops IP-enhanced messaging and communications platforms. The firm Teledata had come up with such innovative fiber optic network technology that it was snapped up by ADC Telecommunications for a tidy $200 million in 1998. The list, of course, continues to run deep and long.

7 Genius Corps

Hebrew University, Jerusalem, circa 1974...

The nation was reeling. The Yom Kippur War of October 1973 had been a terrible shock, putting Israel perilously close to disaster. An inflated sense of military invincibility in tandem with an arrogantly held conviction, known as *Haconzeptzia* (the concept), was at fault. This concept stemmed from the belief that the humiliating blow the Arabs suffered in 1967 would prevent them from engaging in an all-out war they could not win. It did not take into consideration that despite their huge losses, the Arabs could regain their composure and in fact execute a coordinated, motivated attack. Holding fast to this theory had prevented the Israelis from correctly assessing the pileup of intelligence information that showed Egypt and Syria were heading exactly in that direction. Slow to predict the war and even slower to react, Israel's eventual triumph after 18 days of fighting was bitter and hard won. It was a somber victory. More than 2,800 troops were left dead and nearly 9,000 more were wounded.[1] In economic terms, the losses were just as devastating, reaching an estimated $7 billion. The financial price tag was the equivalent of one year of Israel's GNP.[2] The war was a sharp kick to the gut of Israel's military and political leaders. The notably agile and ingenious thinking that had served them well in the past had ossified into an ironclad confidence that had placed the country in serious jeopardy.

In the aftermath of the war, the Israeli government set up the Agranat Commission to investigate the military and political myopia that preceded it. Among the commission's key findings was that the situation was not simply a matter of not having the information at hand or even perhaps not solely a matter of assessing it properly, but rather of not grasping its utter significance. Much of the blame was placed on the head of Aman General Eli Zeira. Following the war, a number of changes were put into motion, among them Zeira's dismissal. The embattled Prime Minister Golda Meir, who was said to have received a direct warning from King Hussein of Jordan of the looming assault less than two weeks before the outbreak of fighting, resigned in April 1974. In a period of introspection, Israel, a nation whose outlook was permanently set at change, was again readying itself for more shifts.

It was time for new approaches, and they would come from all corners. The chief of staff at the time, Rafael Eitan, had put out a clarion call requesting new ways to increase the army's effectiveness. Like many in Israel's academic and industrial sectors at the time, three Hebrew University professors (two in the chemistry department and the third a physics professor) heard the call and were propelled to action. Previously, the professors had helped to devise an electronic simulation system for training soldiers in tanks without having to use live rounds of ammunition.[3] However, these three highly intelligent men now wanted to combine their intellectual powers to turn the tide of a war and save the lives of Israeli citizens and soldiers. They had heard about a French project that selected talented people and trained them specifically to work in military development. Inspired, they thought there might be something in this for Israel. Of course, it would upend one of the IDF's strongest traditions: the closely held notion of the IDF as the people's army, a strong reflection of the country's collective character and one of the greatest forces for social equality.

Under the professors' initiative, the IDF would handpick the most brilliant and capable young people. Instead of placing them in the general pool of recruits to be sorted and placed, these candidates would be separate and not equal from the outset. They would be classified among themselves—

As in business, competing purely on brute strength seldom wins a market; one must outmaneuver and outrecruit a competitor to win.

an assembly of geniuses. They would be singled out for special duty, and they would use their cunning and intellect rather than pure force. Their contributions would be used to outsmart their opponents rather than to just physically quash them. As in business, competing purely on brute strength seldom wins a market; one must outmaneuver and outrecruit a competitor to win. The core of this idea would work on two levels. In the broad sense, it would nurture talent and lay the groundwork for Israel's future leaders. On a more specific, practical level, it would create a core of soldiers dedicated to developing new weapons systems. Their contribution and mission would be a tall one: to change the language of technological warfare. Although Talpiot operates independently of unit 8200 (some Talpiot graduates may end up serving in 8200, however), both Talpiot and unit 8200 have come to represent an important IDF mechanism for identifying individuals with the capacity for innovation on a practical level and the ability to execute it in the advanced systems of weapons and intelligence.

For years, the IDF had a program called the Academic Reserves that allowed a number of incoming recruits—top-flight students—to defer enlistment in order to earn their degrees in various scientific and engineering fields and mathematics. Following their studies, they would be dispatched to a slot in the military where the need was greatest. The catch was a few extra years of service tacked on to the mandatory three. The Hebrew University professors' concept was to turn that proposition on its head: identify and locate the top 1 to 5 percent of high school students, and instead of just sending them to university and then casting them off to fill a spot in some unit that had an opening, these geniuses would go to the army and create their place in it. Existing in a unique capacity as soldiers, they would receive tailored instruction in a variety of disciplines combined with accelerated academic programs, receiving their BS degrees in math and physics (some have also completed Master's degrees and PhDs) and special training in the army. When they finished, they would be officers who would invent new technologies and weapons systems.

The professors submitted their proposal to the Chief of Staff's Office in 1975. A small think tank was formed, drawing from the army, the Chief Scientist's Office, industry, and military R&D to come up with a full-blown concept that might make this idea a viable reality. Hanoch Zadik, a civilian working in the air force with a background in economic statistics and human development systems on the organizational level, was approached two years after the group was formed. He was giving a lecture on creative thinking at the Israeli air force academy when he was asked to join up with the men grappling with this endeavor. It was dubbed *Talpiot*, named for the biblical Hebrew word meaning "to build something strong, impregnable, and impressive." For a year and a half, a committee of 12 met once a month to kick around the Talpiot project. They laid out the objectives and detailed the possibilities of executing what would eventually become the IDF's most elite brainpower summit.

However, for an army that fed off of innovative thinking, even this was a somewhat radical notion. "There were a lot of objections that this was a waste of money," recalled Zadik. At the time, the national discussion centered around closing the gap between those of means and those less fortunate in society. "The idea was equal education for all," Zadik continued. "It was rooted in the county's deep socialist roots. Nobody spoke about taking excellent boys and girls and accelerating their learning and doing something good." There were other concerns as well. "People feared that if we took such brilliant people it was dangerous," he explained. "There could be a military junta. It was against the basic value of Israeli culture to take people and separate them and say 'you are the best,' and if you put the best in the army like this there was a danger of a coup. I was quite sure that they wouldn't do anything with this."

Nevertheless, Israel has always had resourceful military leaders willing to make giant leaps of thought along razor-sharp edges. One such man was Rafael Eitan, the IDF's chief of staff. Sometime in the late 1970s, Eitan launched an education initiative that took kids from disadvantaged circumstances, many living on the periphery, and made sure they had an education—particularly in the basics. Instead of leaving them sidelined, this program greatly improved their future prospects. Talpiot was on the opposite end of the same spectrum; it would take the intellectually elite and enhance their already considerable opportunities with enormous educational and institutional advantages. In 1979, Eitan took that leap and green-lighted Talpiot, although initially he gave it one year. Zadik and Dr. Dan Sharon, who received his PhD in innovation sciences, were asked to look for people to run the project. However, they were so enthusiastic about Talpiot, the pair decided to head it up themselves. To do so, they both reenlisted in the army more than a dozen years after their own compulsory services had been completed. "My wife and I had two kids, and she couldn't believe this move," said Zadik. "It was crazy." For the first seven years of the program (until 1986), Zadik served as Talpiot's deputy commander and chief trainer. Nearly two decades later, he became a management coach at the High-Tech Management School at Tel Aviv University.

The project was daunting from two significant vantage points: A military corps of geniuses was nearly unprecedented, and the military had very little to go on. Most of the recruits, for their part, were just finishing high school and had even less to go on. For the privilege of signing up for this new frontier, they were staring down the barrel of eight years of military duty—five years longer than the standard term (later it would extend to a total of nine years). The inaugural Talpiot class began with a group of 26 high school graduates out of an initial pool of 1,000 potential candidates, and only 20 made it to the end. All of them were male. In the second year, 30 recruits were selected, and 20 graduated. In the third year, the Talpiot class started with 28 soldiers and finished with 20. Talpiot began recruiting female candidates in the mid-1980s.

The process of selection and retention has always been a brutal intellectual survival of the fittest. Each year, tens of thousands of names are submitted to the IDF for Talpiot consideration by school principles and science teachers. Each September, this group is narrowed down to about 5,000 potential candidates who for a period of about six months are rigorously screened. Very quickly, this number dwindles down to 1,000, and then it drops to 180 after written examinations. Another 60 are cut after personal interviews. At the end of the testing period, only 50 candidates are invited to sign up. Among this group, however, only 35 to 40 make it through the entire program and graduate.[4]

With notable exceptions (Orthodox Jews and Arabs), nearly all Israeli men and women are called up to serve in the military. While in recent years the overall number has decreased for a variety of reasons, it still holds in principle, and that means the military has its hands on the nation's entire high school population, which is then scrupulously vetted and sorted. Over the years, the IDF has developed its own methodologies to select, sort, and direct the top conscripts into the most elite and challenging units. Intelligence, above all other military units and branches, has first pick of all of the nation's conscripts.

Talpiot is in a class by itself. It takes about the top 1 percent of the top 1 percent. Without question, it is the most vaunted of the IDF's elite programs, and it demonstrates how Israel's military system in many ways performs the kind of sifting function that academia serves in the United States—and offers the same unparalleled cachet for those who graduate. It is somewhat akin to the Ivy League and other universities, such as MIT and Stanford, that draw the top-tier American high school students. As Professor Shimon Shocken explained, "In America the best and the brightest go into academia. In Israel, the army attracts the top talent."

However, in the case of Talpiot, conscripts don't exactly apply—they are chosen. "I got a letter that said come to be tested in Jerusalem," recalled Yuval Shalom, who was recruited in 1984 at age 17. "Usually nobody believes they will make it. There is a very high prestige, and nobody thinks they are good enough. This is not something you can prepare for." A little more than a dozen years after his Talpiot invitation, Shalom co-founded the wireless technology firm Wiseband communications. Among its initiatives, Wiseband helped pioneer digital signal processing amplifiers for 2.5 and third generation cellular networks.

Once chosen for Talpiot, candidates must prove themselves through a grueling series of tests. One test, developed with a math professor from Hebrew University, required the creation of a new language using words and signs—in half an hour. There is also a battery of questions—more like riddles (for instance, "How long before a cup of coffee turns cold?"). These questions were designed not to be solvable, but to analyze how a candidate would problem-solve, a super-selective filter intended to separate the true genius from the exceptionally gifted. By the end, barely 1 percent of the candidates make the cut. The only mitigating factor a recruit has for selection is his or her ability to perform under the accelerated and pressurized atmosphere of the program. No outside influences impact the selection process. Talpiot goes for quality over quantity, and there is no quota to fill. If someone is not suitable at any point, his or her training is halted.

> *Once chosen for Talpiot, candidates must prove themselves through a grueling series of tests... These questions were designed not to be solvable, but to analyze how a candidate would problem solve. A super selective filter intended to separate the true genius from the exceptionally gifted.*

Lieutenant Colonel Avi Poleg, himself a graduate of Talpiot and the program manager of the IDF's technological manpower, described the testing process as one in which it's not so much the end goal that is emphasized, but the journey in getting there. "There are mainly two instruments, and they are improving all the time," he explained. "The first is the pencil and paper exam for general excellence and thinking in math and physics. Second, we're looking at how candidates think about solutions. Not necessarily that they got the right solutions but that they have an interest in the field and they are curious about things. We pick people who know how to think. There are dozens of criteria. Candidates have basic knowledge in math and physics and the basic potential to be leaders, and they are good at teamwork. They must cross the threshold of each field. We know that not all of them will reach over the prime level, but everyone should excel in one field and in the other fields know at least the threshold level. We profile and do psychiatric tests where six to eight people sit together, and we give them tasks intended to see their social and teamwork capabilities, like is one person dominant? Does he or she have good ideas but can't convince the group to take them?"

The IDF says it is difficult to assess the success of Talpiot in the normal kind of considered, qualitative measures—for instance, outside of the number of its graduates. It does say, however, that the fact the program continues to exist more than 20 years after its inception speaks volumes, as does the fact that the IDF allocates $1 million annually toward it (it is run under the authority of the Israeli Air Force).[5] As Lieutenant Colonel Poleg suggested, "For every one Talpiot graduate, there are five units asking for him."

Talpiot is like a military Mensa. The soldiers of Talpiot begin their military service at Hebrew University. They are housed apart from the main student population, living instead in specially built barracks on the Givat Ram campus in Jerusalem. During the academic portion of the program, they study for their bachelor's of science in physics, mathematics, and computer science, and they take technological courses at an accelerated rate, covering about 40 percent more material than they would in a regular BS degree program. These soldiers are also trained in military strategy and complete an officer's training course. "We expect them all to become officers," said Colonel Yaacov Nagel, the acting head of research and development. "If after three years they fail the officer's class, they won't be Talpiot graduates. In the last class we almost lost one," he said. "It would be very shameful if we lost one after three years. However, until now they've all become officers."

They spend their summers doing 12 weeks of basic training. It is the same tough, no-holds-barred program given to the paratroopers. They train in the desert, hiking with 10 to 20 kilos and rifles on their backs, and they learn to jump out of planes. "We put them through a tough course, the same as paratroopers, because we want them to be strong and brave too," explained Zadik.

Talpiot soldiers take special courses rotating with each force of the army: intelligence, navy, and air force. They learn about the weapon systems from the inside. They sit in cockpits of fighter jets and shoot off weaponry to gain a real understanding of its operational and technological needs. "It's not just theoretical," explained Zadik. "They know what it means to spend cold nights for one month in the Negev in a tank." During the second year, they devise a project of their own choosing for three months. After all, Lieutenant Colonel Poleg reiterated, "The idea of Talpiot is to raise the next generation of R&D." The last six years of the program are divided between two years in field units and four as an R&D officer.

The idea behind Talpiot was to create a unique group of men and women with extremely high IQs and aptitude for performance, and provide this group with an equally unique environment. Talpiot members are exposed to multidisciplinary studies in military strategy, the sciences, computers, math, and physics, and they receive instruction from the nation's elite such as Nobel prize-winning economists. They participate in top-flight security systems both in the field and in the lab—establishing fields of inquiry. "There are many brilliant ideas," said Major Barak Ben-Eliezar, Talpiot's commander. "Most of them have ideas, but not just ideas—they bring about change."

While critical discussion has surfaced in recent years about the erosion of the IDF's mission in light of the Israeli occupation of the Palestinian territories and its long-term characterization as the "people's army," undeniably the military continues to play a crucial and central role in the life of the country. Its influence is an enduring one in ways both obvious as well as latent. From amplifying and refining national character traits such as risk-taking, creativity, and ingenuity to instructing the problem-solving skills of generations of thinkers to creating the backbone of technological innovation, an entire world-class industry is built around the military.

Rafael Eitan's one-year directive has stretched into nearly a quarter of a century. By 2003, nearly 21 classes of more than 440 soldiers have called themselves elite Talpiot alumni. In recent years, the IDF has expanded the Talpiot initiative, creating similarly conceived programs. Although Talpiot remains at the pinnacle, some of the other spinoffs include *P'sgot,* which focuses on physics and electronics, and *Atidim*, which finds recruits with strong potential who come from disadvantaged or overlooked schools and neighborhoods across the country, and who haven't been deeply exposed to science and engineering but have the aptitude for it.

Only a handful of Talpiot soldiers have become military careerists. There are 2 colonels, 14 lieutenant colonels, and 1 brigadier general (as of 2003). "I'd like to have more brigadier generals or plane squadron commanders coming out of Talpiot," said Colonel Nagel. However, Talpiot has served as an important graduation to prosperity. During their years of service, recruits have all been involved intimately in some of the military and defense's most important systems. Although, for the most part, their achievements are left unpublicized, their fingerprints can be lifted off of Israel's UAV program, the Arrow anti-ballistic missile system, and scores of communications, wireless technology, and weapons systems.

Upon entering the civilian world, Talpiot alumni have made equally important contributions. Many have continued to develop technology in the commercial realm, and the program's graduates include a significant list of players in Israel's high-tech world. Marius Nacht, one of the co-founders of Check Point Software Technologies, the company that virtually created the commercial Internet security firewall, came out of Talpiot, as did Jonathan Silverberg, who took his Talpiot background in developing locations systems in the Israeli Air Force to Decell Technologies, a mobile traffic information company. Before co-founding Provigent, a maker of chip systems for fixed wireless broadband, Dan Charash developed digital signal processing telecommunications applications in elite Ministry of Defense and IDF units following his graduation from Talpiot.

One company that clearly demonstrates the influence of Talpiot is Compugen, a pioneer in applying computer science and engineering to the fields of biotechnology, pharmacology, and medicine to develop technology-enabling genomic data mining and to the discovery of new drugs and diagnostic tools. Compugen was founded in 1993 by three Talpiot graduates, Eli Mintz, Simchon Faigler, and Amir Natan, who established the company with a grant from the Chief Scientist's Office at one of its incubators in Sde Boker in the Negev Desert. Two years earlier, Mintz, a physicist and mathematician, was studying in France for his MBA at the INSEAD business school. His wife, Liat, a molecular biologist, was doing her PhD studies at the world-renowned Pasteur Institute. She happened to mention to her husband that the tsunami of data she and her colleagues were working with was beyond the capacity of any computer.

It was during the early days of bioinformation, and laboratories were beginning to spew out vast quantities of information. Only a year earlier, the U.S. government had initiated the ambitious Human Genome Project: a mammoth international endeavor to unravel the genetic puzzle by identifying all of the 30,000 genes in DNA and determining the 3 billion chemical base pairs that comprise DNA. Mintz, who had spent his Talpiot service developing algorithms, signal processing software, and hardware at Israel Aircraft Industries, thought he could apply his experience to managing and sorting through all of the data produced by the upsurge in genomic research. He called his Talpiot pals Faigler and Natan to join him.

In eight months, Compugen had developed its first product: the Bioccelerator, a computer system that identifies similar characteristics in genome and protein sequences 1,000 times faster than any other hardware or software product available at that time. A year later it was sold to pharmaceutical giant Merck & Co. and quickly became the industry standard. In 1998, the U.S. Patent and Trademark Office began using the Bioccelerator to check every patent submission of DNA sequences.

Following closely on the heels of the Bioccelerator, Compugen developed the LEADS platform, a data mining search engine that analyzes genomic and protein data in order to predict their biological functions and lead to the discovery of new drugs to treat them. In short order, the company, which moved out of the desert incubator into its own Tel Aviv headquarters, began announcing collaborations with huge multinational firms such as Novartis and Pfizer. In 2001, Compugen joined forces with Motorola to develop and manufacture DNA biochips: glass slides daubed with thousands of pieces of DNA that will be used to better diagnose specific diseases and illnesses and to aid doctors in tailoring precise drug prescriptions.

Certainly, Compugen's products are breakthroughs in and of themselves, using computer science and mathematics to create new information about biology and to radically transform research methods in the life sciences. The ability to do so can largely be credited to Talpiot's influence. Roughly 10 percent of Compugen's R&D staff are Talpiot grads (there is also a significant number of unit 8200 alumni). "The core innovation is a multidisciplinary way of thinking," explained Mor Amitai, a Talpiot graduate who became Compugen's CEO in 1997. "This is not easy. You don't just put some people in a room and they work well together in different disciplines. Each thinks his discipline is superior. In the army we didn't combine scientists but we did research and development with people in different industries. It is a similar challenge to combine physics engineers and computer scientists with military intelligence."

In 1983, Amitai, then a high school student and Math Olympiad veteran, received a letter from Talpiot inviting him to take an exam in Jerusalem. He earned his bachelor of science degree in mathematics and physics and a master's degree in mathematics while serving in Talpiot, and he gained his PhD in mathematics following his military service. Intense and wiry, Amitai focused on developing algorithm and communications systems for the IDF. After his discharge, Amitai went to work for Comverse Technology, a communications systems company (another Israeli company said to have the the considerable DNA of former unit 8200 soldiers), as a digital signals processing engineer. There he developed speech recognition technologies. His roommate during this time was Compugen co-founder Simchon Faigler, who was developing Compugen at the Sde Boker incubator. "He would disappear into the Negev," recalled Amitai. The two would discuss his progress. Sometimes Faigler would present Amitai with a problem when the Compugen team reached a bottleneck. Amitai met with Mintz and Natan. Soon he began consulting at Compugen, splitting his time between the fledgling startup and Comverse. In 1994, he came on board full time and served as the company's chief scientist and head of research. Amitai led the group that developed the LEADS platform core technology.

There is a great deal of carry-over from the Talpiot approach to Compugen. One of Compugen's hallmarks, however, is one that marks much of the IDF: the exposure of very young people to huge challenges. "When I look at it now, it doesn't make sense," said Amitai, shaking his head. "After earning a BS at 21 in computer science or math you are asked to solve challenges in weapons systems or communications systems that would normally take people with 20 years' experience [to figure out]. And some things I was asked to do with almost zero experience. If I were as mature as I am now, I would have given up." Amitai said that while in Talpiot he was trusted with responsibilities he wouldn't trust to himself. "People relied on us," he said thinking back in awe, "and people's lives depended on us."

"What we are doing at Com-pugen is to challenge people, and sometimes that includes our-selves, to do the impossible or the unlikely," explained Amitai. "To be successful is not to never have failed here. In a sense we must fail; our strategy is to work on difficult challenges that are high risk, and if we always suc-ceed, it is not high risk. In addressing this type of R&D chal-lenge, I think here the army experience is direct."

> *"To be successful is not to never have failed here. In a sense we must fail; our strategy is to work on difficult challenges that are high risk, and if we always succeed, it is not high risk."*
> —Mor Amitai

In the bigger picture, Talpiot is a repository of patterns of thinking and behavior working at mach speed, which has spilled over into society and industry in Israel. "Israeli industry inher-ited a lot of things. This is where I learned that nothing is impos-sible," he said. "Maybe it is in math, but in life you never know."

The counterpart of Talpiot graduates in the United States, for example, would be the kind of people who in traditional cir-cumstances would wind up in academia. In Israel, only a small, unscientifically measured, percentage of Talpiot alumni end up in university careers. Many have continued to develop technol-ogy. "Some people learn computer science or math and get a PhD," said Amitai. "If they are talented, the natural track is for them to end up at the university. But for us it wasn't. This natu-ral track was broken. A significant number of people learned [in Talpiot] that they have alternatives." For instance, Amitai compared a talented PhD graduate in physics from Stanford to a Talpiot graduate. "Ask him what he can do in life, and he [probably] can't give any other answer but to be a professor. What we did in the army was five years of R&D. This program made people think about alternatives. They did very interesting R&D work [such as] developing algorithms and parts of communication systems." He continued, "It is addictive to work on things and see the outcome, not on paper or a discovery but an outcome of a machine or system working for many people. When you know you can do that, you don't want to give up on the creative, material things—the tangible things."

Talpiot functions within the Israel military system in a way like Bell Labs in New Jersey or research-rich academic institutions or even the Defense Advanced Research Projects Agency (DARPA) do in the United States. Its recruitment process would rival or even best the kind of screening done to gain acceptance at Harvard or MIT—or even Microsoft. Talpiot encourages bold moves into new fields of inquiry. However, unlike many of its esteemed companions in U.S. academia, business, or defense, Talpiot has little time to spend on the theoretical—the problems it is grappling with are constantly changing and must be solved at warp speed. Furthermore, Talpiot puts this responsibility on the shoulders of some very young (and heretofore) unproven minds. But in doing so, it provides the keys to future generations of innovators.

8 Soldiers' Stories

The Sinai Desert, the late 1960s...

Sometime around 1968, an engineer from unit 8200 was sitting in a tent somewhere in the Sinai Peninsula, the triangular desert wedged between Israel and Egypt that at the time was part of Israel. His assignment: pick up signals. He had his headset on when he heard something odd and disturbing: a sudden loud and unfamiliar beat. First there were five pulses in a row, equally spaced, then double spaced, and then the frequency rate repeated itself going up and down, becoming stronger and stronger. Troubled, the engineer pulled off his headset and jumped out of his tent. Looking out over the desert toward the horizon he saw a cloud of dust moving toward him. Soon a car emerged out of the swirl of sand kicked up in its wake and two Israeli soldiers disembarked from the vehicle. They approached the engineer, saying they needed a mechanic. He told them they had to leave, immediately—after all, the area was classified. The two soldiers said they were desperate. They explained that they were traveling hard: They were expected in Bir al Gifgafah in the northwest Sinai, and their engine was boiling over.

There was neither a garage in sight nor any mechanic around—just the engineer on duty. Not unsympathetic to their dilemma, the engineer gave a cursory look at the car and instructed the soldiers to lift the hood. If they would reconnect one of the plugs inside, he suggested, they could be on their way. So, the pair pulled up the hood and found that indeed one of the plugs was off. The soldiers, as the story was recounted, thought he was a magician when in fact all he did was correctly assess the situation—albeit one that was not exactly part of his core competency. While the unit soldier was not a mechanic, he was able to understand the problem very quickly. When he looked at the vehicle, he saw it was a six-cylinder car and then put together that he had only heard five pulses on his headset. He simply and quickly deduced that the sixth cylinder was off.

This story, about an unnamed soldier in the Sinai, was told by another former member of unit 8200 as a way to depict in the most simplistic of terms what could best be described as a typical moment—one that illustrates the unit's cultural insignia: creative, idiosyncratic thinking, exposure to a wide variety of disciplines, and the ability to transcend one set of skills in order to identify problems quickly and deploy solutions even faster.

> *...the unit's cultural insignia: creative, idiosyncratic thinking, exposure to a wide variety of disciplines, and the ability to transcend one set of skills in order to identify problems quickly and deploy solutions even faster.*

The success of any endeavor depends on the quality of its people. The top companies, particularly those that venerate innovation, tend to recruit endlessly, canvassing all corners of the world for the best people possible. They look for certain markers, a professional or academic track record or some kind of past experience that could indicate future success. They probe for examples that would reveal desired proficiencies and intelligence, and they take note of significant pedigrees like degrees from select universities.

However, an organization such as the IDF is prospecting for the future of its strategic edge. Each year, the elite units like 8200 must gauge a set of qualities in the unproven minds of kids barely out of high school. There are those characteristics that are at once definable (hard-core abilities in math and science, for instance) and those that aren't as easily quantifiable (creativity, leadership, flexibility, and the ability to reason and work well in a group). Here the historical record is short. Recruiters must also place their bets on raw, untapped potential. So, at the moment of truth (say, sitting in a tent in the desert, developing a system that does not yet exist out of limited resources and under brutal time constraints, or collating information that will support policy-makers), these are the people who are going to perform. Not just perform, but excel.

It's not enough to be smart. These soldiers have to be a certain kind of smart: creative, innovative, and practical. They will be given a remarkable amount of responsibility. All but some of them will serve for five years—five years to make a difference and to turn visions into ideas and ideas into innovative solutions. Solutions that may exist in the future but are needed today. Those in the technological departments may see through the entire lifecycle of six or more systems. Those in the analytical sections will be counted on to find the thread weaving through the information collected by the systems developed by their colleagues to amass raw data, to intuit patterns of intentions, and to make assessments—all of which lives will depend upon.

A unit like 8200 has come to signify the IDF's ability to sort through a population of 17-year-olds and uncover intrinsic talent. Then again, it accepts only the top 1 percent of all potential draftees. The IDF starts with the most brilliant individuals, and then special attention is given to parse out the most creative among them. In describing the unit's typical recruits, one of its former commanders, retired Brigadier General Elie Barr, said they have a special balance: "The simultaneous ability to produce algorithms and write poetry."

It starts with a process. Soldiers are not actually recruited as much as they are identified and plucked out from high schools and technical colleges across the country. "People don't apply to the unit—we send them letters," remarked J.J. Now a psychologist, in the 1980s he served as an officer in

8200 for four years. As a reservist, he deals with recruitment. He himself was discovered, he says, because he "was studying in the best high school in Jerusalem and studying the highest level of Arabic. I wanted to be in intelligence and wanted to be sure that they wouldn't miss me."

In the early days of the unit, soldiers were selected based on a loose, informal referral system that eventually evolved into a highly polished filtering and recruiting machine with its own particular vagaries. Obvious skills like fluency in Arabic were tapped in many Sephardic Jews whose families had originally come from Arab countries and who spoke and understood Arabic like their mother tongue. By the 1960s, however, the unit took a turn toward seriously bolstering its ranks and strengths. According to one account, one of the unit's more influential commanders, a man known as "Shlomo," persuaded Israel's then chief of staff, the equally influential David Elazar, to focus on recruiting individuals with high IQs and to push for more resources.[1] This may have been a turning point that would influence not only the unit for the next generation but the nation as well. As it heightened the importance of the unit, it took in the best and the brightest and turned out individuals who went on to hold leading positions not just in the high-tech industry, but also in academia, literature, and law.

Gilad Goren, co-founder of Native Networks, an optical Ethernet network access company, was recruited in the late 1970s, two years after high school. He was studying at an engineering college affiliated with Tel Aviv University before joining the army. Goren recalled:

> There was a friend of mine at college, and he had a girlfriend who later worked for the Mossad whose brother was in 8200. Her brother told 8200 about me and my friend, and they asked us for an interview. I was about 19, and they were looking for talented people in the usual way. Somebody recommends you. It was very informal. I think the first meeting was in the college cafeteria for one hour. It was around Chanukah, and one of the officers was

eating a jelly donut, and the powder was getting all over his uniform. Then I was asked to take a test in math, English, and mental capabilities—it was almost six hours. I wasn't told what this unit was or that I would be in intelligence, just that I was going to be an engineer.

"Leni," the CEO of a communications networking company, was tapped after finishing his first degree in electronics at Tel Aviv University. He was part of the Academic Reserves. "I had an interview for about 45 minutes," he explained. "They want to see how creative you are. They ask questions that there is no right or wrong answer; it's the method in which you answer. Nothing is specific to the topic that you've learned but you have some knowledge in it. It's how you use your knowledge." He ended up staying in the unit for nine years.

One of the most distinctive paradoxes of the unit is that those in the process of being selected are rarely if ever told what they will be doing, and they are also told very little about the part of the military for which they are being recruited. "I don't know how I was recruited," said Amnon, who was drafted in the late 1980s. Given his high school transcript, however, it is not that difficult to see how he attracted attention. He was head of the student council, active in the scouts, and captain of the volleyball team. Rounding out his talents was his linguistic ability. He could speak Hebrew, Portuguese, English, French, and Italian—he learned Arabic in the unit. "When I joined the unit I knew absolutely nothing except that it was an intelligence force. I talked to a veteran, and he didn't tell me a thing except something about espionage, cryptography, and James Bond. Because I trusted him since I was 17, I said, 'Listen, am I going to the right place?' and he said, 'You will be satisfied, and the unit will make you into something else.' "

In recent years, an enormous amount of time and resources has been invested into locating and training recruits. Army recruiters scour the nation's talent pool. One former officer, "Michael," who spent more than 20 years in the unit, described the current selection process as akin to "NBA scouts tracking kids in high school and college." Now the CEO of a search engine software company, he spent the years between 1972 and 1976 in military intelligence in the Sinai Desert. The army sent him to college, and he received two degrees from Bar Ilan University—both a bachelor's and a master's in mathematics and computer science. "I didn't join through the technology gate," he said. "After my first degree, I was sent to the unit, and then for three years I was in Silicon Valley working on a joint U.S.-Israeli intelligence project. I was not recruited for technology; they were looking for people who were intelligent, plus I expressed a strong desire at the military sorting center. I said I wanted intelligence." He stayed 22 years.

In recent years, the reputation of unit veterans as successful entrepreneurs defining new technological categories in the civilian world has cast a spotlight on the once unknown name of the unit, attracting a large group of potential draftees. Such has been the widespread reputation of the unit despite its cloaked nature. Moreover, given what they have seen, many don't mind signing on for at least two more years of active service above the usual three-year hitch. First, however, they must make the cut, and very few do. It starts with a long and demanding testing process, including both psychological evaluations and simulations. Avi served in the unit from 1988 until 1993, and he is now the principle in a venture capital firm. At the top of the unit's wish list is to select potential innovators, but he warned, "Innovation is hard to articulate." As part of his reserve duty, he is also involved in recruitment. "The unit is very diversified," he explained. "There are thousands of people from all over, and we have different criteria in recruiting. I'm astonished and in fear of these 17-year-olds. They have better curriculum vitae in high school than I have today. They say they have worked for Hewlett-Packard in software testing for three years or were in the boy scouts, were head of a big group, chairman of the school council, volunteered in the community, and did a robotics project."

The bright prospects are sifted through and narrowed down into an elite group. For instance, when looking at candidates,

Avi takes note of their grades in all subjects. He wants to see that they are successful in all areas. "Even in the bad ones," he said. "If I see someone has a 100 percent in math and physics but a 60 percent in another subject, what does this tell me? That he only makes an effort in what he likes?" In addition, Avi explained that recruiters put people in simulated situations to see how they can handle pressure, what leadership skills emerge, how they work with others, and to assess their creativity and their ability to cope with failure. "There are formal courses," he said. "Each of them will learn many things from scratch. I can teach them math at the Msc level very quickly. But I want all kinds of people." Notably, this is a place where connections hold little weight. Indeed, he says, "I personally filtered out the daughter of one of the commanders."

For many, this is the first time they experience a true peer group, and that in and of itself creates an opportunity to see if they are unit material. "Sometimes it is like shock treatment," explained J.J. "All of them come from places where they are identified as the lions in their own vicinity. They are picked up and put in a place where there are a lot of guys like them, and some are even better. It's shocking." Those that see this as a threat don't make the cut. Those that see it as a challenge do.

Once they're in, they're in. They begin an intense 16- to 18-hour a day, 6-month training course. Because of the sensitive nature of the work involved, the washout rate is almost negligible. Once you've begun the course, "no one gets out," remarked J.J., "unless they're on a stretcher."

Heavily indoctrinated from day one, most rarely mention the name of the unit they serve, much less what they are doing inside its corridors. Even years after their discharges, most find it difficult to utter the name of the unit aloud. They'd refer to each other as "one of us" or "one of the guys"—despite the fact that this unit has a large proportion of women serving in it. Some make jokes, referring to the unit, which in Hebrew is pronounced *shmone matayiim,* in the cloaked and rhyming *shmone garbayiim*, which happens to means eight socks. Despite having worked with some of the world's most sophisticated security-related technology and operations, they don't look especially menacing. In fact, they look like a collection of graduate students, mathematics professors, and engineers.

Listening to former soldiers, nearly all of whom have gone on to found companies, develop technology, or excel in a number of categories from business to law, is a lot like looking at a flash rewind in time—a quick snapshot view back to the kid who sat in his or her bedroom dreaming, scheming, and imagining. They sound a lot like "Adam," the CEO of a software company. "I was always inventing things, ever since I was a child of seven years old," he explained. "I said I could make a computer and millions of alternative kinds of transportation. I was even thinking 20 years ago that I wanted to build shoes that converted to have wheels on them." Eventually, "Adam" and his colleagues were pulled from the complicated inner workings of their own brains and placed in a room with other like-minded individuals with whom they would now join forces. All the tinkerers and thinkers who created whole worlds on their own now had a shared universe in which to play.

The unit has been described as a loose confederation of geniuses—some with eccentric edges—firing on all cylinders all the time. It is not uncommon for soldiers to complete their master's degrees and even PhDs while simultaneously serving in the unit. There was the veteran reported by his colleagues to have won the Israeli version of the game show *Jeopardy* until he was finally kicked off because he had already won it three times. "We had one guy in our unit who was genius in math," recalled Gilad Goren. "Also, he was the best dancer, and he never paid to get into a theater. He'd say, 'I'm with the band.' He was so talented. He was even successful with girls. The only thing he failed in was that he was a bad actor." Although he tried to study the craft, he eventually went back to being a brilliant mathematician in academia.

Then there is Itzhik Pomerantz, serial entrepreneur. A large, burly man who would not look out of place in the physics department of some university, he may perhaps be described as the traditional "square," but there is nothing fixed in his thinking. When he was not quite 17, Pomerantz had skipped two grades in high school and was studying electrical engineering at the Technion, considered the Israeli equivalent of MIT, in Haifa as part of the Academic Reserves. He wound up in 8200 almost randomly. He wanted to enlist and serve with the Army Radio but was refused by the IDF. "They said this was unacceptable because I was taking up the space of an engineer in the Academic Reserves," he recalled. "They said if I refused to be an engineer they would send me to an infantry artillery post. All of the other engineers chose intelligence or the air force or the Signal Corps." He ended up in a unit he had never heard of—8200. "It was 1969, and they sent me to a place I never knew. The unit was unknown, mysterious, and most people never asked. I ended up here [in unit 8200] to fill the space of a vacant engineer. I stayed 15 years and left as a lieutenant colonel."

In a place not lacking in genius, Pomerantz earned a reputation as one of the unit's truly brilliant magicians. His ingenious bent quickly stood out, and stories about him filtered through the years to successive generations of soldiers. One of the best-known stories concerns the time he was caught speeding. He avoided paying for the ticket by coming up with an algorithm that disproved the police radar that nabbed him in the first place. In retrospect, he said, it is an episode that he is not particularly proud of. Once, on a trip to Jerusalem to visit an electronics exhibition, he saw an advertisement for a contest to sit in front of a computer and form as many word combinations as possible out of one word. "I happen to have a good imagination," he recalled. "The average was 25 words every three minutes. I did 57 every three minutes. I won the contest and got to take two free weekends in Jerusalem at the Sheraton." In his spare time he came up with a host of ideas. In one, he designed a foldable, collapsible bridge that a truck or tank could go over safely.

Like most, Pomerantz talks little about the details of his time inside of the unit. However, he will admit to a couple of things. One: At age 23 he headed up a team of 30 soldiers and a $10 million budget to build a computer system, the function of which is still under wraps. However, the directive was to build the system to perform one particular task that would run for five years, and then the unit would build 10 copies of it. It worked so well that it was finally retired 21 years later. "We are talking 32 kilobytes of memory," he explained. "That was in the early 1970s. It shows the kind of improvisational skill and flexibility we needed to function with such a small and weak computer." And two: In 1969, a time when television was still a new and rare thing in the world but particularly in Israel, the unit's technicians assembled a TV from an oscilloscope[2] and by tapping into a few signals to intercept television station broadcasts. "It was one of our very favorite challenges," he noted dryly. "It was in order not to have a boring evening."

Pomerantz left the unit in 1984. He was 37 years old. It was, he decided, time to start something new. "I am very entrepreneurial in character and interested in creating new things," he explained. "I was not interested in existing things." In 1985, he went to work for Scitex, the pioneering Israeli digital imaging company. There he invented a complicated system that could create three-dimensional objects that would represent graphic sketches. The design became the model for Cubitel. "The idea was that you would input into a system a sketch and raw data and out would come a very detailed 3-D object," he said. "Today, it is called rapid prototyping. When I invented it there was no solution. It was ahead of time—as was the product.[3] I built a machine that was 5 meters long and weighed 5 tons. It could create any geometry and any object in any size 20 inches by 20 inches by 14 inches." Feeling hamstrung and frustrated by having to deal with the management side of things, he left Cubitel in 1993. After all, he was more interested in being an inventor.

The idea behind his next invention, however, came to him during a trip to Tokyo in 1991 and while he was still at Cubitel. "I was walking in the Akihabara district, and I had to send a fax back to Cubitel to fire someone," he recalled. The problem was that the company had only one fax machine, which meant that anyone in the company could read the contents of the message. Pomerantz figured there had to be some way in which he could send the fax so that only the addressee could read the message. It took him, he said, just one day to come up with the solution. Pomerantz devised a software encryption that secured messages sent by faxes. He obtained a patent for the innovation and put it in his drawer for two years.

When he left Cubitel, he took the idea out of the drawer. It became the basis of Aliroo (a play on a Hebrew word meaning "they don't see"). Pomerantz raised $300,000 from private investors, and a year later, in 1994, he exhibited Aliroo at Comdex. From fax encryptions the system was later expanded to include securing email and photographs. Ten years later, companies all over the world use Aliroo's systems. In 2003, Eastman Kodak Company announced a deal with Aliroo to use its email encryption to securely send all types of patient information and imagery (including bills and lab and radiology reports) over the Internet to doctors, healthcare providers, and patients without the need for software on the part of the recipient.

But, for Pomerantz, it was time to move on—again. He left Aliroo six years after establishing it, a decision he made after concluding that his "creative skills as a technological entrepreneur were no longer useful." A consultant to other startups, Pomerantz runs courses at Tel Aviv University in the field of biometric signal processing. He is also at work on his next invention—one that involves corporate information security.

There are two aphorisms that have been attached to the soldiers of unit 8200. The first: "Give these people a lever, and they will move the earth." The second: "Their heads are so smart they must be tied to the ground with cables, otherwise they will float away." If the exiting conga line out of the unit is any indication, it has indeed succeeded in creating a place in which both adages exist simultaneously—the freedom to make change linked to a solid foundation. Unit 8200 has tapped into the fundamental capacity and faculties of these individuals and has thrown them into a very particular set of circumstances. The result is the ability to steer through the obvious, to calculate a set of possible variables and their outcomes from the most probable to the least, and to always keep the lever turning.

9 Battle Tested

The Suez Canal, circa 1968...

Since ancient times, the Suez Canal has served as one of the world's most vital water passageways. Situated at the mouth of three continents, it has been an enduring symbol of the ever-shifting balance of the Middle East, and its strategic importance has not gone unnoticed. The pharaohs were said to be the first to try to build a canal by connecting the Red Sea to the Nile. With varying degrees of success, later regimes that conquered Egypt would make more ambitious attempts to link the Red Sea to the Mediterranean and shorten the lucrative trading routes among Europe, Asia, and Africa. Around 1798, Napoleon's engineers wrestled with constructing a large-scale canal, but they came up empty. It wasn't until 1857, when the Turkish viceroy governing Egypt commissioned French engineer Ferdinand de Lesseps to build a canal, that the construction of the modern Suez Canal got underway. It took 10 years to complete.

Its construction was cause for celebration. Indeed, Giuseppe Verdi was commissioned to write the opera *Aida* in honor of the canal's inauguration. However, having gone into debt to build it, Egypt was forced to sell its controlling interest in the canal to Great Britain to pay for it. For their part, the British, who regarded it as a crucial gateway to the Far East and its oil interests in the Persian Gulf, stationed troops along the Canal Zone to protect their access to those internests. For almost 90 years, the canal remained under foreign control, operated by the Compagnie Universelle du Canal Maritime de Suez.

That is until July 1956, when Egyptian President Gamal Abdul Nasser abruptly seized it. His nationalization of the canal bolstered his seat of power. It also capped off what became known as the Suez Crisis—increasing the tension swirling around a series of political events that had now come to a head. France, Britain, and Israel, each with their own reasoned motives to bring down Nasser, joined forces. Simply put, within months the three invaded Egypt to open up the canal. The attack, however, earned international censure and harsh rebuke on the part of both the United Nations and the United States. In the end, the ill-fated troika was compelled to withdraw, and President Nasser emerged victorious, fortifying his leadership in the Arab world.

Eleven years later, the Suez was once again the center of a geopolitical storm. As a result of the Six Day War in 1967, Israel was now in possession of the Sinai Peninsula—including the 101-mile waterway. Shut out for years by the Egyptians, it was the Israelis who now held sway over the canal's fate. The Suez Canal, a key artery for international trade and the symbol of Egyptian national pride, was now a strategic buffer between the two enemies. The British and French were out, the Egyptians were pushed back, and the Israeli troops were sitting along the eastern bank of the canal nearly 60 miles from downtown Cairo.

At some point following the war, the storied Suez Canal was once more the scene of action—a clandestine footnote, really, in a body of water that had played so publicly on the international arena. At this moment in time, it would be the launchpad of an Israeli operation. A plan was drawn up. In it, soldiers would secretly cross over to the Egyptian side of the canal on the west. It was decided that they would be ferried over in a small rubber boat. The problem was that the Israelis needed a way to track the commando boat and they had less than a week to come up with one. The solution would require a device that would allow the Israelis to monitor the boat but at the same time remain undetected to the Egyptians, providing the soldiers with safe passage. The task fell to a handful of soldiers in unit 8200. Immediately, they went into action, and in five days they had invented a special transmitter signal that would trail the boat and follow its movements as it crossed the Suez Canal into enemy territory.

The solution—this transmitter—had all of the defining elements that would come to characterize the unit: it was efficient, resourceful, fast to development, quickly deployed, and created under tremendous pressure and time constraints.

This was not a singularly spectacular episode but rather a common occurrence in the life of the unit, observed "Reuven." Although he was not part of the particular group that developed the transmitter signal and would not join the unit until many years later, this was, he suggested, a simple illustration of the nature of the game and the constant churn of events that has established a modus operandi heavily contingent upon self-reliance. "They designed a full solution and installed it in a very few days," he explained. "Sometimes the solution is so unique because there is no such solution on the market. You can't always buy it because then you expose what you are doing. And we don't have the time to go by the book or follow all of the procedures." To underscore his point, without irony, he delivered the unit's motto: *It takes us a few hours to do the odd thing; unfortunately, the impossible will take us a few days.*

Hubris aside, it is not too much to say, however, that it is out of this sense of impossibility that one of Israel's most significant cultures of innovation was created. It is the spark that drives the idea flywheel from which national security has rested, new technologies have emerged, and an entire economy was invigorated. It is a military unit, which by its very definition as part of a military organization should be rigid, disciplined, and compliant to authority, and yet is the exact opposite.

Rather, it is a fusion of motivated individuals working within a military structure—a structure that nourishes creativity and encourages risk-taking and even, to a degree, failure. It is a structure that celebrates leadership but disdains hierarchical authority, advances a spectrum of viewpoints, promotes collaboration, and places equal weight on imagination and experience.

The structure of unit 8200 is what accounts for the caffeinated torrent of ideas that has emerged from it—ideas that have become startups and NASDAQ-traded companies. In some cases, whole industries have been built upon these ideas. The unit's enduring imprint on a large proportion of startups is why the economic pages of the Israeli newspaper *Ha'aretz* declared that it was no mere twist of fate that a number of technological innovations in play in the civilian world had been born and improved in the Israeli military by unit veterans.[1]

Two organizational behavior professors at Tel Aviv University's Graduate School of Business, Drori Israel and Shmuel Ellis, have been examining the root of this link that has emerged from a number of elite military units, including 8200. They determined, initially at least, that soldiers from these units capitalized on both the networks formed in the army and the skills that they learned there. However, the situation runs deeper than just the tangible skill sets obtained in service, such as knowing signal processing or radio connectivity, and the shift out of the unit into commercial applications. Just as influential, they explained, are the values and norms at work. From the intense immersion in what Ellis and Israel term a "culture of improvisation and innovative thinking," these soldiers have developed primordial connections between what they have learned and how to adapt that behavior to the civilian world.

"Startups are highly risky and need quick responses," said Israel. "These people really fit in to this stress. They are not risk averse. They are task-oriented and very loyal. They don't crack under pressure." "On top of that," Ellis added, "they are talented engineers. What more can you want? Even better." That is to say, who better to spend all night in pursuit of developing an idea into a product under the incredible weight of uncertainty? "Each individual is considered a whole world," explained Professor Ellis. "Such a person finishes the army and goes to the market and is considered to have these qualities: creative, accountable, highly motivated, and talented."

With notable exceptions (state security, military training, uniforms, and medalled generals as immediate supervisors), this environment mirrors if not mimics the kind of forces at play in the proverbial startup: the chaos, the sleepless nights, the pressure, and the mix of talent funneling its way through a maze of obstacles toward an end goal. The soldiers trade in systems, information, and analysis; these are the tools of spy craft on which Israel's policy-makers will base their decisions and actions. Intelligence is information, and information is derived in large part from sophisticated communications systems. It may be on the front lines of national security, but it has always been, at heart, information technology.

In his office inside of the Kirya complex, Israel's director of military intelligence, Major General Aharon Ze'evi Farkash, pulled out a computer printout with the names and logos of 34 Israeli companies on it. A partial list to be sure, but all of its entries spun out of the nation's elite electronic intelligence units. A broad and imposing figure, Farkash has spent most of his military career in the Intelligence Corps connecting the dots. In this case, the dots form the converging forces where war and business meet. His no-nonsense assessment is, "Here we have competition—unfortunately—for 55 years. It has brought us to be better, accurate, and shorten the lines."

However, looking back upon the printed list of companies that in no small part came out of this "competition," as he phrased it, explains only part of the story. After all, one would be hard-pressed to find the kind of institutionalized innovative spirit—almost like an incubator—sweeping through a military-intelligence complex and transferring to the civilian world in quite the same way. For Farkash, this unique situation resides somewhere in a more fundamental, pragmatic approach. It stems from a mission and commitment to something bigger than individual glory or monetary gain that is grafted onto a very specific way of doing things. Concerning these units, he said, there is "a mixture of high motivation. We have the feeling they can be creative for their own country. There is a combination of a few disciplines, not just physics, chemistry, and mathematics. You put a few people together and ask questions." He thought about this for a minute and continued: "Sometimes it is the power to ask the right questions and not necessarily have the right answers. Maybe this is too simple a formula, but maybe because of the threat, you have to know that you have to be better than the others. This [need for] superiority forced us to be the best. It is a very high motivator."

It is not unlike the kind of cocktail of self-discipline and creativity established by the Americans as they entered the "space race" of the 1960s or the intense rush of effort to mobilize and crush the Nazis during World War II. However, in Israel, this high level of intensity operates on a continuous, hourly basis.

The unit's creative bent begins with a spark. The spark generates an idea that starts the process. Innovation can come from an operational initiative, from the internal pull to improve upon what already exists, or from a desire to find another way to get there. It is drawn from illuminating ideas and finding the answers in the cracks, the niches, and the dark unexpected corners. Sometimes it comes from uncovering something entirely new, or it is just seeing something from a different perspective: sideways or from the bottom, or a new approach to an old way of doing something. There is no other option: A person is confronted with a challenge, and he or she has to solve it very quickly. One former unit 8200 veteran, who later co-founded a communications company with several other alumni following their discharges, explained that the innovation comes from the fact that there is a need for a kind of machine to function in a way that does not exist: "No problem [like it] arrived before, and you have to come up with a solution very quickly." At the same time, "there is no help because it comes from out of the blue. You have to invent."

There is a relative autonomy and self-determination within the unit that confers a great deal of latitude to create and the means with which to do so. The atmosphere in many ways is deliberately informal. "People have a relatively high degree of freedom to play with technology," said "Reuven." "For an engineer it is like toys. He will always try to experiment with the top-of-the-line technology. In a business they would never let him do that." He then emphasized that "the army is not a business." Freed up from external considerations that bog down a commercial product (quality assurance, stability, and functionality guarantees), the emphasis is on developing a technology at its outer reaches, without a manual, academic literature, or, at times, a tried and true use. "One technology is a kind of magic," he continued. "It does exactly what you say but everything around it doesn't exist. Intelligence develops a one-time solution for one type of problem, and you have only one vendor: the army. The technology center can always take the risk of using top-of-the-line technology." To formalize this process, he noted, would be "to lose this spirit."

Elie Barr, who capped off a number of years in the unit with a three-year hitch as its commander, described an environment resembling something of a high-tech three-ring circus, all motion and blur and moving in time to the syncopated rhythms of circumstance. He said:

> It's like a pendulum. Every minor swing of intelligence sends the whole military into a larger swing. It goes to the heart of training and the mission, coupled with the

creativity needed day-to-day, week-to-week. There is a lot of work in planning ahead. The technology is so advanced, you can't deal with today's problem but you are building a solution for tomorrow's problem. Part of the day is dedicated to the next 24 hours and another part is dedicated to designing issues four to five years at a time in advance.

At its crux is a focus on identifying and solving hard problems. At the same time, there is an accommodating enthusiasm in which brigadier generals keep their fingers loosely on the tap. Their job is not to keep everyone in line, but rather to perpetuate an atmosphere in which they keep

To avoid limiting their subordinates to one perspective, it is a place where commanding officers rarely impose their way of tackling a problem.

the spark lit. To avoid limiting their subordinates to one perspective, it is a place where commanding officers rarely impose their way of tackling a problem. "In my point of view this unit leads the changes and capabilities of the IDF," said Pinchas Buchris, who commanded the unit between 1997 and 2001. "In this unit there are many clever, smart, sophisticated, enthusiastic, and motivated young people," he said. "And the question is how do you lead these kinds of people? In the army you can manage a unit by orders. You can say be here or there at this or that time but you can't order soldiers to think or be motivated. It is more than creating a challenge—you have to create an environment and a spirit."

That environment starts with some tall expectations—encased in a high level of support. "We give young people very big challenges, and we give them the opportunity, the conditions, and the responsibility," said Buchris. "No company is going to give young engineers this kind of responsibility to lead a project." There is a fundamental need to be creative. Following the thread to his own conclusion, Buchris said that the highest order of magnitude of an intelligence organization could not survive without cutting-edge technology:

> To collect very sensitive information you have to have cutting-edge technological capabilities. What has happened in the last decade [is that] the technology world has become very dynamic. These young people find out how to deal with technology. They have to have very creative, dynamic thinking. Sometimes they are dealing with a technology system in front of them, or you have to find a way to deal with something that lends itself to other capabilities. It's not like [if] you decide to create this product you are dealing with something ahead of time, and all the time it's changing.

It is an environment, Buchris concluded, where "the sky is the limit to what they can create."

It would seem the elements required for actionable intelligence in war echo those for success in business. Rapid response time is critical, and new products must be adapted and introduced continuously in a changing marketplace. Like the employees in a startup, the soldiers work independently and yet as part of a team. They are flexible and innovative and capable despite age or experience to apply themselves within a fluid chain of command. "The level of creativity dictates people are willing to rely on the ability to live in a relatively unstable situation," explained Elie Barr. "The startup environment is very paradoxical. One paradox of 8200 is that it is one of the most orderly units in a disorderly army. At the same time it is well-formed from the outside. On the inside it is all free spirits with leeway budgets and the manpower to come up with solutions." Not incidentally, Barr followed up his 27-year military career with his position as executive vice president of the global communications firm Teledata Ltd. (which was acquired by ADC in 1998). Later, when Barr served as a managing partner at technology venture fund Mofet, he estimated that some 70 percent of his portfolio bore the stamp of former 8200 members.

What exists is an informal atmosphere tethered to a military framework. It is a place in which the outlandish is considered OK and is even encouraged—as is the counterintuitive. There exists an inexhaustive ability to ask "What if?" Its ethos is entrepreneurial. On a practical level, it also means next-generation security for the

It is a place in which the outlandish is considered OK, even encouraged—as is the counterintuitive. There exists an inexhaustive ability to ask "What if?"

nation. The battle order is to invent, which may mean creating a new system, improving an existing one, or solving an analytical challenge. These are not just baseline changes but an accumulation of breakthroughs. "There is a special spirit there and a lot of responsibility," said former member Gabi Ilan. "There are young, talented, ambitious people. This spirit, courage, and initiative supports certain new ideas even if they are quite different from what is accepted. Everyone there behaves differently, and the unit accepts it. One of the strengths of the unit is that it doesn't put you in a predefined square job and tell you what to do—the job can be tailored to individual capacities." As Ilan explained it, the ultimate value is not placed solely on creating an end product but on how ideas are generated, as well as on the self-initiative needed to try to change existing procedures, to try to create new systems, and to try to find technical solutions to operational problems—even those that are considered unsolvable and those that are not their own mandate to solve.

Following his discharge from the unit in 1981, Ilan spent 10 years working for the large Israeli telecommunications company Tadiran creating a new signal processing-based communications intelligence system from scratch. Then he asked, "What if?" What if there were a system that could recognize human handwriting and compose it like a digitized tablet? This was, by the way, 1989, long before personal digital assistants (PDAs) became ubiquitous and four years before the introduction of the Apple Newton Message Pad. This was, however, a time when Ilan noticed that his wife, who was studying for her MBA at Tel Aviv University, spent a significant amount of time writing out her homework and typing out her subjects. Ilan helped pioneer handwriting technology as a timesaving gift for his wife.

For a year, Ilan and a colleague, a mathematician, worked on the prototype in his kitchen. They created a system using specific signal-processing algorithms, and this system formed the backbone of what would eventually become Advanced Recognition Technologies, Inc. (ART). The two colleagues first developed an intuitive program, converting handwriting written onto a PDA into digital text that could be stored in a computer and printed out. The handwriting system led to the development of a voice command software program capable of integrating voice commands into a variety of electronic devices. For instance, by adding a software chip into a cell phone, a caller speaks into the phone, and the phone will identify the words and make the call. Both the handwriting and software programs use artificial intelligence to learn the particular voice and handwriting patterns of the user as a means of identifying and recognizing him or her in the future.

Around 2000, Ilan asked "What if?" again. What if one could manipulate electronic and light signals for the common household? Having worked with this type of technology for years, he began to think up ways that it could be commercialized. "I thought there could be an application for the coupon market," he said. "I knew in the U.S. coupons are a huge business." Ilan started brainstorming about the possibility of replacing newspaper coupon inserts by pulling them directly off of television commercials. So began Optinetix, a proprietary technology for optical downloading of digital information from TV screens and monitors.

In his office in a Tel Aviv suburb, Ilan lined up a group of what looks like television remote control devices colored silver, blue, and red. Each of the remotes actually houses a small optical receiver, four double-A batteries, and a printer. Ilan is using these devices to develop a system that downloads coupons directly off a TV. For instance, a Coca-Cola commercial is broadcast, and a user points the remote at the screen and hits a button. The device recognizes light signals from the TV, picks up a bar signal, downloads the message, and prints out a coupon. "The device is quite complicated," he explained. "The operation is simple, just one button, but what's inside is not trivial. There is lots of signal processing."

At its best, unit 8200 summons the brainpower of a group of people who join forces to probe the unknown and push back its limits, and to peer into the unformed future and ask not "Why?" but "Why not?" So, for example, if you can send data over bandwidth, why not speech? And if you can target and intercept enemy frequency hopping, why not expand that knowledge into creating bands of wireless fidelity for two-way paging systems and then integrating systems into single networks…ad infinitum.

Four years after leaving the unit with a rank of full colonel, "Michael" joined a software startup in the late 1990s as its CEO. "The most interesting aspect and real reason I consider the unit to be the biggest and most successful incubator in Israel is that how it behaves and what it does is like no other unit in the military," he said.

It's not a coincidence. If you look at the process of how to build a high-tech company in the civilian world, in the very first stages you find a similar parallel process [of taking an idea and producing a system] in the unit. By definition, by nature, you find very unique solutions. You are taught that from day one. It was the way I was raised and the way I raised those after me. This challenge is difficult but you have to find a way to solve it. You are taught to look at original solutions. They expect you to [do this]. They don't want to hear excuses.

"Assume you have an idea," he said. "A lot of times you see people without a task identifying a challenge or need themselves and coming up with solutions, exactly like a startup does. For instance, we think people like to send text messages between cell phones, so let's develop SMS [short message service] software. However, the kind of ideas the unit provides are linked not to a consumer service, but to an operation that is required by the security needs of the State of Israel." Michael concluded: "Identify a problem and solutions. An idea takes resources and people and money. The main point is to describe the problem and solution, which is close to a business plan in a military environment."

"Michael's" software company was founded by a small nucleus of former unit members. They applied the same causal standard: identify a problem and come up with a solution. At the time—the mid-to-late 1990s—Internet commerce was beginning to emerge with the appearance of the Mosaic Web browser. According to "Michael," a rigid standard called Standard Query Language (SQL) was used to access and manipulate database systems. His company was looking to create a more sophisticated, intuitive search mechanism. It came up with a program that enabled searchers to find information parametrically, intuitively, and associatively. That is to say, it is a program that can identify patterns and links between names and phrases tailored in a way chosen by the user to retrieve a set of information. For instance, the company's programs can help individuals search for movies online even if they have only partial information such as a theme or the name of a character, and even if they have the incorrect spelling of the names of actors or directors, the software will provide them with the correct movie title. It's like recalling a film to a friend with details that you can't quite get right. You start by saying the film takes place in space, and you think there is a character named Luc, a robot, and a princess. It is enough of a link that the friend can connect the information in his or her own personal stored memory to, say, *Star Wars*.

It is not all that different from the kinds of intelligence systems used to pick up, comprehend, and collate pieces of information, and then find the hazy links and collate them into a comprehensible connection. After all, as "Michael" explained, "It is the same idea used to find terrorist links." And it is used by consumers to hunt down wedding gifts, tools, movies, and practically any consumer item on a number of large retail websites.

As significant as the unit's approach to problem-solving is, just as important to the process is the undeniable youth factor. People barely out of high school shoulder a huge amount of responsibility. The process is designed to give equal weight to the ideas forwarded and to the experience and pedigree of the idea generator. At the same time, a constant flow of new recruits each year and the significance placed on each one of their contributions means that the unit's idea culture rarely remains stagnant.

In the whir of the moment, members of the unit have to make decisions that could mean the difference between life and death. This runs across duty lines—whether developing a system, analyzing a situation, or interpreting data. "The unit teaches you two things fast," explained Amnon, who served in the early 1990s doing analysis. "Responsibility and ownership. You are 20 years old, and you are responsible. No one else is responsible for the intelligence product of 200 to 400 people on the base. You have to get that information to headquarters on time. It is your responsibility [to say], 'Are the missiles going east or west?'"

Amnon recalled one episode in which he was just about to finish the night shift on his base at 2:00 A.M. "It was quiet, and then all hell broke loose. A terrorist was trying to go from Jordan into Israel." At 20, and barely out of training and his officer's course, Amnon was in charge of the situation. "We were trained to act under pressure, to meet the task, to act fast and cool and calm. The situation fills you with adrenaline." He continued, "You have seconds to minutes to choose among three to five scenarios: to act, to react, to report, and to whom."

The intense compression of experience has left an indelible mark: an innate sense of one's ability to affect change, to create realities, and to push back boundaries. At 20, Lior was given the daunting task of condensing 15,000 pages containing 20 years' worth of Israeli technological intelligence into a comprehensive summary of 230 pages. "Every day for a year from 8:00 A.M. to 6:00 P.M. I read the pages," he recalled. More importantly, he completed the job successfully. "I learned that there is no subject too big to learn, or period of time that is too short, if you have the right attitude and the skills learned in the unit. When I finished this project I felt there wasn't anything I couldn't do." A recurrent theme that one takes away from soldiers from the unit is this: Anything is possible. Where others see constraints, they see opportunities. Similarly, Ori spoke of his time in the unit as being a period in which he "learned that there are no limits. Nothing is too complicated to solve. They taught us that there is nothing that can't be done or worked on except," he laughed, "maybe budgets. But it makes me question everything."

In turn, the youth factor has created a dynamic that encourages several points of view. In part, it is rooted in the trauma of the 1973 Yom Kippur War when senior intelligence officers held on to predefined concepts and ignored the warnings of their subordinates. However, the unit, like the IDF, is willing to set the bar for entry at a good idea. "It doesn't matter what is your rank," said "Michael." "All people are assigned tasks and expected to resolve problems and come up with ideas." This is one trait that has a deep carry-over into civilian life. Israelis are still astonished by the rote adherence to pecking orders shown in American and European companies. Raised in an environment where a low-ranking sergeant can contradict his commanding officer and in fact is expected to if the situation demands it, there is a healthy encouragement of multiple points of view. "Of all the professional situations in my life," said Avi, who joined the unit in 1988 and served for five years, "the one by far that informed me in my seminal years was the unit. I used to speak almost daily with the office of the chief of staff. He would call me informally to see what was happening when I was 20. Our counterparts in the United States would be 40 years old."

While experts may generate proficiency, combining specialists with the relatively inexperienced produces ingenuity. "We are lucky," explained former Commander Pinchas Buchris.

> Every year the unit gets new soldiers and engineers. There is fresh blood. Some people in an organization may think about a problem one way and get stuck. You look at a problem and your point of view. Suddenly there is a new soldier, a new problem, and a new point of view. People are not stuck in their thinking. There is a constant flow of the way of doing things. When you put young people and sophisticated people together in the same environment to deal with a problem, they invest all of their capabilities into solving it. There is a quality to solving it and getting results."

The diversity of ideas and solutions comes not only from the combination of age and experience but also from the integration of several disciplines combined in pursuit of probing, prodding, and breaking through problems to a joint solution. There is a wide-angle sweep of backgrounds and disciplines that can certainly hold their own separately but that together can create a perspective that is both deep and broad. Take, for example, Pinchas Buchris. Unlike many commanders who started in the unit and moved up the ranks, he came from a totally different background and perspective. In the early 1970s, he wanted to be a pilot and entered the air force's pilot training course. Within a few months, however, the air force decided to let him go. Their reason, according to Buchris, was that he was not pilot material. "When I started to fly," he recalled, "I tried to control the small [training] plane. I was so concerned with everything, they thought I wouldn't be able to see the whole picture." In retrospect, for Buchris, a soft-spoken man, it was the proverbial blessing in disguise. In 1974 he joined the Sayeret Matkal, the elite reconnaissance special-ops unit. Two years later he was part of the elite of the elite—the handful of commandos who were chosen to take part in the legendary Entebbe rescue operation. "It was," he said, "a once in a lifetime operation." Buchris stayed in the Sayeret until 1982. Six years after his discharge he was asked to re-enlist as deputy commander of the Sayeret. He thought he was on track to eventually lead the unit, but instead he switched to another technological unit in intelligence before heading up 8200. Along the way Buchris completed the Advanced Management Program at Harvard Business School— that on top of earning a Bachelor's of Science degree from the Technion and an MBA from Derby University. In 1993 he won the Israeli Security Prize. Utilizing his own deep and broad experience, in 2003 he joined the Israeli office of the British venture capital group Apax Partners as a partner. Fittingly, his area of specialty is information technology.

Approaching its sixth decade, Israel is a relatively young nation. As such, it has yet to fully accept the yoke of tradition. It may be for that reason that much of its practices and institutions remain loose, informal, and open. A significant effect of serving in the unit is the ability to learn by doing—not just how things are done, but how they can be done. While this approach certainly has its disadvantages—a short-term perspective and a propensity toward short cuts is not a real management primer, for example—it has also had a profoundly positive effect on creativity. By the time the soldiers enter the unit, they've gone through mind-boggling six-month immersion training. Sixteen-hour days are dedicated to learning such brain-bending subjects as Arabic, physics, and signals processing. But the real education happens on the job. The practical experience is immediate and constant; the theoretical paper pushing exercises are a luxury. This is a rapid-fire deployment of ideas in real time.

"Leni," who left the unit in the late 1990s and is the CEO of a communications networking company, described it as a kind of ongoing knowledge baton toss. "Young people learn from the people above. You are trained day one from experts in the field scratching the limits of technology. You are working in technology, not in the academy. Much of this is not implemented yet, and you have to be ahead of technology." It is an immersion hothouse. "You are never going to get that information anywhere, and it's hands-on experience. You don't have to get burned to get hot. You don't have to go through an experimental phase."

The rate of speed at which the unit moves is responsible for creating a system that functions within its own calibrated sense of efficiencies, hewing closely to Israel's aversion to hidebound tradition in favor of improvisation. For one thing, the choreography of training soldiers and the development of systems and technology are rarely put down on paper. Most of the knowledge transfer done among and between soldiers is verbal. "Everything is moving so fast," explained "Leni." "We don't have time to document it." While they were deliberately vague on details, many unit members described myriad occasions in which the time between recognizing a problem and solving it would be just a matter of days. For instance, "Leni" suggested, "You design a system, and it works. It does what it should be doing." But, if it goes operational and fails, "You don't have time to go back to the lab and figure out why. You have to fix it now, on the spot, with no tools or components.

It's like *MacGyver*," he joked. "Take a piece of chewing gum and make an airplane—in real time."

This fast deployment of a total solution, as well the ability to adjust quickly to adverse circumstances, is behind, say many, the ability of Israeli companies to best much of the world in terms of the time it takes to complete a near-finished prototype. There was a story that made the rounds at the cafés around the high-tech clusters in Tel Aviv and Herziliya. It was light on specifics but the message's essence left a deep impression. No one who told it was quite sure of its veracity. It may have been a telecom company or a wireless outfit that had a deal with a big European firm, possibly German. What was certain was that the Israeli startup bore the distinctive imprint of former unit 8200 soldiers. The company had been commissioned to develop a solution for the larger European organization. However, a week before the deadline, the Israeli startup was given a completely new requirement to add to its prototype. The Israelis realized the time it would take to redesign it, ship it, and wait for it to go through customs would mean possibly missing the deadline and the commission. After rebuilding the prototype, they decided to disassemble it into 20 small parts. Instead of shipping it, they flew 20 people to Europe, each carrying one part in their hand luggage.

In many cases, one of the most influential factors at play is simply sheer audacity. Stemming in part from the primal urge to fight when you find your back to the wall, a basic tenet that runs deep here is to find a way—any way—and do not stop until you do. Its essence is found in one of the intelligence community's old adages: If a door is locked, go through the window. Gilad Goren, a unit alumnus and cofounder of Native Networks, put it this way: "We have to solve problems. In America, there is a plan. If there is no plan, they don't do it. In Israel we say, 'We will find a solution. Something will happen. We aren't afraid.' " Furthermore, he said, "There is no Thomas Edison or Alexander Graham Bell in Israel. We're not such great minds. We're fighters, and we want to win. We want to show we are better."

And they are not afraid to slip up in the process. One of the biggest obstacles to innovation is a fear of failure. There is an Israeli saying that surfaces constantly: "You don't make a mistake if you do nothing." Success is based on a foundation of failure. The only real failure is a complete and utter breakdown,

> *One of the biggest obstacles to innovation is a fear of failure. There is an Israeli saying that surfaces constantly: "You don't make a mistake if you do nothing."*

or worse, inaction. That could mean extinction. Anything else is merely another step along the way to beating back what many consider impossible.

Former MAFAT (the Defense Ministry's weapons research and development arm) head Isaac Ben Israel described this concept as part of a deeply embedded Israeli character trait, which has been institutionalized in the military. Ben Israel suggested it began at statehood. "Israel was founded as a counterreaction to the old way of the Jews living in the diaspora," he explained. "It was founded as a revolution. Every idea was an innovation. And you put in the Jewish tradition of questioning everything written in the *Torah*. On top of that, we are in a continuous state of war. It forces us to change in order to survive."

Ben Israel then made the link to science. "When you think about the idea of scientific progress, it is based on failure." He went on to say:

> How do you progress in science? You make some hypotheses and then test the hypotheses, eliminating those that are not working. Eliminating means failure. This is the whole process of innovations philosophy. In such a process you have many good ideas and 95 to 99 percent will fail. You continue on with one. The process of failure is not something that is undesired. Once you realize that failure is an inherently scientific process and you understand that the scientific goes with boldness, there is not a fear of failure.

This is, according to Ben Israel, a basic explanation of the Israeli character.

In the end, the stumble before the leap and the flawed concept that precedes the "eureka" moment have rewards of their own. Perhaps because failure is defined differently here, the unsuccessful is not a mark of failure. It is just part of the process. It is part of the accounting of moving forward.

In some ways this unit is like an assembly of dreamers. These are the kids in school who tinkered on ham radios or took apart their father's car engine and put it back together again. As adults they are encouraged to keep that kind of unedited childhood innocence where the future looms larger than the past. As grownups they are not discouraged from playing, tinkering, or fixing—in fact, they are given the best tools to do so. Their scrapes are noted and their achievements rewarded. They are given a sense of ownership in the idea of change and are equipped to make change happen. They are also hyperaware of the environment in which they are operating. It is these very traits that are carried into the civilian world.

C H A P T E R

10 Spy Company

Diamond District, Ramat Gan, 2003...

If the streets of a city reveal its stories, then the story of Tel Aviv is one of reinvention. The façades of once-elegant villas with crumbling plaster share space with trendy coffeehouses on the tree-lined streets of the once-graceful boulevards. Evidence of the formerly dominant Ottoman presence of crenellated balconies and square domes gives way to the squat, dun-colored functionalism left over from the British Mandate period, which in turn has been taken over by the weathered white Bauhaus buildings and the ubiquitous cement apartment blocks on raised columns. The skeletal reminder of a new era is found in the pervasive rebar frames of construction in various stages of completion that mark the city—accompanied as they are by the ever-present building cranes. Established nearly a century ago, the city has yet to settle into its identity. The name itself describes its own inherent tendency to push forward: *tel* is the Hebrew word meaning "hill built on the remains of the past" and *aviv* is Hebrew for the season of "spring." Unlike ancient cities steeped in history where the cracks and crevices reveal epochs in time, Tel Aviv's urban landscape exposes the layered surfaces of tomorrow. In Jerusalem, history is held closely. In Tel Aviv it is the future that is proclaimed.

Tel Aviv may be the physical embodiment of the Israeli mentality, and if there is one static element that characterizes it, it is the inclination toward improvement and change, the constant march upward and forward. Here it announces itself in the clusters of glass—skyscrapers that sprout up at various points disconnected from any kind of city center. Inside of them a spectrum of transformations are taking place. Ramat Gan, a neighborhood on Tel Aviv's eastern flank, is one such cluster. It also happens to be the heart of Israel's diamond exchange and one of the world's largest centers for cutting and polishing diamonds. Until the mid-1990s, when the country's high-tech sector emerged as a global factor, diamonds and oranges remained Israel's main exports. Here in the Diamond Tower high above Jabotinsky Street is a place where all of the dynamics are at work. It is the headquarters of Check Point Software Technologies. It represents a profound shift, a turning point in Israel's future.

Check Point and Gil Shwed, its shy, intellectual co-founder, have come to define the modern Israeli success story: the breathlessly innovative entrepreneur who left his military service with a vision and created a globally dominant enterprise and an entire industry around it. Check Point nearly single-handedly created the Internet firewall, the now generic term for software that protects computer networks from outside attacks and viruses, allowing information to leave the network and keeping all unauthorized users and information from breaching it. Check Point and its groundbreaking FireWall-1 shot out from practically nowhere in 1993 to become what is considered the standard in network security. According to the company, nearly every government and major organization on the planet uses its products, including 80 percent of Fortune 500 firms. Check Point is a symbol of Israeli triumph. It is also likely one of the most valuable, if not the most valuable, Israeli companies traded on NASDAQ. Since going public in 1996, its market capitalization literally took off, reaching $20 billion at one point (in early 2004 it had dropped to $5.69 billion). In 2003, the company racked up $432.6 million in annual sales.

As for Shwed, within a decade, the company he started at age 24 earned him a personal fortune worth some $1 billion. In 2001 he was one of the youngest individuals ever to land on *Forbes* magazine's annual tally of billionaires.[1] Two years later, the World Economic Forum, the yearly summit where the world's most elite and powerful meet in Davos, Switzerland, named him as one of its Global Leaders of Tomorrow. At home in Israel, he is considered one of his nation's heroes. Shwed is viewed as the homegrown Bill Gates, and not long after his enormous success catapulted him to fame, the nation's newspapers began affectionately referring to Shwed as "Gil Bates."

In a nation filled with brash innovators and with a military that despite its main *raison d'être* of defense has come to function as a finely tuned incubator, Check Point's story is one of the most explicit examples of both. At once mythic, it is also the classic Israeli story of finding a niche at the right time and seizing upon the idea of a problem as an opportunity and solving the problem creatively. It is also a prime illustration of a country that clings to its security as a precious resource and has been able to parlay its ability to not only understand threats but also to come up with innovative ways in which to solve them—and to translate these solutions into the commercial arena. In this case it was a keen grasp that if computer networks could be connected, amplifying our ability to communicate, there would also be a need to communicate securely.

Shwed first came up with what would become the world's biggest seller of security software when he was still serving in unit 8200 in the late 1980s. Although he generally shuns discussing his military service, Shwed does concede that the idea for Check Point did occur to him during his stint in the army. He was involved in linking two different classified computer networks together that allowed some users access to classified data while rejecting others entrée. As it turned out, that initial hookup, in what was likely a windowless room on some army base, proved to be a crucial moment. "I looked at the market, and there were no good solutions," he explained. So, as has become routine, he came up with one on his own. It was simple, it came from a real and defined need, and it worked.

Shwed took a look at the changing landscape. It was a matter of time before the computer and the Internet would move from universities to corporations to the mass consumer. So began the formulation of software security for a computer network in a larger context. "I knew it was a good idea, and I kept it for three or four years." When Shwed left the army in 1991, he took the idea with him, although he cautions that he took nothing else. When it came time to develop what would become Firewall-1, he insisted, "I started from scratch. I didn't take a single line of code from the army. The idea was the same but I waited for the market and built a company around it."

The idea of constructing software walls around computer networks sounds positively banal today. However, at the time that Shwed was nurturing the concept in his mind, the Internet was still largely the province of the government and academics. It was, of course, several years before the Internet made its way into millions of homes and before the rise of services and programs that would expose how incredibly unprotected the Net could be and how vulnerable its users were to rogue hackers and damaging viruses. But Shwed immediately saw an opportunity. A phenomenon was starting to take shape in the way people communicated, something he called "an experience that was not a theoretical vision." In the early 1990s, "if you wanted to send mail between the U.S. and Israel, it took two weeks. To talk on the telephone, there was the time difference, and it cost $2 a minute." Shwed saw how email was used in universities and then the beginnings of how it was connecting businesses within a kind of Internet infrastructure. A conversation began about connecting computers securely. "The two things came together," he said.

After finishing his army service, the preternaturally gifted Shwed decided to forgo studying at university. Something of a computer phenom as a child, he was writing programs as a teen and taking computer science classes at Hebrew University in Jerusalem while still in high school. Instead of attending a university, he started working for an Israeli software company. He met Marius Nacht, who was a graduate of the IDF's elite Talpiot program, and the pair joined up with Shlomo Kramer, another programmer. They were all on the same page when it came to Shwed's idea of devising an easy-to-install software program that was designed to work as an impenetrable buffer between the Internet and corporate networks. In 1993, the three began months of intensive round-the-clock programming, writing code for what would become Firewall-1.

In 1994, the fledgling startup they named Check Point received $400,000 in funding from a small Israeli software company called BRM Technologies. The next challenge was to go from writing code to landing business. However, they faced some formidable challenges. Chief among them was that Check Point, starting out, was not a company, but really just a product—and really a prototype at that. Shwed, Nacht, and Kramer were based in Israel, geographically isolated from the main markets in the United States. Moreover, at the time, the Internet was only beginning to take off in terms of its impact on business and communication. Furthermore, Internet connections were just beginning to catch on with the big corporations in the mid-1990s, and Web security had yet to emerge as a major concern.

The first hurdle was to land in the United States. Like every Israeli company, the local market is too small and the regional one, the Arab Middle East, has traditionally thrown up a political and economic barrier. It was important to "penetrate the U.S. market first and then scale the rest of the world," explained Shwed. "It is not easy working the other way around. It is a difficult culture, and when it is different it is always hard and far away." One of the first things Check Point did was to set up an answering service in Boston to give the impression that the company had an American presence. Shwed found the service in the Yellow Pages and chose it because its costs were reasonable and it had email. "It took mail and faxes and forwarded them to us," he recalled. "I had never been there. There wasn't a single employee or office. The phone machine said, 'Gil is not here.' "

Very quickly, Shwed realized that in order to sell the product he had to demonstrate it—particularly since Check Point was so far from its desired customers. "People react to the concrete, not the theoretical," he explained. "I also felt that if we exposed the idea prematurely people might copy the idea." Initially, he met with such companies as State Street Bank, Goldman Sachs, and National Semiconductor. Check Point presented the prototype for feedback and ended up gaining customers. The product's key selling points were that it was easy to use and install, and it was virtually unbreakable. Unlike the big, customized firewalls that were available at the time, Check Point's firewall didn't need an expert to install and maintain it, and it was standardized across systems. The company also lined up some strategic help in the United States to ease introductions into the market. "We were three Israelis," said Shwed. "We had people help us." Among them was a sales representative for a Boston-based ISP—when customers asked about security, he referred them to Check Point. One of Check Point's first big customers was Sun Microsystems, which bundled the Firewall-1 in its UNIX servers.[2]

In 1994, the young company's reputation began to take off. The shrink-wrapped network security software was nabbing clients and a name for itself. This led the CBS news program *60 Minutes* to ask Check Point to appear in a live showdown between its firewall and a group of New York City hackers. Initially, Shwed said, "I was not happy to participate." His thought was that too many entrepreneurs mistake media exposure for business. "It's nice to show your parents and friends but customers don't buy it because you were in the media," he said. After some prodding on the part of an American marketer, Shwed agreed to the test in which the hackers would battle Firewall-1. Regarding the 48 hours leading up to the combat demonstration, Shwed said, "Every hacker asked all of his hacker friends, 'Have you heard you can break Firewall-1?' " When Shwed came into his office before the broadcast, he saw that his system had been bombarded with 60,000 break-in attempts. However, said Shwed, "Not one was successful."

In 1996, Check Point went public on NASDAQ. Practically overnight, an empire was born on a global scale, the likes of which Israel had never seen. Big-name competitors like Cisco Systems, Nortel Networks, and Symantec would jump into the arena. The security technology industry took off, an industry that by some estimates is expected to reach $45 billion in sales by 2006.[3]

Check Point has since added other products to its lineup, seizing opportunities in the growing firewall market such as providing secure access to mobile employees who tap into their firm's network remotely via the Internet by using Virtual Private Networks (VPNs). It has also partnered with some pretty big guns such as Nokia/Ipsilon, Hewlett-Packard, and IBM. More than a decade after the light bulb went off, Shwed remarked, "Security is still the first fear." The challenge is safeguarding against a growing host of threats.

In the intervening years since Check Point launched Firewall-1, it has had to contend with an evolving list of new hazards that pose new threats and vulnerabilities to computer and Internet users. In addition to business rivals and new technology, it also has had to stay ahead of a number of sophisticated hackers and man-made computer viruses that have become more adept and sophisticated in their ability to find the chinks in the growing techno-armor. Perhaps most infamous was the day in February 2000 when eBay, Amazon, Yahoo, and a number of other websites came under assault by hackers who shut them down and crippled service for hours. The "denial of service" attack occurred when a flood of sham requests hit the companies' web servers and disabled their ability to provide information to the sites' users. Then there is the rampant spread of computer viruses. In 1999, the "Melissa" virus disrupted networks all over the world. Emails carrying the virus infected computers when the attached Word document was opened (which then duplicated the email and sent it to the first 50 addresses in the user's address book). "Melissa" was estimated to have caused $80 million in damage. Following "Melissa," a number of devastating computer worms spread throughout the Internet. In the summer of 2002, the Sapphire Worm became known as the fastest computer worm in history because as it spread, it doubled in size every 8.5 seconds, infecting some 90 percent of vulnerable hosts in 10 minutes, causing network and ATM failures and even airline flight cancellations.[4] The Blaster worm followed "Melissa" the next summer, exploiting a vulnerability in Microsoft Windows operating systems and infecting a few hundred thousand computers around the world. Early the following year, Microsoft announced a leak in its operating system and offered a downloadable patch to prevent a worm from attacking.

Looking back on his astonishing success (in addition to the Ramat Gan headquarters, Check Point has an office in Redwood City, California, and its payroll has expanded to 1,200 employees), Shwed said the company started with an idea that came from a real need and the motivation to build a good product. The product happened to be securing the Internet. "There were a few competitors when we started, and they were all bigger than us, which wasn't hard—we were three guys with a few hundred thousand dollars in financing. Then there was a lot of competition. Today we are in the third generation of competition."

The fact that Check Point's stunning success came out of such humble origins is not very remarkable to Shwed. He repeated what is something of a national mantra. "People look at high tech as new thing but [Israeli] entrepreneurialism goes back 100 years. People started Israel and built the country from scratch. Everyone is an entrepreneur. They all invented something that didn't exist before. People came to Israel. People want to succeed. Look at Israel. Everyone has five ideas to improve things. Everyone wants to innovate and change."

The initial idea for what would eventually become Check Point was ahead of its time. But Shwed and his partners had the fortitude, persistence, and vision to see it through. They were a step ahead but had the foresight to see that the market would fall lockstep behind their concept. In that sense,

> *"I tell people innovation is not a process. Ideas can come from everywhere."*
> *—Gil Shwed*

not much has changed. The hyper-kinetic Shwed who built a small empire on an innovative idea is always on the lookout for another good one. Not surprisingly he says it starts by identifying solutions. "I tell people innovation is not a process. Ideas can come from everywhere. One source is the customers—they tell us what they need. We hear hundreds of partners and thousands of customers. I'm not an easy person to convince. I can come up with 20 ideas myself. I hear a lot of ideas—most of them I rule out." Not every idea has to be a revolution. "One-third of the ideas are fine; they are not an improvement," explained Shwed. "One-third are an improvement and not a reinvention, and one-third are a complete reinvention." Often it's a case of people looking around and just doing things differently. Shwed likened it to a chef in a kitchen who makes a new dish out of the same ingredients. There are five people in the kitchen, and they all have the same ingredients—some of the dishes turn out bad and some are good, and some are really innovative. "To run a business you need to have those who know how to make the same dish every day, those who know how to improve it, and, on the other hand, those people that know how to make new things."

Check Point is an inescapable touchstone in Israel. It emerged at the cusp of time when the Internet was coming into sight as a major indispensable part of the lives of tens of millions of people. The appearance of Israel as a global high-tech center did not happen overnight. It evolved because Israelis had always had a fascination for technology, science, education, and taking risks. The innate mentality here is one of solving problems creatively. It happens to be a way of life honed by security threats and military service. Certainly top-level development in agencies like the American NSA goes on, but the NSA is not part of the military structure. In the case of unit 8200, except for those soldiers who opt to stay in the unit following their mandatory service, many are discharged after they've completed five years of service. During that time, they've gained the kind of knowledge and practical experience that, if it were to be measured in time, would probably equal 15 to 20 years and would be backed up with an academic degree. They are in their mid-twenties, and their minds have been shaped to view the world as a ball of clay waiting to be formed. They had little idea of what was not possible. Their job was to execute their visions—visions that were limited only by their own imaginations.

At the time, however, that the world stood up and took notice of the kinds of innovations that were taking place in Israel, which did not make headlines, there were other advantageous factors that came into play in the larger context. It is instructive to step back and examine the grander swell of issues and challenges from which Check Point and a host of others emerged. There was, of course, the explosion of information technology, the Internet, and telecommunications. This, however, dovetailed with a variety of factors and influences that would open the floodgates for Israeli innovations.

Almost from the start, Israel was always a volatile piece of real estate which many investors had shunned. However, as the 1990s began, a number of positive shifts took place. The first was a government program called *Yozma*, Hebrew for "initiative." The Yozma Management and Investment Fund began in 1993. "There was a lot of potential here," explained Yigal Erlich, Israel's former chief scientist at the Ministry of Industry and Trade and the director of Yozma. "That was not the difficult part. We are known as a country of entrepreneurs, people who can invent and work fast. But it was a place [where] you couldn't make money." The idea was to create an Israeli venture sector by coaxing foreign venture capital into the country. The Israeli government would subsidize foreign investments of $12 million with another $8 million. Within five years, the private investors could purchase the government's investment at a discounted price. In its first round, Yozma succeeded in raising $200 million and creating 10 funds, many of which went on to become Israel's top investment houses. By the late 1990s, during the high-tech boom, the funds were running returns of around 40 percent. According to Erlich, in 10 years Yozma had inflated to include 60 to 70 funds that had raised $10 billion. This helped fund Israel's burgeoning high-tech industry and brought in foreign investors who were quick to see the potential and talent that was in the country. The Oslo peace process that began in 1993, and the easing of the Arab boycott against Israel, which was formally declared in 1945, also stimulated investment. Suddenly, investment jokes about Israel (like the old chestnut, "How does one earn a small fortune? By investing a large one in Israel") were turned on their heads.

In 1996, Yozma went private. The success of the program brought in not only investors but queries from a number of nations that have come to Erlich's offices in the Ramat Aviv Tower that is adjacent to a Tel Aviv shopping mall. Representatives came from as far afield as the European Union, New Zealand, China, Mexico, Denmark, and Japan. "They want to know how we did it," said Erlich, who 10 years on is still pretty pleased with the results. "Why the government was involved. Mostly they are surprised at the success and surprised the government took the risk."

Yozma also happened to occur in the midst of a huge wave of Russian immigration to Israel. During this decade about one million Russians arrived in the country. Most of them were well-educated, providing Israel with a large new talent pool. The boon was also a challenge: The large numbers arriving over a short period of time threatened to strain the resources of the nation. The country now had a greater number of job applicants than open positions. Specifically, it had more scientists and engineers than labs. To cope with the thousands of technically knowledgeable immigrants who were at risk of ending up as janitors, short-order cooks, or—worse—drags on the social welfare system, the government funded an incubator program under the Chief Scientists Office. Launched in 1991, the program helped immigrants develop scientific and technology-based startups, giving them $150,000 a year for two years to do so. The strategy behind it was not simply to establish an employment agency and dole out jobs but to tap into the wealth of talent at hand and give immigrants a chance to create new opportunities.

Now, acutely aware of the kind of innovations going on, within a few years, Israel became a go-to stop for investors from all over the world. Large multinationals such as Microsoft, IBM, Intel, and

Motorola established or enlarged significant research and development facilities. Again, all of the deficits of resources and manpower had converged into an opportunity.

However, before Check Point and before the turn of events fell into step with the wealth of ideas cropping up in Israel (making it possible to nurture them into something bigger than a dream), there were a few pioneers who braved a much less hospitable climate. The common thread was that they, too, created their own opportunities. One such groundbreaker was NICE Systems. Seven former communications engineers from unit 8200, with years of experience in telecommunications systems and communications intelligence, founded NICE in 1986. Like Check Point and scores of other startups and companies that emerged, they were able to translate their considerable military intelligence background to identify a need and adapt it to a civilian use. In this case it was the digital recording of information such as voice conversations and video monitoring for use in what is known as Customer Experience Management (CEM). In plain English, NICE is the company behind the ubiquitous "This call may be recorded for quality assurance."

In the early 1980s, the group that would eventually establish NICE worked on a project with American defense contractor TRW in Silicon Valley. It turned out to have made a highly influential impact on the group of communication engineers. "In Israel then, there was no high-tech culture," explained Benny Levin, one of the group of seven and NICE's former CEO. "There were government companies but not the entrepreneurial startups. We were seven people from the unit, we all worked on a project for more than four years, we knew each other very well. We had very good complimentary skills. I was the project manager. Working there we were exposed to high tech in the Bay Area." Levin recalled the eye opener they shared at the congenial atmosphere, the relaxed, no punch cards kind of place, the humming work environment: "There was email, there were classes at Stanford." It was what he called an open environment. "We got a lot out of being there, and we said to ourselves, 'Let's build our own high-tech industry in Israel.' " At that point the engineers had no product in mind, they didn't know how to build a company, and they didn't understand the market or customers. Still, Levin said they decided to try it for one year. They did know that they wanted to build a company that was fun to work for.

Initially they traded in on what they knew best, intelligence, and partnered with those with whom they had a good relationship, such as TRW and Israeli defense contractor ELTA. They developed a transmitter locater system, and they plowed the profits from this product into the new communications company they were building. In the late 1980s through the 1990s, a confluence of events surfaced that would make a marked change: Digital signal processing and the PC kick-started what would become the IT revolution, transforming communication and bringing on the information age. The newly hatched NICE wanted to develop a commercial communications product but had little knowledge of the market and even less in the way of capital.

NICE approached Ed Mlavsky, a former material scientist who had produced crystalline semiconductors. In 1960, the British-born Mlavsky co-founded Tyco International. When Levin went to see him he had moved on to become the executive director of the Israel-U.S. Binational Foundation Research and Development Foundation. BIRD, as it is best known, is an organization that partners an American company that is strong in its market with an Israeli company that has a complimentary innovative technology. In a cost-sharing arrangement, BIRD funds half of the development of a commercial product. Mlavsky started at BIRD in 1979, and over the course of 14 years he had overseen about $100 million in investments for more than 300 joint projects between U.S. and Israeli high-tech companies. Levin told Mlavsky who he and his group were and what they were about. "I said we want to do a commercial communications business," he recalled. "Mlvaky asked, 'Why is a government business like sex?' When it is good it's good, and when it's not so good, it's still good. Why go commercial?' He directed us to a concept and a company to develop with in America."

Levin and his team spent several months meeting with various companies, trying to understand what they needed and what Levin and his colleagues could offer them. Eventually, they hooked up with Tekelec Inc., a telecommunications signal solutions, packet telephony, and network monitoring company based in the Los Angeles suburb of Calabasas. Together they would develop and market a protocol for a fiber optics analyzer. Levin and the other engineers worked 20-hour days developing a prototype. It was 1991, and it also happened to be during the first Gulf War. Recalling this period, Levin said, "We took a lot of risk. In the afternoon everyone in Israel left work early because the SCUDS were coming in the evenings. Our wives would watch our kids and we, the men, the engineers, would work through the night." At one point Levin recalled that Tekelec told the NICE engineers they should decamp to Los Angeles to finish the product. "I said the war is our problem—we'll deliver." In the end, NICE did as promised and at breakneck speed—in less than 12 months.

Their partnership with Tekelec also delivered, and NICE carefully studied how the company did business. "This was like a school for us," Levin recalled. "We learned how to develop a product and introduce it into the commercial market—how to position it." Levin said that NICE saw a return on its investment in a year. Within a year, NICE set up a separate company called Nicecom Ltd. and developed additional products, including an ATM Switch used for network routing.

With an intense education in doing business, NICE Systems was ready for its next step. The process was instructive. "Once you understand what the market needs you either compete with a giant or sell it," explained Levin. "It helped us refocus. We actively came up with a strategy." This is how they learned their next and seminal lesson. They didn't want to be a "me-too" company and realized at that time it would be difficult to compete head-on with such heavies as Cisco. "We didn't want to be a player in a big playground," Levin explained. "Our strategy was to cooperate and develop a niche product—something that is too small for the big guys but is attractive for an Israeli company." In 1994, they sold Nicecom to 3Com Corporation, the software and networking hardware giant, for $60 million. "3Com needed the technology instantly," said Levin. "And they opened a 3Com in Israel, and for three years they were exporting $100 million to $300 million a year."

NICE's next entry into the market solidified it as a global player. It also showcased its trademark ability to identify a solution and come up with an innovative product and a rapid deployment. Up until then, the commercial data and voice recording business was a slow, clumsy process. The NICE engineers had military experience in developing communications systems. They came up with a commercial, digital recording system that was a vast improvement over the large reel-to-reel analog and magnetic tapes in use at the time.

NICE engineers adroitly recognized the need for better, faster digital recording applications. They set their sights first on the financial markets of Wall Street, which relied on huge analog tapes to record transactions. The process was hugely inefficient: To find a piece of information, the user would have to listen to the tapes from start to finish. It could take hours to retrieve the desired word or conversation, and the big and bulky tapes also required storage space. NICE offered a way to digitally record on a PC and established a beachhead in the United States, opening up a small subsidiary in New York. This allowed the small Israeli company to work closely with its customers. Levin said they did everything to overcome the geographic and cultural obstacle of being an Israeli company: "We even gave our home phone numbers to customers." Their first client was Deutsche Bank. "They really took a risk with us," said Levin. Soon, NICE expanded its client base to include other financial trading institutions, banks, and big call centers.

NICE's big break came around 1995 when the U.S. Federal Aviation Administration (FAA) announced it was looking to implement a new recording system. It received bids from nearly every company in the world, including the giant at the time, Dictaphone. In the end, NICE won the FAA account. "It really gave us a stamp when the FAA chose us," said Levin.

And, by 2003, the FAA had installed NICE's systems to record all conversations between pilots and air traffic controllers at nearly 700 control towers and radar rooms across the nation.[5] "Our strategy was to go into the American market. If you can take the United States, you can take the world," said Levin. Headquartered in Ra'anaana, north of Tel Aviv, NICE expanded to include subsidiaries in Rutherford, New Jersey, as well as in England, Germany, France, and Hong Kong. Business took off quickly: Between 1994 and 2000, Levin said revenues grew 50 percent annually.

The acknowledged market leader in CEM, the company says it provides call-recording software to 65 percent of Fortune 100 companies. NICE's software digitizes, compresses, and archives recordings on hard drives. These recordings are encrypted and can only be played on proprietary software. NICE's recording products, however, go beyond the scope of quality assurance. The company has also constantly updated its offerings. For instance, its software performs functions that actually give the companies that use it a competitive advantage. These functions include word spotting, sifting through sound files for such phrases as "cancel my order" or "cancel my account." The software also can signal when a competitor's name is mentioned. Should either the customer service agent or a caller become angry or tense, NICE's program can pick that up, too. In that case, the call can be sent to a supervisor.[6] The software can be used to analyze conversations in a variety of ways, providing companies with a kind of customer behavior profile that includes information such as why a customer might purchase something or cancel his or her relationship with the client altogether. At the same time, it lets call center managers monitor how their agents are doing, helping them to determine who needs help or who is doing a great job. Moreover, the software compresses the amount of time needed to analyze a day's worth of calls, which could number in the thousands.

NICE's client list represents a range of industries, and its clients include FedEx, Carnival Cruise Lines, Time Warner

Cable, and British retail giant TESCO. In 2003, NICE's revenues rose 44 percent to $224.4 million.

In addition to CEM, NICE has not strayed altogether from its military-intelligence roots. It offers a suite of products aimed at homeland security and communications intelligence, including real-time communications monitoring, short-term and long-term archiving, in-depth analysis tools, and advanced information management systems. Its Big Brother-like capabilities include the ability to identify, locate, monitor, and record transmissions from various sources and the ability to monitor Internet traffic such as emails, web chats, instant messaging, and voice over IP. In 2003, the company demonstrated a video surveillance camera that monitors and analyzes activity. Based on technology reported to be used by government agencies, it can tell whether a bag has been left unattended in a public space such as an airport by memorizing scenes and understanding repetitive movements.[7] Less than a year after its unveiling, NICE announced that it had received a large contract to install its digital video security solution to a major, unnamed U.S. airport.

Clearly the military has had an incredibly large influence in the development of Israel's high-tech industry. In Israel, the military is like a metaphor for a way of life, and high tech is its manifestation. It starts from the battle-tested ability to address real problems and turn them into solutions, first for operational needs and then for commercial applications. This, of course, has led to an internal discussion about what kinds of knowledge have exited the military in general and unit 8200 in particular. Many of the companies that have been formed with a core of former soldiers deal in peripheral fields to what is done inside the military. There has been some circuitous discussion over the transfer of military technology to the commercial sector. The military itself maintains patents in particular areas—for one, encryption. But working in tangential areas has become something of a talking point. There is a law preventing the dissemination of military technology patents, but, as Israel's Military Intelligence Director, Major

General Ze'evi Farkash, jokingly remarked, "These engineers are so clever they find ways to get around the patents."

There are many in Israel who think these soldiers should pay royalties to the military, and there are also those who think ultimately the country benefits from the success of these individuals. In a latent sense, the success of many has created a continuous talent crank on both ends. It has established such an aura around unit 8200 in particular that it has become one of the units most coveted by young recruits. They want to enter the unit because of what they have seen come out of it on the civilian side.

Most former members are at pains to explain that the connection between technological development in the unit and the kinds of innovations devised in the civilian world is a superficial one. That is to say, more than taking computer code or a software system and commercializing it, it is the kind of critical

> *"Creative people throwing ideas in the air and brainstorming with friends, and then they decided they had a great idea, and then they make it happen."*
> *—"Leni"*

thinking and approach to problem solving in a technological arena that they have taken with them into the civilian world. "Look, there is no real need to duplicate what we did in the unit," said "Leni." "Only other countries would want it, and I hope nobody would do that. You learn stuff. Creative people throwing ideas in the air and brainstorming with friends, and then they decided they had a great idea, and then they make it happen. Sometimes it has nothing to do with what they did in the unit. It is part of the culture. It is what you are."

It is exactly this notion that has taken hold in the Tel Aviv neighborhood of Bnei Brak, a mostly industrial area with a large enclave of Orthodox Hasidic Jews. However, in one small building near the Bnei Brak train station is the modest office of ADKiT, short for advanced kit. In 1988, Israeli-born Hezie Lavi, a former copy editor and advertising executive in the United States (he worked on the Hebrew National campaign "You Should Be So Lean"), returned to Israel and set up ADKiT. He was in the information business, mining market data and selling it to companies. This, of course, was before the Internet exploded and with it data mining and search engines. ADKiT did the labor-intensive work of sifting through encyclopedic volumes of information, financial reports, and data about markets and businesses and compiling thick reports for clients seeking information on their competitors in the global market. Then the Internet burst onto the scene and gave anyone with a keyboard and online access a window into a nearly endless stream of information. The phenomenon virtually rendered ADKiT irrelevant. "My company was facing a terrible time," recalled Lavi. "Clients were saying, 'We don't need you.' It was a crisis." Perhaps as has become the Israeli approach, Lavi added, "There was an opportunity in a bad time."

In 1996, Lavi laid out his dilemma with a strategy consultant group and looked at the future of ADKiT. The Internet was becoming a major threat, but one of the consultants suggested that the Internet was also an opportunity. If you had the right people who could take the massive amount of information available on the Net and pick out the most relevant data and compile it for clients, it could be a major asset rather than a liability. This particular consultant, as it turned out, was an alumnus of unit 8200. "I had no clue what 8200 was at the time," recalled Lavi.

The consultant asked Lavi if he knew about "these special kids that could take a lot of information and make sense of it and summarize it. They could," he said, turning the dictum on its head, "see the trees from the forest." These "special kids" happened to be young discharges from the unit who worked in analysis, sifting data large and small and processing it into a picture that makes sense for policy-makers. It was the reformulation of ADKiT.

"He gave me the telephone [number] of one kid," recalled Lavi. "We talked about two clients." One was a company that sold equipment and services for UAVs, and the other was a large Israeli clothing retailer. The "kid" was about 23 and had recently finished his service in unit 8200. He was a university student and was looking for a way to help support himself during his studies.

Lavi gave him a mission: He was to digest everything he could that was open source and off-the-shelf information on the UAV industry and identify what was important. Then Lavi took him to meet his client. "I didn't sleep the night before the meeting," said Lavi. "It was a case of what can you do for me, what can you teach someone about UAVs who has spent his whole life doing nothing but UAVs." As it turned out, quite a lot. "We were able to show them things they'd not paid attention to."

Immersed in the day to day, the company didn't see important opportunities. For one there was an opening in the Canadian market. "We showed them that there was this huge potential contract," said Lavi. At the same time they had already lost out on a bid for another contract. "When a company puts out a request for a bid," explained Lavi, "in most cases it's already too late. We came up with the idea to try and get information about a contract before it comes up for a bid. One of my people set up a website created around the whole UAV market, products, everything." The site included all information that was coming down the pipeline, rumors that turned out to have nuggets of useful information and those that were false alarms. "There is a lot of information out there." By chasing it all down, they could analyze it and pick and choose the most useful information to get a leg up on business opportunities even before they became public.

It was the beginning of a new business. Lavi set up a group called *KAMAN* (the Hebrew acronym for intelligence officer). The "kid" led to other newly discharged soldiers from the unit. It was all done by word of mouth. Today, Lavi works with a core group of 15 former members of the unit and assigns them to a specific client in a diverse group of industries from telecommunications to dairy products. ADKiT describes the *KAMAN* group as "personal knowledge managers in the world of business," and as the "intelligence eyes and ears for the entire world of business." These *KAMAN* members "assimilate and digest all of the relevant information and translate it into a wider, potentially more objective perspective." In doing so they pour through mountains of data, ideas, advertisements, and promotions, including broadcast and print mediums. Then they filter the data down to its most important points and put together a cogent presentation tailor-made to each client. Basically, Lavi established a corporate intelligence corps applying the same approach and methodology to analyzing and ferreting out the activities of Israel's enemies into disseminating and presenting a picture of actionable, need-to-know activities of a company or businesses global competitors.

Following September 11th, a small Israeli government-owned company involved in commercializing science-based technologies contacted ADKiT. "We covered the market looking to see what was available to alert people to dirty bombs," explained Lavi. "We found that there was the potential in the market for small-sized radiation detectors." Within one month of the request, ADKiT had a presentation and recommendations on the client's desk. Today, the company sells these detectors all over the world.

Ori, Lior, and Jonathan all left the unit within two to three years. All are studying at universities in Tel Aviv or Jerusalem. They all ended up at ADKiT through the recommendation of a friend who came through the unit and landed on Lavi's payroll. All three see certain significant parallels between the crucial need

> *"You make sure the intelligence product is adequate. There is an ocean of information, and you can produce information, but the most important thing is resource organization to make sure that who is supposed to gets the most important information."*
> —*Jonathan*

to capture intelligence in the military and in the civilian world of business. When he was in uniform, Ori described the situation as one in which "we were managers of the process of creating intelligence. It was our responsibility that that information was perfect." Jonathan added, "We are resource managers of the base. You have your clients here. It is the army, and they need information. You make sure the intelligence product is adequate. There is an ocean of information, and you can produce information, but the most important thing is resource organization to make sure that who is supposed to gets the most important information."

Now in the trenches of corporate intelligence, the trio is astonished at how the business world lags behind the military in understanding its significance and the crucial role it can play in advancing, getting a leg up, or succeeding. "Business intelligence is really behind the army—even the giant companies," said Jonathan. "They don't understand how beneficial it is." Ori drew an analogy: "The army is spending less on soldiers and more money on knowledge on finding out what the enemy is doing." "In the army," continued Jonathan, "the main battle is changing from conventional warfare to terror. And the management of terrorism is more information-based than in the past. With terrorism you have to be on the top of your toes all of the time to collect information—and fast—and accord it a priority. In terrorism no decision is undertaken without information." Trained in this kind of approach, Jonathan found it difficult to think otherwise. "A decision made that is not intelligence-based," he said, is, well, "weird."

None came through an MBA program or a business experience. None of them have any practical experience in any of the industries in which they now consult with executives on a regular basis. What they do have is the ability to absorb a mountain of information, to cherry pick what is crucial, and to connect the dots. "I can read about a project, 600 to 700 pages of financial magazines," explained Lior. "I know not to panic. I need to read it and take important lines and organize it in a readable way. I need 50 hours for a new subject and to make a presentation." Moreover, they've applied a lot of the mentality that's been ingrained in the army to the business world. Because, simply, "This was similar," explained Jonathan. "It was a very easy adjustment. What they are asking for is providing information in business."

For example, in one project that Jonathan and Ori both worked on for a large telecommunications company, they found that half of their time was spent scouring media for articles that related to the industry and were particularly pertinent to the company, and then summarizing them and writing them up. "Time is a valuable resource," explained Jonathan. "I shouldn't be doing that." So, Ori wrote up a small software program that performs the same function automatically, freeing the two up to spend their time in other areas. Ori credits his time in the unit not so much for the ability to come up with the program, but for the understanding of doing it. "We don't just accept things. We work like this: If you are spending half your time doing something, then you come up with a solution that will save 50 percent of your time. This is very strong in the unit. I came from a way to improve things."

ADKit, not incidentally, borrows a phrase from Albert Einstein: "Genius is knowing where to look."

11 Soldiering On

Tel Aviv, the Twenty-first Century...

At the turn of the Millennium, the IDF and its select technological intelligence agencies, particularly unit 8200, went into battle. The elite vanguard of the nation's security went to war—over talent. The unit had done such a stellar job of shaping the raw potential of some very smart men and women that it now found itself in the position of having to compete to retain its soldiers, who despite the unit's deliberate policy of ambiguity were now in high demand by investors and companies both in Israel and around the world. Having produced the foundation of the nation's high-tech sector by honing generations of its innovators, it had become an unqualified *hamemah,* or greenhouse, and there were many outside forces that wanted to benefit from the talent engine the unit had developed over the decades. The big generals of the IDF now had a critical new directive on their hands: launch a course of action that would allow them to hold on to their top brains.

Originally intended to defend the nation (and to that end its fundamental mission has not abated), Israel's redoubtable national defense had at the same time also catapulted the country onto the global stage as a significant high-tech center. In some ways, the unit, which had come to represent one of the nation's most significant brainpower incubators, had become too much of a success. The dynamic processes that had churned out scores of inventors and thinkers under fire had ended up as some of the seminal factors in transforming the army's resourceful and independent mentality into a prolific industry of innovators. As it turned out, this incubator also became the catalyst for an innovation-oriented economic blast-off. The world stood up and took notice of Israel for something other than war, conflict, and competing narratives of victimization and statehood. And it wanted a piece of the action.

A nation of just six million had generated at its peak something like 4,000 startups and high-tech firms. Its strength derived in no small part from its unceasing military and defense needs and the ability of individuals to take technology and infuse it with new ideas and applications. The kinds of secure codes and applications that were critical for privacy in electronic communications and necessary for business trans-actions in the digital age had roots in the kind of technology initially developed for military systems. While the United States has always had a significant edge in skills, manpower, and resources, the minds the Israelis regularly applied to their own unique situation had found profound and resourceful ways to commercialize a number of good ideas. Applying mili-tary technology to the civilian sector discharged a pellet resulting in some of the world's top wireless and telecom tech-nologies, including bandwidth compression, digital recording and data retrieval systems, search engines, security software, small satellites, radio frequency identification tag technology, and signals processing and high-speed broadband digital transmissions products.

A host of significant factors had also come together. In 2000, a number of transformations took place. The Oslo peace process was well into its seventh year. In July, Israeli Prime Minister Ehud Barak met with Palestinian Chairman Yassir Arafat and U.S. President Bill Clinton at Camp David in Mary-land to forge what many expected to be a final peace agreement between the Israelis and the Palestinians. Foreign investors, who only years earlier had viewed an investment in Israel as tantamount to tossing a quarter in a sink and watching it circle the drain, were now spurred on by the promising political developments and by the frisson caused by the kind of innovations they saw coming out of the tiny nation, and they began pouring money into Israel. The conjunction of investment, political developments, and innovations was like an expanding accordion. At the height of the rising new economy, in 2000, 513 Israeli high-tech companies raised $3.3 billion.[1] Just eight years earlier, in 1992, they barely registered $81 million.[2] Orna Berry, Israel's former Chief Scientist and a venture partner in Gemini Israel Funds, told an audience of Silicon Valley executives that during this period, sales of high tech went from 5 percent to 15 percent of Israel's GDP.[3]

In the most simplistic terms, a few good ideas had turned the nation around in just a few short years. Israel's economy had for decades suffered under the burdens of one of the world's largest per capita foreign debts and staggering inflation—which at one point had hit the 500-percent range. The economy remained standing in no small part because of American foreign aid. The nation's economic misery was behind an oft-told verbal tease in which Israelis would joke that the country was the 51st state of the union. Israel's new economy, hauled up by "the new economy" and powered by innovation, changed all that. Indeed, the nation had produced a large number of engineers in its very capable universities as well as well-thought-out and timely initiatives to harness the talent of the incoming Russian immigrants, but there was an undeniable font to a great deal of this activity—the IDF. And, from it came a set of recurring numbers: 8200.

For perhaps the first time, early in the twenty-first century the talk of peace overshadowed that of war, and the newspapers were filled with stories of big deals between Israeli outfits and large western corporations with a vertigo-inducing number of dollars. A current of change was in the air. With an end to the static hostilities with the Palestinians seemingly around the corner at that time, there was open talk that the mandatory military service would be cut by six months. The fierce determination to serve the country through military duty had suddenly given way to an equally intense pursuit of individual gain. It was a time when career soldiers saw their former colleagues developing products, starting companies, and making millions (although at the time many remained paper millionaires). The number of engineers available could not keep up with the dizzying growth and activity. Companies openly advertised for soldiers from the elite units, particularly 8200, and many of these soldiers who saw their former brothers-in-arms striking it out in the civilian world and becoming rich heard the call.

It was a time, recalled retired Major General Amos Malka, who was director of military intelligence, when "keeping the brains in [the army] became very complicated." The call to patriotic duty, especially in the looming horizon of a real, negotiated peace with the Palestinians, did not burn as bright as the potential to be the next Gil Shwed. The army found it exceedingly difficult to compete with the civilian sector and its higher salaries, stock options, bonuses, and promise of future riches. A number of soldiers were lining up at the exit door. To the dismay of more than one commanding officer, companies actively called the army to ask who was about to be discharged. Many enlisted soldiers began shopping their ideas to venture capitalists while still in uniform. Soldiers toiling on military systems all night would awaken to read in newspapers about former colleagues and a peripheral civilian application of a technology being sold for millions.

Looking at the pileup of soldiers leaving the military, Major General Yehuda Segev, the head of the IDF's personnel directorate, saw a battle at hand between the army and the commercial world, and he remarked publicly: "We are in the middle of a war. The civilian economy has gone all out."[4] The professional problem-solvers had a quandary of their own to crack. The IDF's success had in some respects cannibalized itself; as a result, the IDF took appropriate action.

The IDF's most secretive units did something almost unimaginable—they began opening up in order to recruit. One of the most overt moves turned out to be from one of the most furtive agencies: the Mossad. Only a few years earlier, it was illegal to publish the name of the Mossad chief, and then, in the spring of 2001, the agency openly advertised in Israeli dailies for 13 electronic engineers and computer science graduates for what it obliquely termed its "technology department," a division the spy agency had kept under wraps for three decades.[5] The want ad asked potential applicants, "Do you dream of developing sophisticated technological instruments? Are you looking for work that provides a challenge every day? The technology branch of the Mossad invites you to become a partner in the production of clandestine technology." Those interested were asked to send their resume noting citizenship and their ID number to a specific fax number or email address.

Unit 8200 also quietly engaged in its own headhunting activities. In a seemingly uncharacteristically brazen move, it set up a booth at a job fair at Tel Aviv University, as if it were a bank or an accounting firm, looking for solid university graduates. It was also said that the unit's alumni, along with Aladdin, the Israeli software security company, and the prestigious Weizmann Institute of Science, are among the sponsors behind CodeGuru, the nationwide computer competition aimed at 15- to 18-year-old high school students. The annual contest attracts a few thousand teenagers who must first submit to answering a computer riddle over the Internet to gain a point of entry. Only 100 to 150 get past this initial stage. Those that do are then invited to a competition in Tel Aviv where they take another round of tests in math, computer skills, logic, and programming. There are three first-place winners, and the top 10 are awarded prizes that can include laptop computers and printers.

However, another long-term—although tacitly acknowledged—prize is the exposure these young computer whizzes get to the unit through the contest. Alumni of unit 8200 have been known to attend competitions. Clearly, the association with CodeGuru helped polish the elusive allure of the unit. "The competition supports talented youngsters," explained one of CodeGuru's organizers. "If you support and encourage and help them develop their talent, they can eventually contribute to the high-tech industry." However, he also added that the competition has formed an important unofficial link to the unit. "It even allows some of them to present their data to the army authorities. In some cases it helps their army classification for the intelligence units. The army can't run a competition, so we are a buffer."

The military's real trial, however, was not so much in finding fresh recruits but in retaining enlisted soldiers. It became a strategic imperative, and it was coming down from the top. The challenge was to strike a delicate balance between keeping the most talented officers in uniform without shutting off the spigot entirely to those who wanted to exit. After all, the army had acknowledged on some level the important function it had served in delivering technological innovators onto the civilian scene. It had to come up with a way that made a military career an attractive and rewarding proposition in the face of the big carrot that dangled before their soldiers pointing to a civilian career. The army initiated a slew of incentives, starting with improving the working environment from drab, functional, typical army setups to interiors that more closely resembled the startup aesthetic. It also offered bonuses for officers who extended their enlistments, and cars that previously were only given to officers of lieutenant colonel rank were now used as enticements to help keep talented and desired soldiers who served at lower ranks. The IDF was competing on a monetary playing field that was hardly level. It could not exactly match private enterprise dollar for dollar (or rather shekel for shekel). Its one major draw, as has always been the case, was patriotism, duty to country, and the satisfaction of having the ability to work on the kinds of systems only available in this type of environment—which itself became a stepping stone to the civilian rewards that awaited some.

At issue was motivation. While offering monetary inducements was an undeniable incentive, it was also a limited one. The military did some research and realized there were other important mitigating reasons to stay in uniform. The kinds of challenges found only in the particular military environment were unmatched. Then there were issues of personal satisfaction, engagement, and advancement. The chief of staff recognized the importance of paying special attention to technological warriors. As it turned out, one of the lynchpins for retaining soldiers was to shorten the time up the promotional ladder. There was a bottleneck around the rank of lieutenant colonel: Career soldiers, who like everyone began serving at age 18, were looking down a distant horizon before achieving the coveted stripes on their epaulets. "I took two brilliant guys and made them lieutenant colonels," recalled Major General Malka. "Three years later they should reach full colonel." The idea was, according to Malka, to send a ripple down the ranks. The message was to show the talented and up-and-coming enlisted soldiers at age 27 or 28 "that if they look to the future, they could be a lieutenant colonel in 4 years instead of 14," explained Malka. "It was a turning point in promotion in the technological units, which were like the startups. If you are good, you can be promoted even if you are young—you don't have to wait eight years."

Discussion about initiating other ways to keep soldiers satisfied and in uniform was kept open. There was talk about forming some kind of relationship with the private high-tech community that would be beneficial to both sides. "We succeeded in understanding the problem and the challenge," explained Malka. "We decreased the damage and kept enough good and brilliant officers, and lowered the trend of the exiting strategy."

Then it all came crashing down. In just under two years everything changed course. Just as the army had effectively found a way to staunch the flow of soldiers running off to start their own companies, the boom turned to bust and the hoped-for peace once again turned to conflict. While powering the country's wealth upward, Israel's high-tech sector also tied itself up into the most fickle part of the global economy. When the market rose, it pulled Israel up with it, and when it crashed, it took the fledging explosion of Israeli high tech down with it. Especially hard hit was the telecommunications sector in which the Israeli IT community excelled. In an alarmingly short period of time, companies that were once practically levitating on their success were now fighting to stay afloat. Gilat Satellite Networks, the number two maker of satellite-based communication networks—once heralded by a Merrill Lynch analyst as the Cisco of satellites[6]—had news of a different kind to announce. In 2003 the company said it was working on a deal to restructure some $300 in bond debt. Perhaps most dramatic is the story of Chromatis, a metro optical networking systems company. In May of 2000, Chromatis raised the bar for all Israeli acquisitions when Lucent Technologies purchased it for $4.5 billion in stock. However, within months Lucent's own stock took a massive death spiral, leaving the Chromatis buy a desiccated one worth only 10 percent of its original value. Less than a year after the trumpeted deal was splashed across the headlines, Lucent announced it was shutting Chromatis down altogether.

Like the economy, a durable peace with the Palestinians that appeared on the horizon had also collapsed quickly—bracketed by the disastrous Camp David meeting and, closely on its heels, the eruption of the second Palestinian intifada. Israel was now fighting a war on two fronts: NASDAQ and Nablus.

If there is one certainty in Israel, it is the dynamism of change. Backs to the wall as a matter of course, the Israeli mentality was honed on living in an incessantly changing environment. And the environment had again taken a considerable turn. Living under a constant threat of war has produced a population of fighters who refuse to lose. High tech flourished because it matched the country's military-intelligence mindset

and, by extension, Israel's. It was polished on the act of rou-
tinely solving problems quickly and innovatively, and also on
the belief that being told something is impossible was an opening rather than a dead end. In Israel the word "no" is viewed
not as a finality, but as a goad, a prod, a challenge. A new season of problems had settled on Israel, and with these new challenges came another set of opportunities.

During this period of being under siege, the Israelis
hunkered down. Israel was not entirely immune to the greed
that had permeated Silicon Valley throughout this time, but
when paper fortunes turned to dust, many Israelis stayed on to
fight to the bitter end. It was not uncommon for employees to
remain working without pay for stretches of time. Israel was in
a better position in some ways to withstand the profound hits.
Many wanted to stay and build strong companies. Furthermore, the companies they were building were based on technology, the infrastructure that made the Internet and
communications businesses and their services run faster and
better. Besides, Israelis are used to working under pressure
and with their backs to the wall. Indeed, Israel's back was
pressed against a tall and thick one. Its economy was decimated, unemployment numbers were registering a northern
trajectory, and the nation was once again engaged in war, a
low-intensity conflict with the Palestinians that appeared to
deepen with each passing month.

In the parade of crises that have wracked Israel and the
prospects for opportunity that have emerged out from under
these crises, one of the most prominent is the calamity over
the Lavi project. In 1980, Israel announced it would develop

its own advanced fighter craft, the Lavi (Hebrew for "lion"). Israel had developed fighter jets in the past, the Nesher and the Kfir, both based on versions of the French Mirage warplanes, but because of the exorbitant economics involved, the Israelis had over the years switched to the practice of purchasing planes, like F-16s, from the United States. They then adapted these planes for their own particular uses and outfitted them with their own specific avionics systems.

The Lavi, an Israeli-designed fighter with an American jet engine built specifically for it, is the most ambitious and costly weapons development project in Israel to date. At the outset, the United States became directly involved in the development of the Lavi, both in the financing of it and in the transfer of very specific technology needed for building such an advanced aircraft. The U.S. government approved technology transfers and an annual budget of $250 million of U.S. military aid money to be spent on the project instead of the customary arrangement known as foreign military sales, or FMS.[7] The initial rollout called for 300 planes beginning in 1990, with 24 planes manufactured each year thereafter.

Almost from the start, the Lavi was a lightening rod for dissent. A mounting Babel of concerns and criticism piled up on both sides of the globe. Three years into the program, the estimated outlay for the Lavi had increased from $750 million in development costs and $7 million per aircraft to manufacture to approximately $2.3 billion in development and $15.5 million per aircraft.[8] Disparaged as a possible boondoggle, the focus of American ire was the increasing amounts of money it was pouring into the project and the unprecedented state-of-the-art technology transfer. The U.S. Department of Defense was reportedly opposed to the project over re-export concerns. In Israel, the project created a swell of immense national pride. However, the pride over the project did not deflect the internal squabbling and criticism over its necessity and of course its expanding costs. Chief among the criticisms was that the pricey project was slow to develop and ate up an inordinate amount of the military budget. The prohibitive cost of continuing the Lavi was questioned in light of the price of purchasing American fighter jets.

In 1983, the U.S. General Accounting Office (GAO) launched a study that said the Lavi was looking a lot like the F-16 or F-18, and that Israel did not possess the technology or the money for such a massive undertaking.[9] The GAO and the Office of Budget Management commissioned studies outlining the fact that cost estimates would well exceed initial projections. Pressure to cancel the Lavi was heard all over the place. In Israel, the threat of its cancellation sent shockwaves through the nation because of the fear that abandoning the project would cripple the Israeli economy. This was primarily because Israel Aircraft Industries, which was directing the project, was the country's biggest employer. The main trepidation was that when it was hit, the crash would reverberate like an echo chamber. It had been reported that some 4,000 IAI employees were assigned to the Lavi, and another 1,000 worked on Lavi-related systems.

In 1986, the first Lavi prototype took flight, but a year later the entire project fell out of the sky. The Israeli cabinet voted to cancel the project in the midst of heavy political pressure and infighting in both the United States and Israel over its prospects and problems. As feared, IAI had to drastically downsize its workforce as a result. Yet, far from the economic paralysis that was predicted, the cancellation of the Lavi turned into a significant opportunity. It was behind a wave of technological innovation that spilled out of Israel. During the Lavi's short lifespan, a few thousand engineers worked on the cutting edge of aerospace technology, electronics, and weapons systems. The Lavi was like a high-tech boot camp for engineers; it stood at the apex of the country's technological infrastructure. Let loose from the project, its personnel were dispersed onto the marketplace and went looking for places to utilize their fine-tuned talent and experience. Many emigrated from Israel and washed up on such shores as Silicon Valley.

Others stayed in Israel. The Lavi's influence is acknowledged to be in place in a number of advanced radar systems, precision weapons systems, UAVs, Israel's satellite program, and a number of commercial technology companies. The end of the Lavi was the beginning of a new era. While the project itself is still lamented in some quarters, it has also been described as one of the best drivers of Israel's high-tech industry.

The Israelis wanted to develop their own sophisticated state-of-the-art fighter jet, but their desire to do so exceeded their grasp at the time. The effort fell victim to cost overruns, politics, and a chorus of opposition of what could and could not be done. There was a gloomy forecast of what would happen if the project succeeded and, moreover, what would happen if it all fell apart. Neither prediction turned out precisely as anticipated. This serves perhaps as an example of what Dr. Zvi Lanir says is "history is not the future."

A former 20-year senior intelligence officer in the IDF, Lanir is the founder and president of the Praxis Institute. Established in 1994, Praxis works with individuals, businesses, governments, and military clients to "reframe their mindsets and create new knowledge in order to remain relevant through fundamental changes." Praxis's small offices are on the top floor of an apartment building in the north end of Tel Aviv, near the old port. The atmosphere is decidedly unlike an institute. Rather, it is homey with its soft lighting, comfortable couches, and stone fireplace. From its perch on Ussishkin Street, there are clear views of the city sprawl and, beyond it, both the Yarkon River and the Mediterranean Sea. Slight and grandfatherly, Lanir looks like a college professor in his loose sweaters and corduroy trousers.

Praxis evolved from the theory Lanir developed while working as an intelligence analyst assigned to investigate Israel's failure to anticipate the joint Egyptian and Syrian surprise attack that resulted in the Yom Kippur War. Initially, the full weight of finger-pointing was leveled at intelligence. Lanir was given complete discretion to view all of the intelligence data and detailed analyses before, during, and after the war. He concluded otherwise. "We had the information," he explained, "but we failed to make the right analysis. Research and collection was blamed. It was very typical. It was the same following September 11th." After evaluating all of the information, Lanir explained, "It was an almost perfect situation. By definition there is never a perfect situation mathematically, but you can come very near to it." He continued, "It was almost perfect information, and despite this we were surprised." Lanir studied and compared the Yom Kippur debacle to other ignominious events in history such as Pearl Harbor and Operation Barbarossa, the Nazi invasion of the Soviet Union during World War II. In each situation, Lanir found that although the nations that were attacked had near-perfect information regarding what was about to happen, they were still surprised when it occurred.

This gap between surprise and near-perfect information was Lanir's point of departure. "The more information you have," he said, "the more the degree of uncertainty decreases. So I went on to find out an answer for this paradox." He came up with two types of surprises. The situational surprise is a type in which one has relative information but misses the data or doesn't analyze it correctly, such as a car accident. "I know a car can come from side to side, but I am still surprised when I am hit." The second is fundamental surprise: This is the situation that occurs not as a result of absence of information but rather because of a mindset that was not relevant to the environment or to the understanding of events. In the case of the Yom Kippur War, the buildup of Egyptian and Syrian troops, the intensified "chatter" the Israelis picked up that Egypt had the military divisions in place to cross the Suez Canal and the surface-to-air missiles to protect it from the Israeli Air Force was all in evidence—and yet the Israelis still did not believe they were about to go to war. Despite a heap of clear indicators of mounting aggression, the Israelis clung to the concept that the Arabs would not fight a war in which they could not win overwhelmingly. Lanir described this kind of situation as one in which "suddenly the mindset is not relative to the environment; the information wouldn't solve it. You are judging the information by the concept you have." In other words, history is not the future.

Lanir coined the term "Fundamental Surprise" to describe this phenomenon and published a book by the same name in 1983. As in war, the element of fundamental surprise manifests itself in many areas— most notably in business. Over the years, several tools have been developed in order to

> *As in war, the element of fundamental surprise manifests itself in many areas—most notably in business. Over the years, several tools have been developed in order to enhance and enable the methods to collect and analyze information, while, for the most part, the mindset and the approaches to understanding information have remained relatively stagnant.*

enhance and enable the methods to collect and analyze information, while, for the most part, the mindset and the approaches to understanding information have remained relatively stagnant. "We value information that is relative to the concept," explained Lanir. "It is always subjective to the information that you have. If I have a proper concept to interpret information, I say it's a reinforcement of my concept but not necessarily of the information I have. If I have information, but not a proper concept, then I say the information is not important or I don't see it at all. If we want to be relative to a changing environment we have to be relative." He continued, "We have a measurement of everything we do except thinking, until recently." The problem is, he explained, "You can't deliberately change something you don't see."

It is, of course, human nature to look at the strange or the unusual and define it as questionable or dubious. Contemplating the implausible means to give it equal credence to what is already

> *"You can't deliberately change something you don't see."*
> —Zvi Lanir

considered plausible. The Yom Kippur War, Pearl Harbor, and

September 11th were not solely failures of intelligence, but, as has been tirelessly described, they were failures of imagination. Those failures in no small part came from a fixed set of expectations. The American mindset could not conceive of the possibility of the Japanese attacking the U.S. headquarters of the Pacific Fleet, just as it did not envisage 19 hijackers taking over commercial airliners and crashing them into the World Trade Center towers and the Pentagon. The Americans had the information but they just didn't consider the probability of it, and they weren't prepared for it when it happened. Likewise, when the new economy imploded, many of the warning signs were in place. Indeed, as far back as 1996 Federal Reserve Board Chairman Alan Greenspan had cautioned that stock prices might be rising too high when he made his famous "irrational exuberance" speech. Personal fortunes were made and lost in hours. The divergence in price-earnings ratio between new and old economy stocks was staggering. Companies with no revenue streams were hitting the market with huge valuations. Then again, there was the law of gravity: What goes up must come down.

Innovation traffics in change. Part of that is the ability to divine the unknowable—and if not divine it, at least be aware of it. One of the hallmarks of Israeli thinking resides in this twilight—the ability to be hyperconscious of the rapid-fire nature of change to trade in

> *Innovation traffics in change. Part of that is the ability to divine the unknowable—and if not divine it, at least be aware of it.*

the unknown. A large part of this, of course, comes from the unique and precarious geopolitical situation with which Israelis have always lived and the military system that Israel has developed around it. It is not, however, failsafe. The main thing Lanir does when he meets with his clients is give them tools to, as he says, "re-frame" their perceptions of situations. "We work with top generals and managers, and we have only a condensed timetable: six to ten [sessions] of three hours each to change their minds. Small groups come here, and we elicit ways in which they solve problems and raise problems." For instance, he explained that in decision-making they "choose the best alternative among many alternatives." The problem is to know the end result with the highest payoff. But, he said, "In most cases managers find themselves in a situation where they have a problem. They don't know how to define the problem, [and] they feel something is wrong based on end result."

Lanir continued, "When we are talking about innovation, there are two levels of understanding." There is a kind of "know what you know" innovation that exists within the borders of existing knowledge, such as adding a new feature to a product. However, Lanir said, the second, deeper stage of innovation comes from being aware of the existence of what you don't know. "Our lives are an extensive experiment. We are on edge always, and we have to use the 'I don't know what I know.' " He went on to make the comparison to unit 8200. "In 8200, the technology point is to take all of these signal codes and decode them and make sense of them. It demands a lot of thinking qualities to be innovative, because we are always feeling like it is World War II. For years here there are so many fronts—we are always having to shift the mindset. Technology devises a secret competition between the enemy and us: They produce, we detect, and they defend. It is very intense."

For instance, when the intifada broke out, Israel's mindset had to change on a dime. Within months the country went from the precipice of peace to war—an asymmetrical conflict in which the accepted wisdom of battle is irrelevant. "In low-intensity conflict all this thinking is worthless," insisted Lanir. "You don't have something to attack or defend." Here the language of thinking had to change. Lanir described it as a situation in which the army had to be extremely flexible. "They had to learn very, very quickly the cycle was very short. If one tactic doesn't achieve the target, then they had to switch to another." There is, of course, the famous example of the Patriot Missile batteries, originally developed as anti-aircraft systems, that were highly ineffective at deterring SCUD missiles from coming into Israel from Iraq in 1991 during the first

Gulf War. During that time, as the SCUDs were landing in populated areas, the military and its teams of engineers were writing software and making tweaks to see what would work. They didn't have time to test the software because the missiles were coming in nightly. They didn't wait for the next hit. They immediately and simultaneously switched their thinking. Whether one agrees or disagrees with Israeli policy or the tactics Israel has used during the second intifada, it is arguable that Israel has succeeded in quickly moving from facing conventional warfare to guerilla insurgencies to low-intensity conflict. Apparently, Israel isn't alone in this thinking. The IDF organized its first ever "Low Intensity Conflict" conference, held in Israel at the end of March 2004, which was attended by more than 100 representatives from governments and militaries from around the world—including the United States, Russia, Japan, Italy, and Turkey.

In every arena, whether war or business, Lanir said, "The most valuable source is knowledge. Not just knowledge management but knowledge creation—the ability human beings have to create knowledge. Knowledge that goes beyond what is known." Lanir continued, "We can't predict the future, but we can build up a very sensitive concept of early warning detection in order to have the ability to see new trends."

> "We can't predict the future but we can build up a very sensitive concept of early warning detection in order to have the ability to see new trends."
> —Zvi Lanir

The opportunity for innovation lies in understanding the need for new approaches—just as the business community and investors had to make a huge shift after the stock market crash in 2000, and the general public of the United States had to readjust its thinking following September 11th and the post-war in Iraq. The major changes and downturns politically, militarily, and economically can be perceived as a time either to maintain conventional thinking, or to sever linear thought patterns and to readapt. The mind-set of the citizens in Israel is that they are in a permanent state of war. There are wins and losses, and the enemy will always find a way to try to defeat you. You must constantly be alert and a step ahead. This reflexive mentality is pervasive: You move fast, you improvise, and you know what you know, but you are on the watch for what it is that you don't know. In 2003, *Forbes* magazine named Amnon Landan, the CEO of Mercury Inter-active, an Israeli software firm with a Silicon Valley headquar-ters, as its "Entrepreneur of the Year." In an expansive interview with *Forbes* he credited his time as an IDF para-trooper stationed in southern Lebanon as one of the most sig-nificant factors that shaped his management ability—which, by the way, helped push Mercury's revenue up 36 percent annually between 1997 and 2002.[10] It was while hunting down terrorists in nightly raids as a platoon commander at the age of 20 that he says he learned his fundamental management principles, which include taking chances, staying behind and risk getting killed, or, worse, not getting anywhere.

Israel is a hyper-reality of the concept that the life and death of daily life has trained people to look at things from a different angle. There is an exceptional appreciation for understanding what is different, improbable, and unknowable. Moreover, it is this set of circumstances that creates a new set of opportunities.

Following the watershed events that marked the end of the twentieth century, suddenly much of the world was faced with knowing what it didn't know.

Few, if any, of the old rules applied. Technology, which had powered a new economy, imploded. Technology that had advanced an information society was a double-edged sword because it also advanced an information war. The defense industry had led the way in technology and communications, but with the rise of the digital era, the private telecommunica-tions market was now pulling technology. And it was available to everyone, including terrorists. A year after the September 11th attacks, the director of the NSA, Lieutenant General Michael V. Hayden, told *The New York Times* that Osama bin

Laden and his minions were the beneficiaries of a $3 trillion a year telecommunications industry.[11]

Only a couple of decades ago, telecommunications was a pretty straightforward affair, as was the ability more or less to eavesdrop. Communications were between two participants at fixed points connected between one link, and in order to listen in, one had only to tap in somewhere along the link. Today both the volume and methods of communication have expanded greatly. There are cellular and satellite phones and text messaging, virtually undetectable calling cards, email, and chat rooms. Inexpensive encryption is readily accessible. Digital signals have practically rendered analog communication obsolete, while a number of telecom companies are turning to fiber optic cables that transform signal pulses into light waves. Presently, there is simply more communication traveling over an infinitely wider array of paths.

During most of the 1990s, when much of the world was reacting to this new information age, Israel immediately seized upon it, finding ways to adapt and commercialize it. In much the same way a decade later, when the United States and other nations began to grapple with orange codes and homeland security and the detritus of companies that have fallen apart, Israelis went into fight mode and began making the quick change again. All over the country, small companies had moved on to begin solving the new problems, and they were doing so under immense domestic, regional, and international chaos.

Israel once again began reengineering itself. New ideas were being nurtured on rooftops, in garages, and in offices. The army had opened the floodgates. The next wave of small startups and entrepreneurs was spurred on by the early successes and the lessons learned in tandem with the talented classes of scientists and engineers earning degrees in the Technion and other Israeli universities. If telecommunications surged in the 1990s, Homeland Security innovations were also beginning to rush forward. There was a newly defined need, and it was global and urgent. Moreover, this is an area in which Israel has been identified as a pioneer: Homeland security came into focus. America, which established its own Office of Homeland Security with a $36 billion budget, was still figuring it out. Israel, on the other hand, was quick to assert its unusual expertise. Tal Keinon, the director of homeland securities technology at the Israeli firm Giza Venture Capital, said he began surveying Israeli companies in this sector over a four-month stretch. "After reaching 100, I stopped counting."

Israelis, who have always been good at being nimble and finding a niche to improve upon, began moving forward in a number of areas such as biometrics, data streams that can detect money laundering by analyzing the billions of transactions at 1,000 a second, explosive detection devices, and smart fences that can sense intruders and identify the type of breach as well as whether the intruder itself is an animal or a human. In the early part of 2004, a small company called Nemesysco, headed by mathematician Amir Lieberman, which had developed voice analysis and lie-detection technology for the military, police, and insurance industry, debuted a pair of eyeglasses outfitted with a tiny lie-detector chip. The chip uses 3,000 algorithms to read and analyze the voice frequency of the person the wearer is speaking with. Color-coded lights indicate if the person is telling the truth or lying.[12] Around the same time, another small company called Ha'argaz unveiled a device and a pilot project to detect suicide bombers on buses.

Israel had once again hunkered down and switched gears to a host of new ideas. Foreign investors again began sniffing at Israel's front door.

For all of the discussion and talk being thrown at the newly urgent concept of America's homeland security, there was equal discussion and concern directed at a slow-moving U.S. defense infrastructure. Various sites and installations in the country, including airports, seaports, oil refineries, and power stations, remained vulnerable to attack. A pronounced fear was that by the time the big U.S. defense contractors and integrators started building prototypes for devices intended to foil and thwart terrorist attacks, the threat that they hoped to quash would have already become old hat, and a new one would appear. Indeed, a pair of U.S. congressmen, Jim Turner (D-Texas) and Curt Weldon (R-Pennsylvania), sought to remedy that on some level. They introduced the United States-Homeland Security Foundation Act to Congress on March 2, 2004. Acknowledging the vast wealth of experience and know-how on the part of the Israelis in developing technology to prevent and respond to terrorism, the bill would earmark $25 million for research and development of homeland security technologies carried out jointly between American and Israeli private firms.

As the twentieth century passed into the twenty-first, Israel did what it has always done: It soldiered on. As one Israeli after another put it simply, in Israel change was a visceral fact of life. And change, of course, is a powerful factor for transformation. It is not dissimilar to the larger theme of the nation itself, which is one of creation and reinvention. In an interview with the *Jerusalem Post,* Oz Almog, a Haifa University sociologist, described modern Israel and the modern Israeli as the height of Israeli invention. After all, he offered, not many cultures had invented themselves out of an ideology.[13] Israel made a virtue of necessity, dipping into a well based on need that has not abated over time and in turn has become an engine all its own. The negative factors that would cripple most societies galvanize here. There are major fault lines and fissures to be sure, but this is not a complete and perfect success story. It is, nonetheless, a story about successful innovation.

Endnotes

Chapter One—The Intercept

1. Robert Satloff, "The Peace Process at Sea: The *Karine-A* Affair and the War on Terrorism," *National Interest*, The Washington Institute for Near East Policy, Spring 2002.
2. The Oslo accords refer to the process of negotiations between the Israelis and the Palestinians that began in September 1993, establishing a framework for resolving the conflict between them.
3. Netty C. Gross, "Israel: When Arafat's Ship Sailed," *The Jerusalem Report*, September 9, 2002.
4. Michael Kelly, "It All Points to Arafat," *The Washington Post*, January 9, 2002.
5. Yaakov Erez, "A Perfect Operation," *Ma'ariv*, January 6, 2002, and Arieh O'Sullivan, "Quick and Short, Without Any Opposition," *The Jerusalem Post*, January 6, 2002.
6. Amir Rappaport, "Security Officials: 'Arafat Knew and Approved,' " *Yedioth Ahronoth*, January 6, 2002.
7. Alex Fishman and Amir Rappaport, "It's in Our Hands," *Yedioth Ahronoth*, January 6, 2002.

8. IDF Spokesman's Unit, press conference, January 4, 2002.

9. Statement made by IDF Chief of Staff Lieutenant General Shaul Mofaz regarding the interception of the ship *Karine-A*, IDF Spokesman's Unit, January 4, 2002.

10. Ibid.

11. Yaakov Erez, "A Perfect Operation," *Ma'ariv*, January 6, 2002.

12. These remarks were made during a press briefing held at the Eilat port after the seizure of the *Karine-A*. The briefing was attended by the Prime Minister, the Minister of Defense, the Chief of the IDF General Staff, and the Commander in Chief of the Israeli Navy, IDF Spokesman's Unit, January 6, 2002.

13. IDF Spokesman's Unit press briefings, January 4, 2002, outlining the operation and the affair, including those involved in the incident following the seizure, and Ministry of Foreign Affairs statement, "Seizing of the Palestinian Weapons Ship *Karine-A*, January 4, 2002.

14. "Israel Intercepts Palestinian Arms Shipment," International Policy Institute for Counter-Terrorism, Interdisciplinary Center Herziliya, January 5, 2002, and Robert Satloff, "The Peace Process at Sea: The *Karine-A* Affair and the War on Terrorism," *National Interest*, The Washington Institute for Near East Policy, Spring 2002.

15. "Israel Intercepts Palestinian Arms Shipment," International Policy Institute for Counter-Terrorism, Interdisciplinary Center Herziliya, January 5, 2002.

16. Robert Satloff, "*Karine-A*: The Strategic Implications of Iranian-Palestinian Collusion," The Washington Institute for Near East Policy, *PolicyWatch*, No. 593, January 15, 2002; Douglas Frantz and James Risen, "A Nation Challenged: Terrorism: A Secret Iran-Arafat Connection Is Seen Fueling the Mideast Fire, *The New York Times*, March 24, 2002; and Isabel Kershner, "The Changing Colors of Imad Mughniyah," *The Jerusalem Report*, March 25, 2002.

17. Alex Fishman and Amir Rappaport, "It's in Our Hands," *Yedioth Ahronoth*, January 6, 2002.

18. From a speech given by Prime Minister Ariel Sharon in Eilat, following the capture of the *Karine-A*, January 6, 2002.

19. This evidence has not been made public, although a number of news reports indicated that Israel had supplied the Bush Administration with such undeniable proof. For instance, a report in *Debkafile Intelligence Reports*, on January 9, 2002, "Palestinian Security Chief Dahlan Supervised *Karine-A* Loading from Dubai," said Israeli intelligence officers were heading to Washington, D.C., to lay out their evidence of Yassir Arafat's direct link to the operation to Assistant Secretary of State William Burns, intelligence officials, and U.S. defense department officials. According to this report, evidence showed that Mohamed Dahlan, the Palestinian Authority's Preventative Security Chief in the Gaza Strip, was present in Dubai when the arms were loaded onto the ship.

20. Ben Caspit, "Israel and U.S. Exchanged Intelligence Regarding Arms Ship," *Ma'ariv*, January 6, 2002; see also Jonathan Marcus, "Analysis: The CIA and the Arms Ship," *BBC News*, January 15, 2002, and "Major Israeli Haul of Palestinian Arms," *Debkafile Intelligence Files*, January 4, 2002.

21. Lee Hockstader, "Iran Implicated by Captain in Seized Weapons Shipment: Comments Appear to Back Israeli Allegations," *The Washington Post*, January 9, 2002.

22. Transcript provided by the Center for Special Studies at Glilot.

23. For more on this episode refer to Michael Oren, *Six Days of War: June 1967 and the Making of the Modern Middle East*, Oxford University Press, Oxford, 2002, and Ian Black and Benny Morris, *Israel's Secret Wars: A History of Israel's Intelligence Services*, Grove Press, New York, 1991.

24. Ian Black and Benny Morris, *Israel's Secret Wars: A History of Israel's Intelligence Services*, Grove Press, New York, 1991, p. 298.

25. Based on material published in *The Washington Post*: William Claiborne, "Israeli Port Called Goal of Gunman," October 10, 1985; Fred Hiatt and Dale Russakoff, "Four Bunglers Shake the Global Community," October 13, 1985; William Claiborne, "Israeli Text Quotes Order by Abbas," October 17, 1985; Howard Kurtz and Joe Pichirallo and Richard Harwood and John M. Gashko, " 'Hard Evidence' Against Abbas," October 17, 1985; and Ian Black and Benny Morris, *Israel's Secret Wars: A History of Israel's Intelligence Services*, Grove Press, New York, 1991, pp. 457–458.

Chapter Two—In the Beginning…

1. Howard Sachar, *A History of Israel: From the Rise of Zionism to Our Time*, Alfred A. Knopf, New York, 1986, p. 311.

2. Declaration of the Establishment of the State of Israel, May 14, 1948, Israeli Ministry of Foreign Affairs.

3. Ian J. Bickerton and Carla L. Klausner, *A Concise History of the Arab-Israeli Conflict*, Prentice Hall, Upper Saddle River, New Jersey, 2002, p. 103.

4. Amos Oz, "Under This Blazing Light," *Under This Blazing Light*, Cambridge University Press, Cambridge, 1995, pp. 31–32. Reprinted with the permission of Amos Oz and Cambridge University Press.

5. http://www.us-israel.org/jsource/Immigration/Immigration_Since_1948.htm.

6. This data comes from articles published in the Israeli daily newspaper *Ha'aretz*, March 6, 2003, and from the National Security Studies Center, Haifa University, http://research.haifa.ac.il˜focus/2002-summer/17security.html.

7. The Geneva Accord, announced on November 24, 2003, has not been officially recognized by the government of Israel or the Palestinian Authority.

8. Ephraim Kishon, "Happy Birthday to the State of Israel," *The Atlantic Monthly*, November 1961, Vol. 208, No. 5, pp. 92–93.

9. Upon leaving office in 2001, President Bill Clinton granted Al Schwimmer a presidential pardon.

10. Israel Aircraft Industries figures as cited by Hoover's Inc., http://www.hoovers.com, as of 2002.

11. Netafim corporate website: http://www.netafim.com.

12. Yivsam Azgad, *Shaping the Future: The Weizmann Institute for Science, Scientific Milestones During Israel's First Half Century*, English edition, 2000, p. 191.

13. Israel Ministry of Foreign Affairs, "The High Tech Sector," http://www.mfa.gov.il/mfa/go.asp?MFAH0jdq0.

14. Ibid.

15. Israeli Ministry of Foreign Affairs, "Looking at Israel: Economy," http://www.israel.org/mfa/go.asp?MFAH0hg10, and data from Israel's Central Bureau of Statistics report: "National Expenditure on Civilian Research and Development, 1989–2001," published October 2002.

16. Michele Gershberg, "Identical Twins Crack Face Recognition Puzzle," *Reuters*, March 9, 2003; "Two Faces," *Ha'aretz*, March 17, 2003.

17. Haganah Museum, Tel Aviv, Israel.

18. Howard Sachar, *A History of Israel: From the Rise of Zionism to Our Time*, Alfred A. Knopf, New York, 1986, pp. 270–271.

19. Ian Black and Benny Morris, *Israel's Secret Wars: A History of Israel's Intelligence Services*, Grove Press, New York, 1991, p. 48.

Chapter Three—Security Is the Mother of Invention

1. Amos Harel, "Soldiers Capture Two Islamic Jihad Men on Their Way to a Suicide Bombing Inside Israel," *Ha'aretz*, February 7, 2003.

2. Roni Singer and Jalal Bana, "Police Find Explosive Belt to Be Used by Jihad Militants in Taibeh Mosque," *Ha'aretz*, February 7, 2003.

3. Ibid.

4. Margot Dudkevitch, "IDF Nabs Would-be Suicide Bombers," *The Jerusalem Post*, February 7, 2003.

5. Statistics as reported by the IDF Spokesperson's Unit and Israeli Ministry of Foreign Affairs for the time period between 9/29/00 and 3/23/04.

6. Statistics as reported by the Israeli Ministry of Foreign Affairs: "Suicide and Other Bombing Attacks in Israel Since the Declaration of Principles," September 1993.

7. Figures from the Palestinian Central Bureau of Statistics for the time period between 9/29/00 and 2/29/04.

8. According to the Israeli Ministry of Foreign Affairs: "Suicide and Other Bombing Attacks in Israel Since the Declaration of Principles," September 1993.

9. Bradley Burston, "Who's Next? 'Israel's Most Wanted...and Hamas,' " *Ha'aretz*, March 25, 2004.

10. Statistics as reported by the IDF Spokesperson's Unit and Israeli Ministry of Foreign Affairs for the time period between 9/29/00 and 3/23/04.

11. Amos Harel and Arnon Regular, "IDF Kills 13 Palestinians in Biggest Operation in Gaza Since Start of Intifada," *Ha'aretz*, January 27, 2003.

12. According to B'tselem, the Israeli human rights organization, http://www.btselem.org.

13. Amos Harel, "IDF Places Territories Under Full Closure," *Ha'aretz*, February 11, 2003.

14. After Israeli policemen killed 47 Arabs in Kafr Kassem in 1956, an Israeli law was enacted in which a soldier can refuse an order to kill if the order falls outside of very specific circumstances and is considered "patently illegal." For more on this incident and the subsequent law, see Joel Greenberg, "School Official Wants to Mark Israeli Atrocity," *The New York Times*, October 7, 1999.

15. Based on material published in "Rumblings in Unit 8200," *Ma'ariv*, January 28, 2003; Amos Harel, *Ha'aretz*, Janu-

ary 31, 2003; and as reported by Chris McGreal, "Israeli Officer Tried for Sabotaging Raid," *The Guardian*, February 3, 2003, and Ed O'Loughlin, "Officer's Stand Splits Israeli Military Intelligence, *The Herald*, February 4, 2003.

16. Margot Dudkevitch, "Six Hamas Men Killed While Packing Drone with Explosives," *The Jerusalem Post*, February 17, 2003.

17. Ian J. Bickerton and Carla A. Klausner, *A Concise History of the Arab-Israeli Conflict*, Prentice Hall, Upper Saddle River, New Jersey, 2002, p. 334.

18. For more on the Israeli-Lebanese border situation and IDF responses, see Anthony H. Cordesman's draft of "Israel and Lebanon: The New Military and Strategic Realities," Arleigh A. Burke, Chair in Strategy, Center for Strategic and International Studies, August 2000. http://www.csis.org/stratassessment/reports/IsraelLebanonRealities.pdf.

19. Bradley Burston, "Suicide and Sisyphus: Israel's Dwindling Anti-Terror Arsenal," *Ha'aretz*, May 20, 2003.

20. Federation of American Scientists, Space Policy Project, Special Weapons Monitor, http://www.fas.org/spp/starwars/program/arrow.htm.

21. Hilary Leila Krieger, "The Creation Story," *The Jerusalem Post*, July 10, 2003.

22. Samuel M. Katz, *Soldier Spies: Israeli Military Intelligence*, Presidio Press, Novato, California, 1994, pp. 128–129, and an interview with former senior Israeli officer, Tel Aviv, December 31, 2002.

23. The United States military began developing a UAV program during the Vietnam War but eventually scrapped it because initially the information was too slow in coming to be of vital importance. Also, American systems were quite expensive and the design extremely complicated.

24. Amnon Barzilai, "IDF Unveils Rear Gun for Tank, Miniature Airborne Camera," *Ha'aretz*, March 24, 2003.

25. "Israel Develops Credit Card Sized 100g Aircraft," *Agence France Presse*, March 8, 2003.

26. Hilary Leila Krieger, "The Creation Story," *The Jerusalem Post*, July 10, 2003.

27. Walter Pincus, "U.S. Strike Kills Six in Al Qaeda," *The Washington Post*, November 5, 2002.

28. CIA World Factbook, 2002, www.cia.gov/ccia/publications.factbook.geos.

29. CIA World Factbook, 2002, www.cia.gov/ccia/publications.factbook.geos (figures for 1999).

30. Stacy Perman, "Danny Yatom," *Business 2.0 online*, December 2001, www.business2.com/preview.articles/mag/0,1640,35218/2,FF.html.

31. Samuel M. Katz, *Soldier Spies: Israeli Military Intelligence*, Presidio Press, Novato, California, 1994, pp. 334–335; and Ian Black, "Lockerbie: At Last the Trial Begins," *The Guardian*, May 3, 2000.

32. Dan Breznitz, "The Military as a Public Space: The Role of the IDF in the Israeli Software Innovation System, Industrial Performance Center," MIT Media Lab Europe, Dublin, Ireland, MIT Department of Political Science, Massachusetts Institute of Technology, 2002, and G. Ariav and S.E. Goodman, "Israel: Of Swords and Software Plowshares," *Communications of the ACM*, Vol. 37, No. 6, June 1994.

33. Ian Black and Benny Morris, *Israel's Secret Wars: A History of Israel's Intelligence Services*, Grove Press, New York, p. 48.

34. Stanley Blumberg and Gwinn Owens, *The Survival Factor: Israeli Intelligence from World War I to the Present*, GP Putnam's Sons, New York, 1981, pp. 104–105.

35. Howard Sachar, *A History of Israel, Volume II: From the Aftermath of the Yom Kippur War,* Oxford University Press, New York, 1987, p. 251.

36. Based on material from the IDF's online archived history http://www.idf.il/english/organization/iaf/iaf5-2.stm, and an interview with a former senior Israeli officer, 1/4/03, Tel Aviv. Also see Samuel M. Katz, *Soldier Spies: Israeli Military Intelligence*, Presidio Press, Novato, California, 1994, pp. 125–126.

Chapter Four—Brains

1. Accounts of the uranium ship incident have been chronicled by Dennis Eisenberg, Eli Landau, and Menashem Portugali, *Operation Uranium Ship*, Signet, New York, 1978, and by Elaine Davenport, Paul Eddy, and Peter Gillman, *The Plumbat Affair*, Deutsch, London, 1978.

2. Arieh O'Sullivan, "MI Slammed for Failing to Assess Iraq WMD Threat," *The Jerusalem Post*, March 28, 2004, and Ze'ev Schiff, "Failures and Mistakes," *Ha'aretz*, March 29, 2004.

3. Alan Cowell, "The Daring Attack That Blew Up in Israel's Face," *The New York Times*, October 15, 1997.

4. There are several accounts of both Operation Moses and Operation Solomon, including material available from "The History of Ethiopian Jews" by The Israel Association for Ethiopian Jews.

5. The Israeli military censor kept this incident under wraps for more than 10 years, releasing the information only in 2003, following the capture of Saddam Hussein by U.S.-led forces in Iraq.

6. JPOST.com Staff, "Elite IDF Sayeret Matkal Unit Trained Saddam Hit in 1992," *The Jerusalem Post*, December 16, 2003.

7. "Report: Mossad Has Assad Urine Sample Indicating He's 'Living on Borrowed Time,' " *The Jerusalem Post*, January 10, 2000.

8. Stewart Steven, *Spymasters of Israel*, Macmillan Publishing, New York, 1980, p. 169.

9. James Bamford, "Eyes in the Sky, Ears to the Wall and Still Wanting," *The New York Times*, September 8, 2002.

10. Richard Deacon, *The Israeli Secret Service*, Hamish Hamilton, London, 1977, p. 122.

11. Ibid, p. 125.

12. Op. cit, p. 129.

13. Stewart Steven, *Spymasters of Israel*, Macmillan Publishing, New York, 1980, p. 189.

Chapter Five—Listening In

Yehiya Ayyash's capture is based on material published in Samuel M. Katz, *The Hunt for the Engineer: How Israeli Agents Tracked the Hamas Master Bomber*, Fromm International Publishing Corporation, New York, 1999; news reports; and interviews.

The statistics on the number of casualties and wounded come from news reports; Ministry of Foreign Affairs report: "Suicide and Other Bombing Attacks in Israel Since the Declaration of Principles," September 1993; and Katz's *The Hunt for the Engineer: How Israeli Agents Tracked the Hamas Master Bomber.*

1. Samuel M. Katz, *The Hunt for the Engineer: How Israeli Agents Tracked the Hamas Master Bomber*, Fromm International Publishing Corporation, New York, 1999, p. 178.

2. Jeffrey Bartholet, Tom Masland, and Gregory Vistica, "Spooking the Spooks," *Newsweek*, March 18, 1996.

3. Serge Schmemann, "Palestinian Believed to be Bombing Mastermind Is Killed, *The New York Times*, January 5, 1996.

4. Samuel M. Katz, *The Hunt for the Engineer: How Israeli Agents Tracked the Hamas Master Bomber*, Fromm International Publishing Corporation, New York, 1999, p. 249.

5. Ian Black and Benny Morris, *Israel's Secret Wars: A History of Israel's Intelligence Services*, Grove Press, New York, 1991, p. 470.

6. Victor Ostrovsky and Claire Hoy, *By Way of Deception*, St. Martin's Press, New York, 1990, p. 151.

7. Yuval Dror, "Intelligence Unit Fights for Tomorrow's Engineers," *Ha'aretz*, November 8, 2000.

8. Benny Morris, *Israel's Border Wars*, Oxford University Press, New York, 1993, p. 336; Interview, Yossi Melman, Tel Aviv, January 17, 2003; and Samuel M. Katz, *Soldier Spies: Israeli Military Intelligence*, Presidio Press, Novato, California, pp. 108–109.

9. Robert Hotz, "Changing Egypt," *Aviation Week*, June 30, 1975.

10. IDF Spokesperson's Unit online archive, http://
    www.idf.il/english/organization/iaf/iaf5.stm, July 30,
    1970, Israel *vs.* USSR, www.geocities.com/capecanav-
    eral/hangar/2448/operate5.htm; Eric Hehs, "Israeli Air
    Force: 50 Years of Air Superiority," *Code One* magazine,
    July 1998; and an interview with a former senior Israeli
    officer.

11. Ibid.

Chapter Six—The Collection Agency

1. Arieh O'Sullivan, "Anatomy of an Air Force Raid in
   Syria," *The Jerusalem Post*, October 26, 2003.
2. William Safire, "Adding Up Evidence Against Assad's
   Syria," *The International Herald Tribune*, October 10,
   2003; Douglas Jehl, "Construction Was Spotted at Syrian
   Camp Hit by Israel," *The New York Times*, October 10,
   2003; and David Ensor and Andrea Koppel, "U.S. Con-
   firms Construction at Israeli's Syria Target," *CNN*, October 10, 2003.
3. Matt Rees, "Northern Exposure," *Time*, October 13, 2003.
4. Dan Raviv and Yossi Melman, *Every Spy a Prince*, Houghton Mifflin, Boston, 1990, p. 206.
5. Interviews, Tel Aviv, 2003.
6. http://www.isayeret.com.
7. While the drone filmed the entire event, broadcasting the
   precision hit of the missiles fired, the number of victims
   that were wounded or killed did not eliminate the dis-
   crepancies between the IDF's and the Palestinians' version of the fallout. Following this episode there was an
   inquiry made by members of the Knesset—both Israeli
   and Israeli-Arab. They asserted that the high number of
   victims that resulted from the missile strike was due to
   the use of a "banned secret weapon" that was more lethal
   than the Hellfire missile reported to have been used. For
   many, the issue remains unresolved.

8. Thomas W. Lippman and Barton Gellman, "U.S. Says It Collected Iraq Intelligence Via UNSCOM," *The Washington Post*, January 8, 1999. For more on the Israeli-UNSCOM link, see Scott Ritter, *Endgame: Solving the Iraq Crisis*, Simon & Schuster, New York, 1999.

9. Wayne Madsen, "Crypto AG: The NSA's Trojan Whore?" *Covert Action Quarterly*, No. 63, Winter 1998.

10. Ibid and Scott Shane and Tom Bowman, "Rigging the Game," *The Baltimore Sun*, December 10, 1995, and "Swiss Firm Denies Allegations of Rigging," *The Baltimore Sun*, December 15, 1995.

11. Although speculation continues, in 2003 Libya publicly accepted responsibility as the major player behind the Lockerbie disaster.

12. Seymour M. Hersh, "The Deal," *The New Yorker*, March 8, 2004.

13. Ian Black and Benny Morris, *Israel's Secret Wars: A History of Israel's Intelligence Services*, Grove Press, New York, 1991, p. 232, and Zeev Schiff's *History of the Israeli Army: 1874 to the Present*, Macmillan Publishers, London, 1987, p. 200.

14. Matt Rees, Jamil Hamad, and Aharon Klein, "The Enemy Within; Beset by the Israelis, Palestinians See Collaborators All Over," *Time*, August 27, 2001.

15. JPOST.com Staff, "Rantisi: I May Have Helped Israel Target Me by Phoning a Friend," *The Jerusalem Post*, June 17, 2003.

16. Ian James, "Critics: Israeli Strikes Doing More Harm," *Associated Press*, September 2, 2003; Michael Holmes, "Civilians Living in Fear in Gaza," *CNN*, August 28, 2003; and "Hamas Men Hide to Avoid Instant Death," *Reuters*, August 27, 2003.

17. Margot Dudkevitch, "11-Year-Old Boy Used as Human Bomb," *The Jerusalem Post*, March 16, 2004, and "Child Sacrifice," *The Jerusalem Post*, March 16, 2004.

18. Lou Dolinar, "Cell Phones Jury-Rigged to Detonate Bombs," *Newsday*, March 15, 2004, and John J. Lumpkin,

"Electronic Road Bomb 'Jammers' Help Protect U.S. Convoys," *Associated Press*, January 31, 2003.

Chapter Seven—Genius Corps

1. Ian J. Bickerton and Carla L. Klausner, *A Concise History of the Arab-Israeli Conflict*, Prentice Hall, Upper Saddle River, New Jersey, p. 175.
2. Howard Sachar, *History of Israel: Volume II from the Aftermath of the Yom Kippur War*, Oxford University Press, New York, p. 3.
3. Interview, Hanoch Zadik, Tel Aviv, January 29, 2003.
4. MAFAT Directorate of Defense Research and Development.
5. Ibid.

Chapter Eight—Soldier's Stories

1. Batya Feldman, "Nerds in Uniform," *Globes*, August 2, 2000.
2. An oscilloscope is a device that uses a cathode ray tube to produce a visual record of an electrical current on a fluorescent screen.
3. In 1986, a Valencia, California, company called 3D Systems was founded. It is considered the world leader in rapid prototyping.

Chapter Nine—Battle Tested

1. Yuval Dror, "Intelligence Unit Fights for Tomorrow's Engineers," *Ha'aretz*, November 8, 2000.

Chapter Ten–Spy Company

1. Lea Goldman, "A Fortune in Firewalls," *Forbes*, March 18, 2002.
2. Ibid.
3. Data from a survey released by IDC, see Paul Roberts, "Security Market to Reach $45 Billion by 2006," *IDG News Service*, February 4, 2003.
4. "The Spread of the Sapphire/Slammer Worm," http://www.cs.berkeley.edu/~nweaver/sapphire/.
5. Jeffrey Gold, "NICE Systems: Company Behind 'This Call May Be Recorded,'" *Associated Press*, August 10, 2003.
6. Claudia H. Deutsch, "Monitoring Calls in New World of Quality Assurance," *The New York Times*, July 28, 2003.
7. Seth Schiesel, "Security Cameras Now Learn to React," *The New York Times*, March 3, 2003.

Chapter Eleven–Soldiering On

1. Israel Venture Capital Research Center.
2. Israel Venture Capital Research Center.
3. Rick Radin, "Orna Berry Charting a Course for Israeli Business," *Israel21c.com*, August 12, 2002.
4. Yuval Dror, "Intelligence Unit Fights for Tomorrow's Engineers," *Ha'aretz*, November 8, 2000.
5. Josh Wander, "Mossad Opens Doors to Techies," *The Jerusalem Post*, April 17, 2001.
6. Merrill Lynch analyst Tom Watts in 1999 as stated in Gilat corporate timeline.
7. Lt. Col. James P. DeLoughry, "The United States and the LAVI," *USAF Airpower Journal*, Vol. IV, No. 3, Fall 1990.
8. John T. Haldane, "The Lavi Fighter: Lion or Lemon?" *Trade and Finance*, August 11, 1986.
9. Lt. Col. James P. DeLoughry, "The United States and the LAVI," *USAF Airpower Journal*, Vol. IV, No. 3, Fall 1990.

10. Bruce Upbin, "Higher Ground," *Forbes*, October 27, 2003.

11. James Bamford, "Eyes in the Sky, Ears to the Wall, and Still Wanting," *The New York Times*, September 8, 2002.

12. Colin Johnson, "Lie-detector Glasses Offer Peek at Future of Security," *eetimes*, January 18, 2004, and *Israel High-Tech & Investment Report*, February 2004.

13. Hillary Leila Krieger, "The Creation Story," *The Jerusalem Post*, July 10, 2003.

Select Bibliography

Bamford, James, *The Puzzle Palace, Inside the National Security Agency*, Penguin Books USA, 1983.

Bickerton, Ian J., and Carla A. Klausner, *A Concise History of the Arab-Israeli Conflict*, Prentice Hall, Upper Saddle River, NJ, 2002.

Black, Ian, and Benny Morris, *Israel's Secret Wars: A History of Israel's Intelligence Services*, Grove Press, New York, 1991.

Breznitz, Dan, *The Military as a Public Space—The Role of the IDF in the Israeli Software Innovation System*, Industrial Performance Center, MIT Media Lab Europe, Dublin, Ireland, MIT Department of Political Science, Massachusetts Institute of Technology, 2002.

Cohen, Avner, *Israel and the Bomb,* Columbia University Press, October 1999.

Cordesman, Anthony H., *Israel and Lebanon: The New Military and Strategic Realities* (draft), Arleigh A. Burke Chair in Strategy, Center for Strategic and International Studies, August 2000.

Deacon, Richard, *The Israeli Secret Service*, Hamish Hamilton, London, 1977.

Dobson, Christopher, and Ronald Payne, *The Dictionary of Espionage*, Grafton Books, London, 1986.

Dvir, Dov, and Asher Tishler, *The Changing Role of the Defense Industry in Israel's Industrial and Technological Development*, *The Place of the Defense Industry in National Systems of Innovation*, Judith Reppy, ed., Peace Studies Program, Cornell University, Occasional Paper #25, April 2000.

Fridell, Ron, *The Modern World of Espionage Spying*, Twenty-First Century Books, Brookfield, Connecticut, 2002.

Friedland, Roger, and Richard Hecht, *To Rule Jerusalem*, Cambridge University Press, 1996.

Katz, Samuel M., *Soldier Spies: Israeli Military Intelligence*, Presidio Press, 1992.

Katz, Samuel M., *The Hunt for the Engineer: How Israeli Agents Tracked the Hamas Master Bomber*, Fromm International Publishing Corporation, New York, 1999.

Morris, Benny, *Israel's Border Wars, 1949–1956: Arab Infiltration, Israeli Retaliation and the Countdown to the Suez War*, Oxford University Press, Oxford, 1993.

Oren, Michael, *Six Days of War: June 1967, and the Making of the Modern Middle East*, Oxford University Press, 2002.

Ostrovsky, Victor, and Claire Hoy, *By Way of Deception*, St. Martin's Press, New York, 1990.

Oz, Amos, *Under This Blazing Light*, Cambridge University Press, New York, 1995.

Raviv, Dan, and Yossi Melman, *Every Spy a Prince*, Houghton Mifflin, Boston, 1990.

Ritter, Scott, *Endgame: Solving the Iraq Crisis*, Simon & Schuster, New York, 1999.

Rouach Daniel, and Jeff Saperstein, *Creating Regional Wealth in the Innovation Economy: Models, Perspectives and Best*

Practices, Financial Times/Prentice Hall, Upper Saddle River, NJ, 2002.

Sachar, Howard, *A History of Israel: From the Rise of Zionism to Our Time*, Alfred A. Knopf, New York, 1986.

Sachar, Howard, *A History of Israel: From the Aftermath of the Yom Kippur War*, Volume II, Oxford University Press, New York, 1987.

Steven, Stewart, *The Spymasters of Israel*, Macmillan, New York, 1980.

Index

The Power of Impossible Thinking

You don't live in the real world. You live in the world inside your head. We all do. Our invisible mental models shape everything we do. Often, they keep us from seeing what's right in front of us, and prevent us from changing our companies and society...even our *lives*. *The Power of Impossible Thinking* is about fixing your mental models, so you can *see* reality and *act* on it. Based firmly in neuroscience, it shows how to develop new ways of seeing...understand complex environments...even how to do "mind R&D" to keep your models fresh and relevant. Whether you need to beat the competition or lose weight, your mental models may be the problem...and *The Power of Impossible Thinking* is the solution.

ISBN 0131425021, © 2005, 336 pp., $24.95

Failsafe Strategies

In the 1990s, in the name of "revolutionary business models," businesses took on massive risks almost without concern. Today, many companies have become powerfully averse to taking the risks that are essential to long-term success. Now, there's a whole new way to think about risk: one that liberates you to act, while protecting you against danger. Dr. Sayan Chatterjee shows how to identify high-risk high return opportunities, and then systematically manage and reduce those risks up front, as you design your initiative...not after you operationalize it. Chatterjee discusses specific new techniques for neutralizing risk up-front, so you can leverage opportunities your competitors are walking away from. Using his techniques, you can safely pursue opportunities your competitors will walk away from—and sustain profit growth far into the future.

ISBN 0131011111, © 2005, 320 pp., $26.95